AF593584

Nine Lives
Visionary Artists *from* L.A.

Lisa Anne Auerbach
Julie Becker
Llyn Foulkes
Charles Irvin
Hirsch Perlman
Victoria Reynolds
Kaari Upson
Jeffrey Vallance
Charlie White

Ali Subotnick
Hammer Museum, Los Angeles

This publication accompanies the exhibition *Nine Lives: Visionary Artists from L.A.*, organized by and presented at the Hammer Museum, Los Angeles, March 8–May 31, 2009.

This exhibition has received major support from The Andy Warhol Foundation for the Visual Arts. Additional support has been generously provided by Linda and Jerry Janger, Barbara and Peter Benedek, David Teiger, the Pasadena Art Alliance, Joel Portnoy, John Rubeli, and Alisa and Kevin Ratner.

The catalog is published with the assistance of The Getty Foundation.

Published by the Hammer Museum
10899 Wilshire Boulevard
Los Angeles, California 90024-4201
Tel: 310.443.7000
www.hammer.ucla.edu

The Hammer Museum is operated and partially funded by the University of California, Los Angeles.

Occidental Petroleum Corporation has partially endowed the Museum and constructed the Occidental Petroleum Cultural Center Building, which houses the Museum.

Available through D.A.P./Distributed Art Publishers, Inc.
155 Sixth Avenue, 2nd Floor
New York, NY 10013
Tel: 212.627.1999 | Fax: 212.627.9484

ISBN: 978-0-943739-36-6

Library of Congress Cataloging-in-Publication Data

Subotnick, Ali.
Nine lives : visionary artists from L.A. / Ali Subotnick.
p. cm.
Publication accompanying an exhibition held at the Hammer Museum, Los Angeles, Mar. 8–May 31, 2009.
Includes bibliographical references.
ISBN 978-0-943739-36-6 (hardcover)
1. Art, American--California--Los Angeles--21st century--Exhibitions. 2. Fantasy in art--Exhibitions. I. Armand Hammer Museum of Art and Cultural Center. II. Title. III. Title: Visionary artists from L.A.
N6535.L6S83 2009
709.794'9407479494--dc22
2008055851

Editor: Karen Jacobson
Designer: Purtill Family Business
Proofreader: Dianne Woo
Printer: Shapco Printing, Inc., Minneapolis

Dust jacket: Llyn Foulkes. *The Lost Frontier* (detail), 1997–2005. Mixed media. 87 x 96 x 8 in. (221 x 243.8 x 20.3 cm). Courtesy the artist and Kent Gallery, New York.

Contents

Foreword

Nine Lives: Visionary Artists from L.A. is the fifth in the Hammer Museum's biannual exhibition series highlighting work created in greater Los Angeles. We are fortunate to be situated in a city so rich in talented artists. Our community is constantly being fed by the region's outstanding art schools as well as by the continual stream of artists drawn here from across the country and around the world.

Each of these biannual exhibitions has provided the curator with an opportunity to approach the task of sorting through the creative output of Los Angeles in a different way. Ali Subotnick began work on this exhibition almost immediately after joining the Hammer in late 2006. I suspected that she would have an interesting take on the L.A. art world. Having just moved to town, she had the unique perspective of someone with a deep knowledge of contemporary art but a fresh view of Los Angeles. A particular experience that Ali had while conducting research for the show—a visit to Llyn Foulkes's studio—guided her, providing the nucleus and inspiration for her exhibition. This is Ali's first major exhibition for the museum, and I could not be more pleased with the results.

Nine Lives brings together nine artists ranging in age from thirty-six to seventy-four. Foulkes, the senior artist in the group, holds a special place in the history of Los Angeles art, and his influence on younger generations is unquantifiable. Here his work is reintroduced, along with that of eight similarly idiosyncratic emerging and midcareer artists who share several tendencies, including a penchant for storytelling and building alternative private worlds. I want to offer my deepest thanks to Lisa Anne Auerbach,

Julie Becker, Llyn Foulkes, Charles Irvin, Hirsch Perlman, Victoria Reynolds, Kaari Upson, Jeffrey Vallance, and Charlie White for sharing with us their moving and imaginative work.

Special thanks are due to all the lenders of works in the exhibition: Tanya Bonakdar, The Buck Collection, Beth Rudin DeWoody, Ann Faison and Dave Muller, Foundation 2021/Nyehaus, Blaine Halvorson, Karol Howard and George Morton, Laguna Art Museum, Libby Lumpkin and Dave Hickey, Ed Moses, Museum of Contemporary Art San Diego / Gribin Family Trust, Tim Nye, Patrick and Soo Jin Jeong-Painter, Alan Power, Richard S. and Alita Rogers, Ann and Mel Schaffer, Norton Simon Museum of Art, Barry Sloane, Ernest and Eunice White, and several private collectors who prefer to remain anonymous. I am indebted as well to the galleries that represent the artists, which have been especially helpful in so many ways: Blum & Poe, Los Angeles; Gavlak, West Palm Beach, Florida; Greene Naftali Gallery, New York; Richard Heller Gallery, Santa Monica, California; Kent Gallery, New York; Craig Krull Gallery, Santa Monica, California; Margo Leavin Gallery, Los Angeles; Loock Gallery, Berlin; and Maccarone Gallery, New York.

As usual I want to extend my deepest appreciation to the extraordinary staff of the museum for bringing their consummate professionalism to this project. Their dedication and abilities never fail to amaze me. And finally we are profoundly grateful to the funders, especially The Andy Warhol Foundation for the Visual Arts for providing early and substantial support, followed by the generous and enthusiastic support of Linda and Jerry Janger, Barbara and Peter Benedek, David Teiger, the Pasadena Art Alliance, Joel Portnoy, John Rubeli, and Alisa and Kevin Ratner. In addition, our gratitude is extended to The Getty Foundation for underwriting this publication.

Ann Philbin
Director

Lost in Thought

ALI SUBOTNICK

Despite the cloud of imminent destruction that lingers over Southern California—which has been the subject of innumerable works of literature, film, and art—as well as the region's countless real-world natural disasters—including wildfires, earthquakes, mudslides, and floods—millions continue to flock to the promised land of sunshine and renewal to start over, find themselves, or become someone else entirely.

The seminal southerner William Faulkner spent a short spell in Los Angeles in the 1930s, writing screenplays for MGM. In a 1945 letter, he wrote: "I don't like this damn place any better than I ever did. That is one comfort: at least I cant [*sic*] be any sicker tomorrow for Mississippi than I was yesterday."[1] Faulkner's short story "Golden Land" (the only piece in which he used California as a setting), reprinted in this volume, reflects the city's bipolar nature, encompassing high and low, dark and light, good and evil. According to one anecdote, Faulkner asked the studio if he could take his work home, and when his request was approved, he did just that and returned to Oxford, Mississippi.[2] "Golden Land" conveys his disdain for the city and the damage it inflicts on the innocent. This tale of a truly dysfunctional family (written before the phrase "dysfunctional family" had become a cliché) portrays the ugly side of paradise but also reveals the city's undeniable allure, its gritty magic and glaring sunshine. The story concludes with the lament of the main character's mother, who is homesick for her native Nebraska: "I will stay here and live forever." Only in L.A. is death so strangely celebrated, for it's a city where perhaps nobody really dies and everyone is constantly reborn and reinvented.

As Faulkner discovered, there's an inherent loneliness to living in L.A. Some treasure the privacy and anonymity that come with such a sprawling city. We drive on jam-packed freeways, and yet we're totally alone, secluded, isolated in our cars. In other urban metropolises people are forced to interact with one another on subways or busy sidewalks, but in L.A. meeting people requires intention and planning. For these nine artists, this aspect of the city is a blessing. Behind closed doors, day or night, there is a freedom here for artists to tinker, research, explore, and dig into their work and ideas without distraction. While the rest of L.A. keeps Hollywood's dream factory running, artists here have the luxury of space and freedom and time to develop their ideas and nurture their imaginations. But how does one capture the independent spirit of an incredibly dispersed city that encourages disappearing acts and reinvention?

Not having a couple of decades to sink my teeth into the city and meet every artist in town, I chose instead to concentrate on nine idiosyncratic, extraordinarily audacious artists who struck me as being especially hard to define and categorize: Lisa Anne Auerbach, Julie Becker, Llyn Foulkes, Charles Irvin, Hirsch Perlman, Victoria Reynolds, Kaari Upson, Jeffrey Vallance, and Charlie White. They are steadfast individuals whose visions can sometimes be considered myopic because they can be so focused on their work that the rest of the world falls away. One of the unique qualities of Los Angeles is that if you don't make an effort to get out of your head once in a while, you can easily disappear. And sometimes that disappearing act is exactly what allows these artists to build their private universes. It's a luxury to have an abundance of mental space or breathing room (as well as physical space), but too much space can make it hard to pull oneself out of one's private world, so it's a bit of a double-edged sword. The artists in this exhibition intrigue me because they're able to straddle that sword and dive into their own headspace and create works that communicate their fears, dreams, anxieties, fantasies, curiosities, and moral and existential concerns—without disappearing completely.

Fueled by sharp humor and untraditional curiosities, these nine artists share an almost magical talent for seduction and storytelling. They are amateur anthropologists, behavioral profilers, and passionate collectors. Following their obsessions, they conduct weird science experiments and in-depth inquiries into everything from popular culture to the occult, alternative lifestyles, subcultures, conspiracy theories, folk and urban mythology, forgotten rites, and obscure traditions. They have uninhibited imaginations, and like children crafting a fortress of blankets and pillows, they fearlessly construct their make-believe worlds around them. In the process, they bring viewers into these other dimensions. These aren't virtual realities and digital avatar–like universes; they are spaces grounded in obsession and built on fantasy and unbridled creativity. Maybe this is why these artists choose to live and work in and around Hollywood, the ultimate land of make-believe. Or perhaps the fantasyland of Hollywood has bled into their work. Or maybe it's a bit of both. Either way, each of these nine artists has consistently followed the path of Peter Pan, never letting go of the innocence and awe and inspiration of being a kid.

Most artworks contain some degree of self-reflection, and here, even if it's distorted or disguised, the artists give us a little insight into their motivations and interests, whether they intend to or not. We feel Foulkes's angst and unbridled energy. We fall headfirst into Becker's cloud of mysticism and otherworldliness. Irvin leads us through his own private twilight zone, or we can escape into Perlman's mad laboratory. We meander through Reynolds's fleshy paradise and enter Upson's fantasyland grotto and psychotherapy session. In Vallance's world we play pirates digging through a ship of hidden treasure chests. We experience White's insatiable curiosity and fastidious attention to detail, and like a Pied Piper, Auerbach leads us on a parade of sassy women unafraid to speak their minds.

The works in this show trigger visceral reactions, in turn eliciting unease and discomfort, ecstasy and unbridled laughter. These artists are provocative, calling into question their own self-awareness and place in the immense landscape of the city and society at large. They forge head-on into their work and let it consume them entirely. Their artworks are aggressive and commanding, compelling and thought-provoking, weird and confusing, disturbing, funny, and strange. They inspire you to question yourself and your place in the world at large, and also the here and now of this specific moment. And like the frisky feline implicated in the show's title, these artists continue to reinvent themselves and reinvigorate their work. They may stumble and fall, but they always land on their feet and push themselves in new directions, never settling, never compromising their visions. In a land of renewal and reinvention, and in a town revolving around an industry of fantasy, it's a natural impulse to build alternative universes. I hope you enjoy the trip.

NOTES

1. David L. Ulin, *Writing Los Angeles: A Literary Anthology* (New York: Library of America, 2002), 131.

2. Ibid.

The Artists

ALI SUBOTNICK

Llyn Foulkes

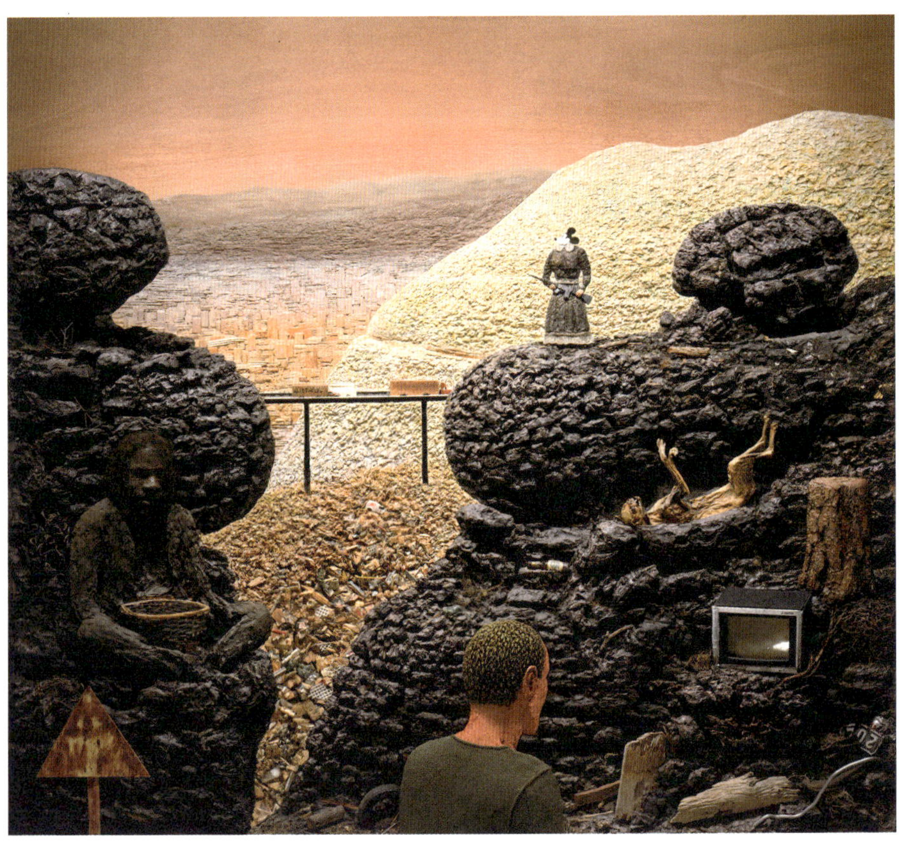

The Lost Frontier, 1997–2005. Mixed media. 87 x 96 x 8 in. (221 x 243.8 x 20.3 cm). Courtesy the artist and Kent Gallery, New York.

Llyn Foulkes has been exposing the hypocrisies and absurdities of American life since the 1960s, and his influence is vast and unquantifiable. From early constructions like the seminal charred blackboard and chair (*In Memory of St. Vincent School*, 1960) to his epic rock landscape paintings and his "bloody heads" and construction paintings, he continually challenges his audience and himself. Having watched the city grow and change significantly over the last fifty years, he dynamically captures the bleakness and the beauty of Los Angeles in his artwork and music. And at seventy-four he's still kicking and screaming.

Foulkes began playing the drums at the age of fourteen and played in an army jazz band when he was stationed in Germany (1954–56). While serving in the army, he painted watercolors and drew, and visited the major museums, where he discovered Italian, Spanish, and Flemish painting. Supported by the G.I. Bill, he moved to L.A. in 1957 to attend Chouinard Art Institute,[1] where he won first prize in drawing and painting.

Foulkes's first wife happened to be the daughter of Ward Kimball, Disney's head animator, and soon after he met Kimball, Foulkes began incorporating Mickey Mouse and other Disney icons into his work. Kimball gave him a copy of the first page from the 1934 Mickey Mouse Club handbook, which shocked Foulkes for its blatant attempt to "implant beneficial principles" into the minds of children through marketing and merchandising.[2] The entire first page from the handbook is featured in Foulkes's tableau painting *Made in Hollywood* (1983). For Foulkes, Mickey Mouse and Walt Disney represent everything that is wrong with American society. As Foulkes reminds us, when foreigners visit America and buy souvenirs, for example, they more often take away an image of Mickey Mouse than one of the American flag. In the artist's world, Mickey Mouse and Walt Disney play the villains in an ongoing battle between good and evil, and Foulkes is the hero liberating us from the tyranny of big corporations.

Foulkes had a solo show of his paintings at the Ferus Gallery in 1961, which featured *In Memory of St. Vincent School* along with several paintings and his portrait photos smeared with white paint.[3] His 1962 show at the Pasadena Art Museum was dominated by tableau paintings built up with assemblages of painted wood and found objects, such as *Flanders* (1961–62), *Geography Lesson* (1961), and *In Memory of St. Vincent School*—very tough, dark, visceral works that were nearly all black and stood in stark contrast to the pop art being lauded at the time (and celebrated in curator Walter Hopps's concurrent survey of American pop art at the same museum, *New Painting of Common Objects* [1962]). *In Memory of St. Vincent School* consists of a charred blackboard and chair that Foulkes found in the basement of a burned-down schoolhouse in South L.A. He took the child's chair and a section of the blackboard home and sprayed the ashes with a fixative, so that the tableau was essentially frozen in time. He added a swastika in the upper-left corner, as the blackboard reminded him of the bombed-out buildings he had encountered in postwar Germany. *Flanders* similarly grew out of a found object, as Foulkes explains: "I went into a plastics place, and identified this huge white plastic mess with the pictures that I had been making, painting white on the faces." He took the plastic home and turned it into a construction painting, adding a landscape, and all the plastic that spilled out became fine, like lace. The piece weighs about a hundred pounds.

Foulkes then moved on to paintings inspired by the rocky landscapes of Los Angeles. These enormous rock paintings became increasingly popular for their photographic quality, but for Foulkes it became too easy to keep churning them out: "If I hadn't stopped making the landscapes, I would have gone crazy." He felt as if he'd lost his soul.

Foulkes never even thought about making self-portraits until he started doing what he calls the "bloody head paintings," which were a direct result of going into therapy in 1971. "I went into the studio, and the magic was gone. I had a big ten-by-twelve-foot red rock painting that was just a copy of a photo, and I knew it. I destroyed the painting. I had one painting left, and it was a portrait that became *Who's on Third?* (1971–73). I just went in there and did something to the face, and that became my first bloody head." He started getting into more political subjects, making a bloody head painting of Nixon and one about the Battle of Wounded Knee. He also returned to the dark construction works that he had been making before he came onto the art scene—like *In Memory of St. Vincent School* and *Flanders*.

Foulkes started making the dimensional tableau paintings in 1983. *The Last Outpost* (1983), a western tableau, features a dying Lone Ranger, and *Oh Pablo* (1983) depicts a dead art critic with a hard-on. Foulkes started doing landscapes on canvas again around the same time because the construction works didn't sell, and as he expected, the landscapes sold immediately. These were more colorful than his previous efforts, featuring huge, mountainous rocks. All the while he continued to work on the tableaux. In 1985 he began the seminal painting *Pop* (1985–90), which was featured in the groundbreaking exhibition *Helter Skelter* at the Museum of Contemporary Art, Los Angeles, in 1992. Art critic Peter Plagens dubbed the piece the show's "lone adult soliloquy," and Peter Kosenko called it the "theme piece" of the exhibition.[4]

Foulkes can spend years or even a decade on a single painting, building up the tableaux with wood scraps, paint, and found objects such as bottles, guns, fabric, and animal skeletons. He continually alters the pieces over time with additions and subtractions. He cuts into the picture plane and then builds it out, so that elements that are actually on the surface appear to be deep back into the picture. It's unlike anything anyone else is doing, and the works are astonishing when viewed in person. He has always worked on his own in the studio, with no assistants or fabricators.

Sometimes the tableau paintings start out enormous, and he cuts them down over time: "Working with a dimensional painting, once you change one thing, you have to change the entire structure; any alterations have huge consequences." He's always looking at the outside and how that relates to the whole thing spatially. As he starts making it smaller, he squeezes things in and focuses on the plasticity, which makes things move. "It's that old push and pull—things that look like they're out are really back in, and it's about getting the light in the right place. It's both an object and something in deep space." Foulkes's work is rooted in abstract expressionism originally, so he thinks a lot about space—and he knows that he can actually get his pictures to look quite deep as long as he keeps pushing. "I'm trying to make the deepest paintings that anybody has ever seen: that's my primary purpose." Figures are also an important aspect of his work, which presents a further challenge in his quest for spatial depth and movement, since it's easier to achieve that depth with abstraction, but this hasn't deterred him. "I want to make it seem like it's moving, so it almost feels like it could come alive. There's something boring about dead, flat art."

This aspiration is exemplified in the monumental tableau painting *The Lost Frontier*, which Foulkes began working on in 1997. This epic, multidimensional painting could be a vision of the future or a depiction of a Wild West dreamland. We see death (a real cat skeleton), destruction, and desolation—with bits of trash and an oddly discarded television (it's real) and dying tree stumps—and the ominous landscape is populated by a seated Native American, a Mickey Mouse–headed pioneer woman cocking a rifle, and a self-portrait, but we see only Foulkes's back, almost as if we are put in his place, staring out at the wasteland. It is a memorial to the dream of the West that began to fall apart in the gold rush and has been steadily eroding since. It's a baffling vision: the cat skeleton is actually on the surface of the piece, but it appears to be deeply recessed and looks quite large. Another remarkable aspect of the dimensional works is that the light looks as if it is coming from within the painting rather than simply coming from above.

Foulkes built an entirely new structure for the tableau *Deliverance* (2007) just six weeks before it went on view: it had gotten so heavy that he couldn't lift it anymore. His obsession with Mickey and Disney continues in this painting, which depicts Mickey Mouse lying dead on the floor, with steam (a tuft of cotton) rising from a bullet hole in his stomach, and a portrait of Foulkes (with a chalk outline head) wielding the gun. *Deliverance* also features a small wax child's head peering through a window within the room depicted in the painting, which features a small landscape of a wave crashing against a rock. We see a child in a painting within a window in the room in the painting—yet another confounding optical marvel.

At this writing, Foulkes is working on what he refers to as the "bedroom painting," an emotionally charged picture of the artist and his second wife (from whom he is now divorced) in bed. Originally nine feet wide and now closer to four feet across, the painting began like most of his works do, with a self-portrait. Foulkes starts with himself and then works out from there. He is awake, sitting up, and his ex-wife lies asleep, cradling an egg. The picture encapsulates the anxiety of life, marriage, and family. He began the painting when he and his ex-wife were still married: "I knew that things were going wrong and tried to work it out in the painting rather than with her."

After the success of *Helter Skelter*, Foulkes was pressured to keep up the momentum and sell work, so in 1994 he reluctantly showed the bedroom painting at Patricia Faure Gallery in Santa Monica. He pulled it out a week later, embarrassed because he knew it wasn't finished. It wasn't what he wanted it to be; it didn't have the depth. The work has plagued him ever since: he stopped working on it after the show in 1994 and then worked on it again for about a year and then left it untouched until 2008. Finding his own image staring him down every day has forced him to face his demons: "It's opening a wound, but it's a good thing. The hard part is making it look like me now."

Foulkes's music is as important to him as his art. He stopped playing music seriously after he left the army and got back into it about ten years later. He played in a rock band for a short while, but he was much more interested in jazz, so in 1973 he started his own band, Llyn Foulkes and the Rubber Band. Nine months later they appeared on *The Tonight Show* with Johnny Carson. He finally gave up the band around 1977 and began building his one-man-band machine, which he completed in 1979. It's a spectacular red contraption equipped with around thirty-five bulb horns, three octaves of animal bells, drums, a xylophone, organ pipes, and a string bass (the artist plays the latter two instruments with his feet). For Foulkes, music doesn't have the angst that art does, and he has more freedom to improvise, plus he gets instant feedback from the audience and the practices benefit each other. "When I get better on the machine or make some move in the painting, I make a big move in the music."

Foulkes perseveres in spite of himself; he never compromises his integrity and always says what's on his mind. He is a true Los Angeles legend, an artist who unabashedly forges his own path and embraces his vision wholeheartedly. "I always had such deep feelings about Los Angeles.... A lot of my songs are about L.A. My music is about L.A. My paintings are all about L.A. It's like I should be here."[5]

NOTES

Unless otherwise noted, all quotations from the artist are from conversations with the author.

1. In 1961, under the guidance of Walt Disney and Roy O. Disney, Chouinard Art Institute merged with the Los Angeles Conservatory of Music to form California Institute of the Arts.

2. The notebook introduction explained: "Everyone knows how strong the 'gang' instinct is in children. The Mickey Mouse Club is unique in that it furnishes entertainment of the most popular nature (stage and screen) and at the same time, implants beneficial principles, the latter so completely shorn of any suggestions of 'lessons' of lecturing, that children absorb them almost unconsciously."

3. The photographs with white paint obscuring the subjects' faces were inspired by Willem de Kooning's *Merritt Parkway* (1959), with its big white splash of paint, as well as Emerson Woelffer's paintings.

4. Plagens and Kosenko cited by Howard Singerman, "Howard Singerman on Pop Noir," *Artforum* 43 (October 2004): 126.

5. Oral history interview with Llyn Foulkes, conducted by Paul Karlstrom, June 25, 1997–December 2, 1998, Archives of American Art, Smithsonian Institution, http://www.aaa.si.edu/collections/oralhistories/tranSCRIPTs/foulke97.htm.

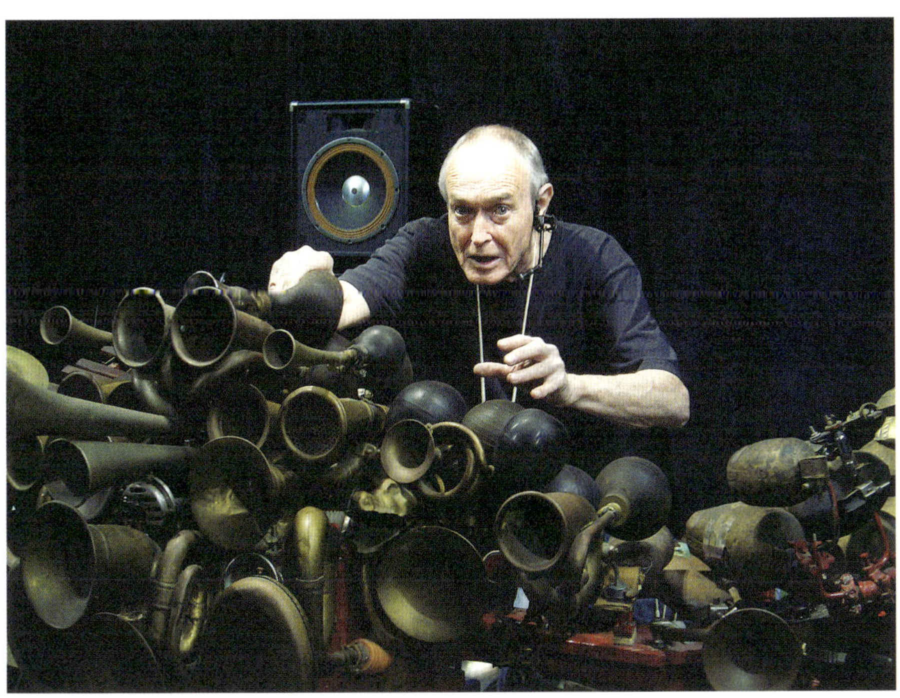

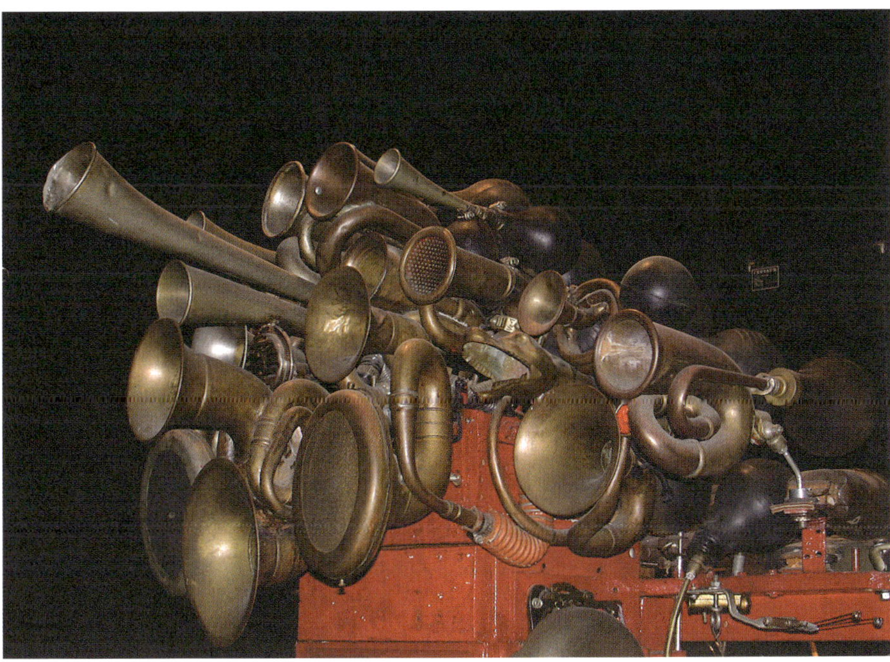

Top: Llyn Foulkes Live at the Church of Art, 2008.
Bottom: Llyn Foulkes's machine at the Church of Art, 2008.

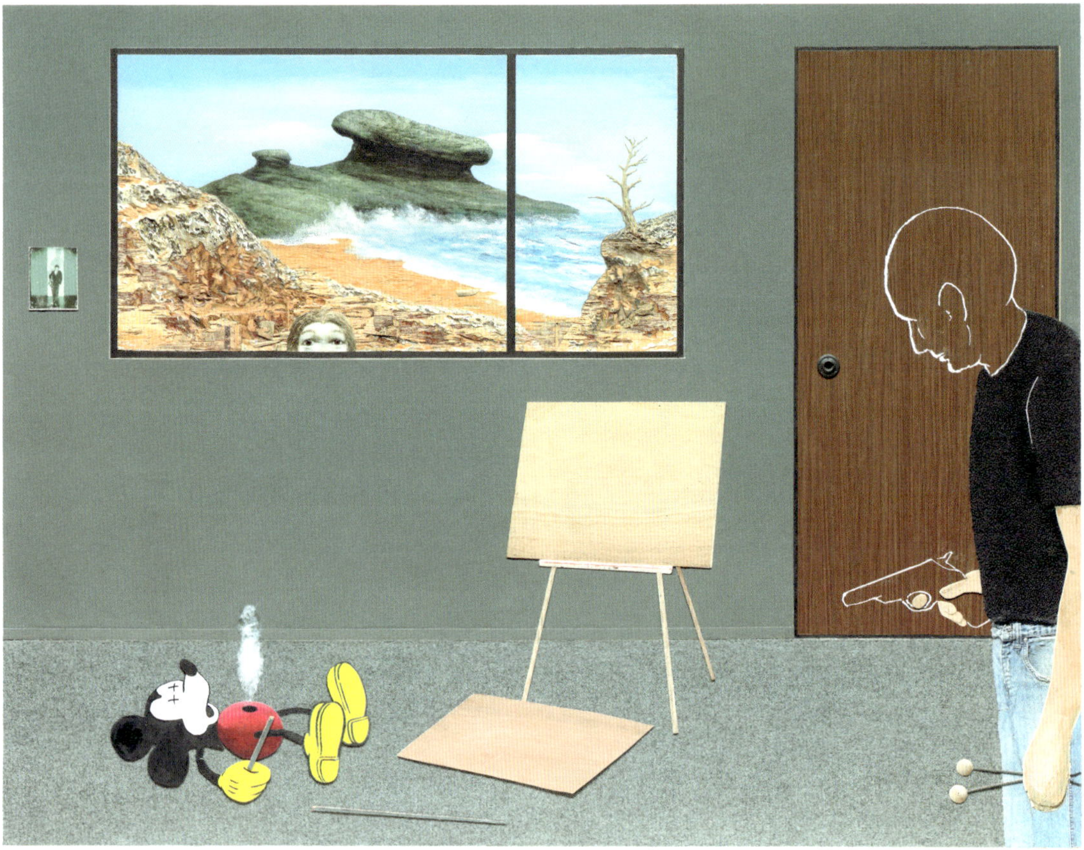

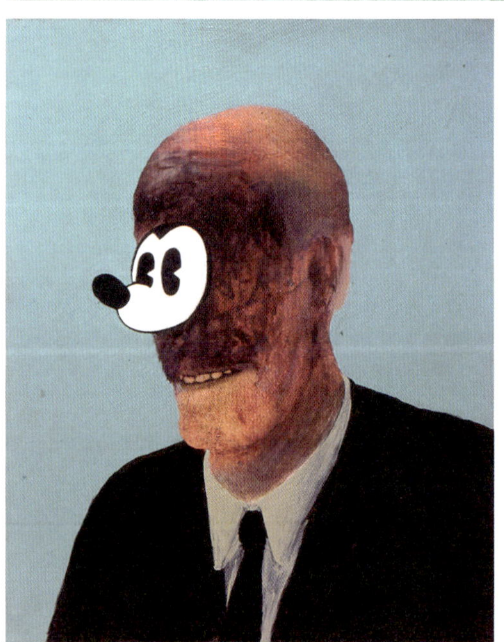

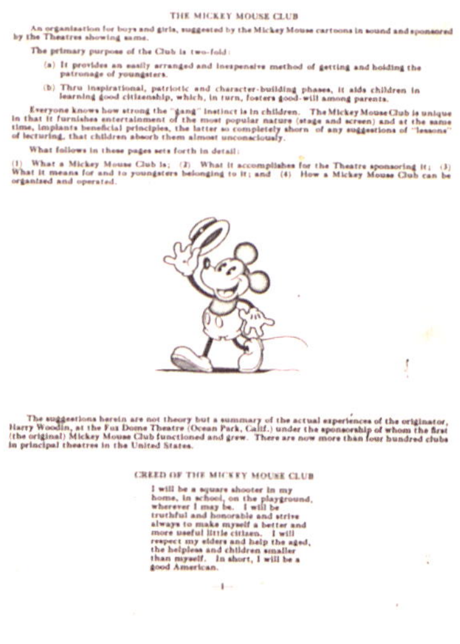

THE MICKEY MOUSE CLUB

An organization for boys and girls, suggested by the Mickey Mouse cartoons in sound and sponsored by the Theatres showing same.

The primary purpose of the Club is two-fold:

(a) It provides an easily arranged and inexpensive method of getting and holding the patronage of youngsters.

(b) Thru inspirational, patriotic and character-building phases, it aids children in learning good citizenship, which, in turn, fosters good-will among parents.

Everyone knows how strong the "gang" instinct is in children. The Mickey Mouse Club is unique in that it furnishes entertainment of the most popular nature (stage and screen) and at the same time, implants beneficial principles, the latter so completely shorn of any suggestions of "lessons" of lecturing, that children absorb them almost unconsciously.

What follows in these pages sets forth in detail:

(1) What a Mickey Mouse Club is; (2) What it accomplishes for the Theatre sponsoring it; (3) What it means for and to youngsters belonging to it; and (4) How a Mickey Mouse Club can be organized and operated.

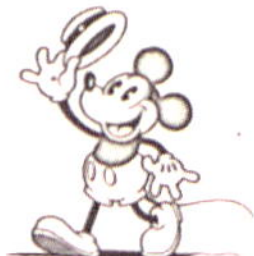

The suggestions herein are not theory but a summary of the actual experiences of the originator, Harry Woodin, at the Fox Dome Theatre (Ocean Park, Calif.) under the sponsorship of whom the first (the original) Mickey Mouse Club functioned and grew. There are now more than four hundred clubs in principal theatres in the United States.

CREED OF THE MICKEY MOUSE CLUB

I will be a square shooter in my home, in school, on the playground, wherever I may be. I will be truthful and honorable and strive always to make myself a better and more useful little citizen. I will respect my elders and help the aged, the helpless and children smaller than myself. In short, I will be a good American.

—1—

Top: *Deliverance*, 2007. Mixed media. 72 x 84 in. (182.9 x 213.4 cm). Courtesy the artist and Kent Gallery, New York.
Bottom left: *Portrait of Walt Disney*, 2004–5. 20 x 16 in. (50.8 x 40.6 cm). Private collection, Chicago.
Bottom right: First page from the 1934 Mickey Mouse Club handbook.

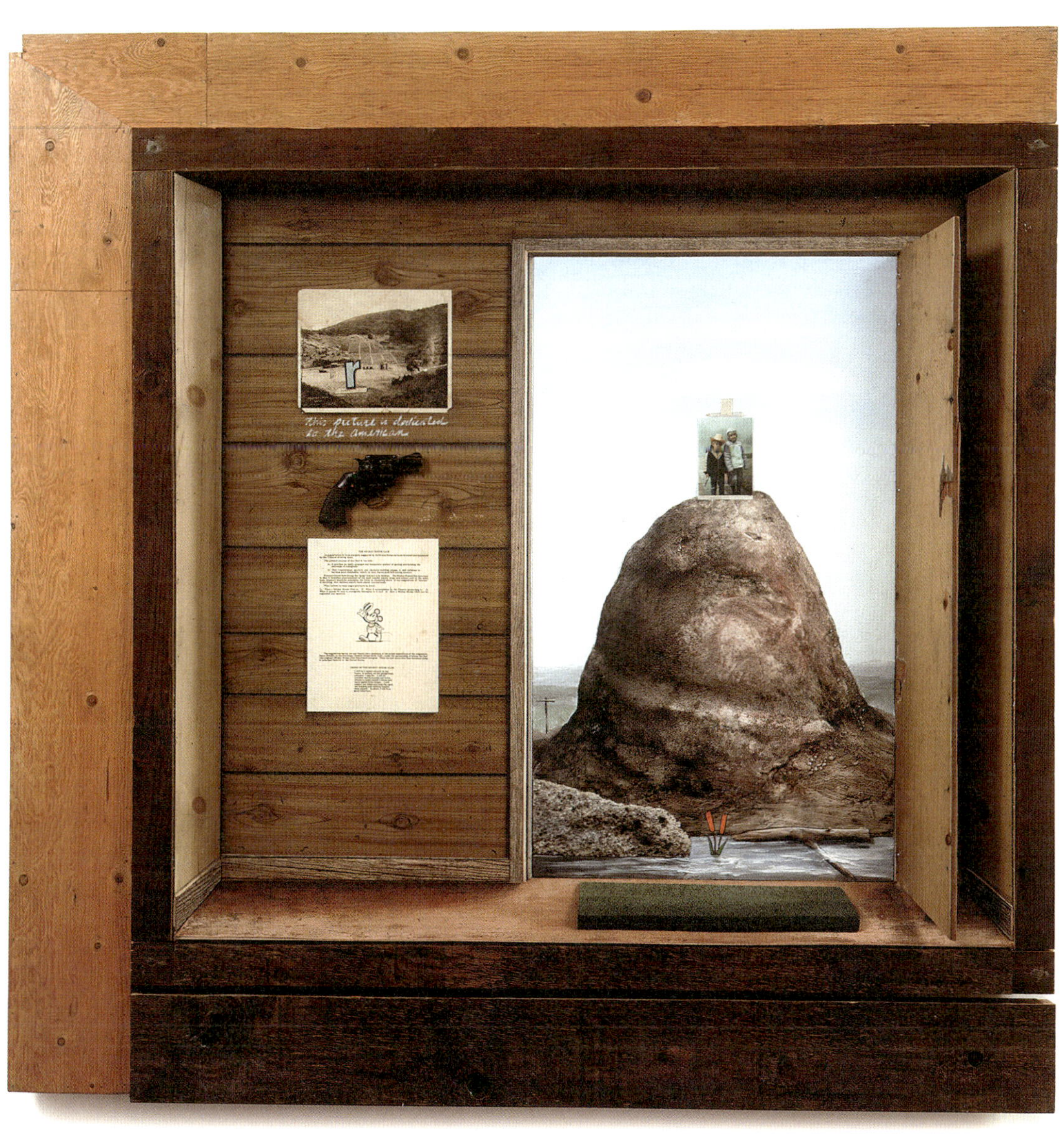

Made in Hollywood, 1983. Mixed media. 66 5/8 x 66 7/8 x 7 1/4 in. (169.2 x 169.9 x 18.4 cm). Museum of Contemporary Art San Diego; Promised gift of the Ruth Gribin Non-Exempt QTip Marital Trust; courtesy Gribin Family Trust.

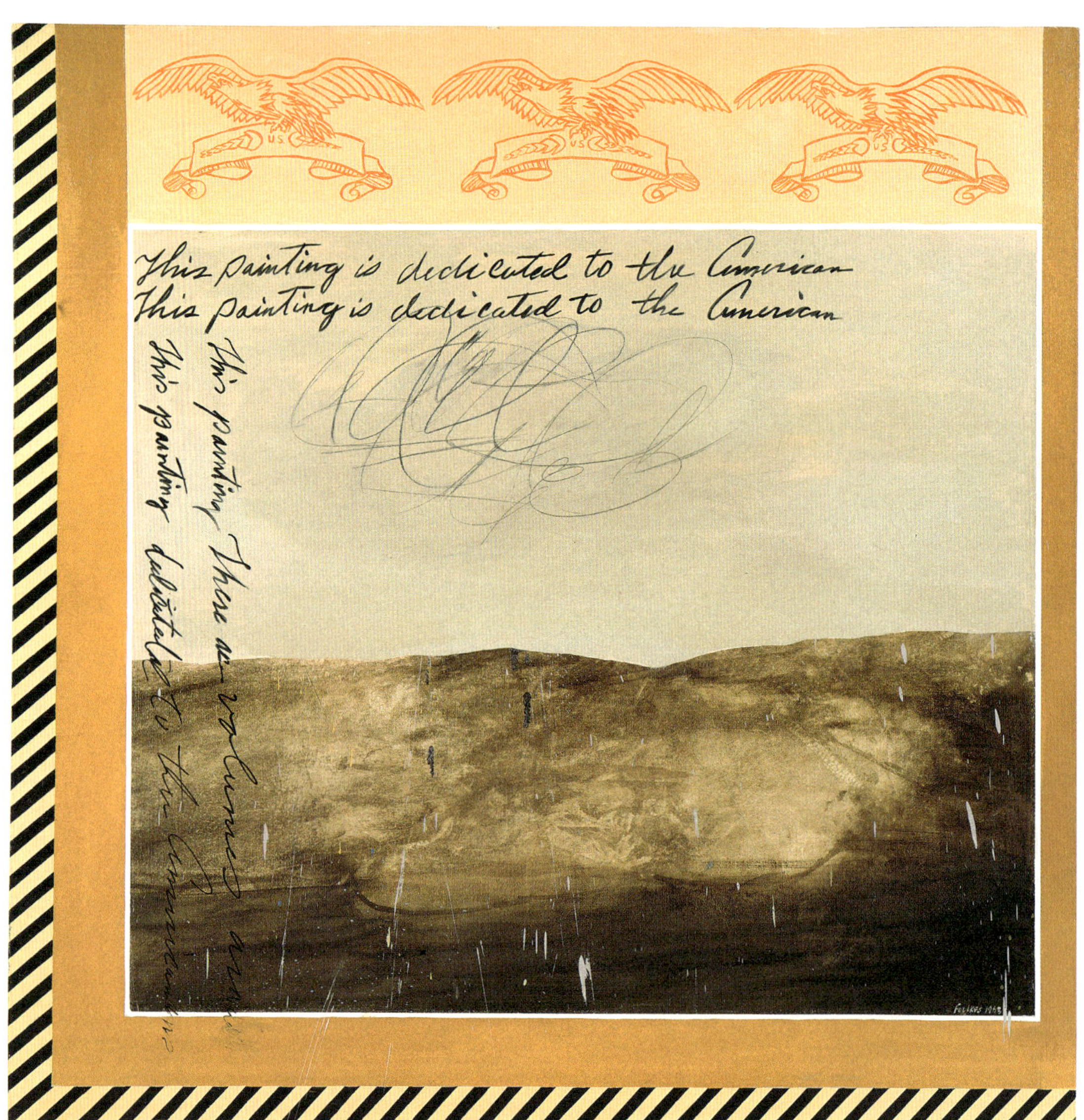

Death Valley, USA, 1963. Oil on canvas. 65 1/2 x 64 3/4 in. (166.4 x 164.5 cm). Betty and Monte Factor Family Collection.

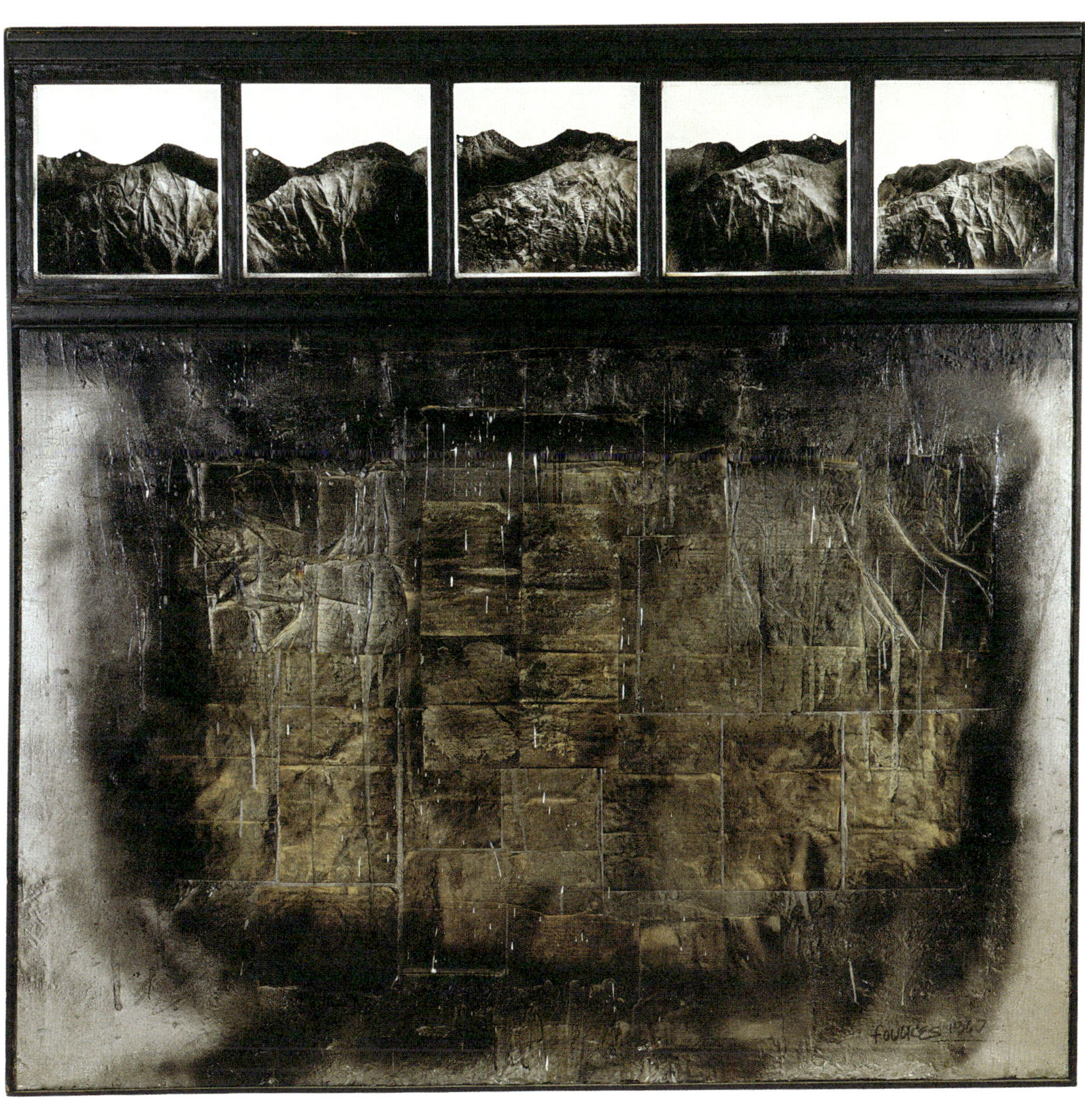

Geography Lesson, 1961. Oil and collage on canvas and Masonite. 64 x 66 1/2 in. (162.6 x 168.9 cm). Diana Zlotnick, Los Angeles.

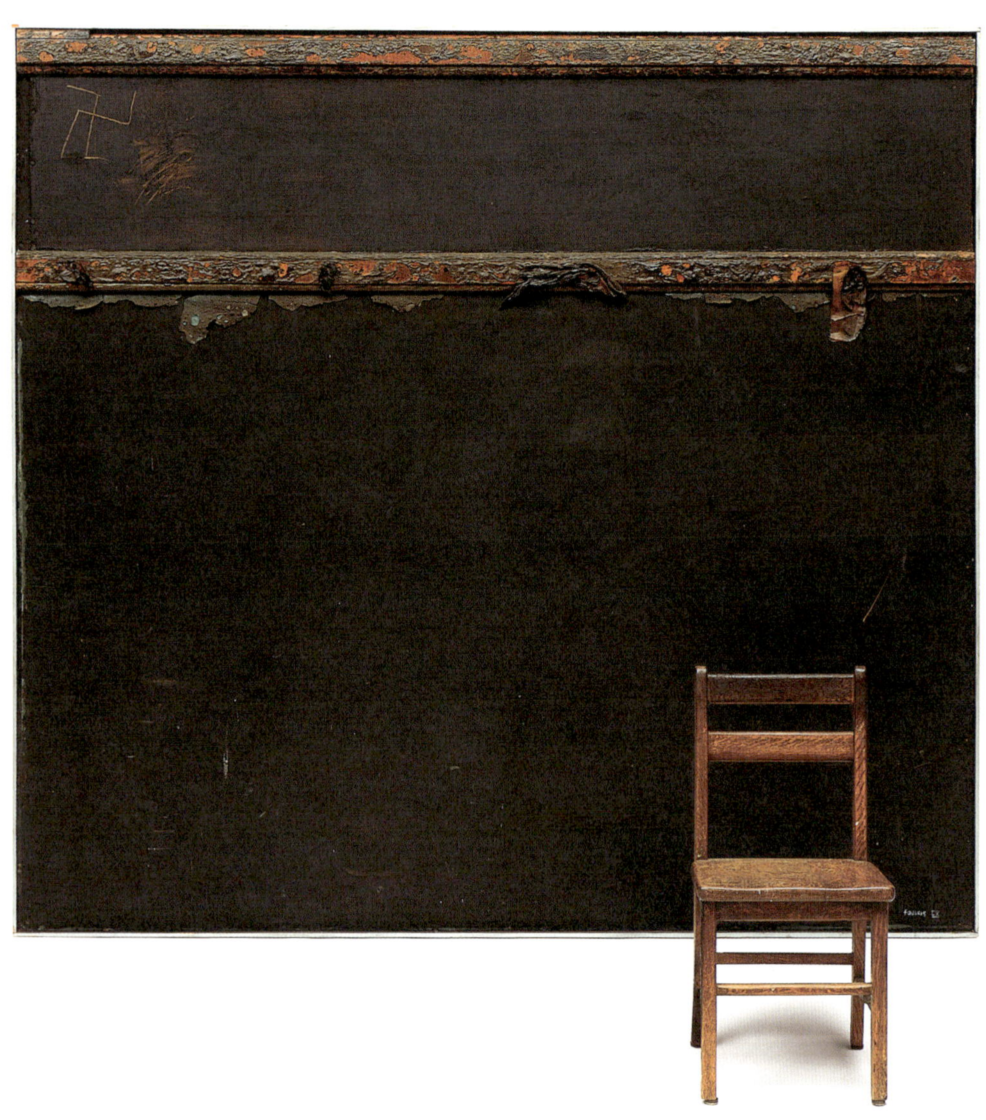

In Memory of St. Vincent School, 1960. Assemblage: oil, charred wood, and plasticized ashes on blackboard, with chair. Blackboard: 66 x 72 1/4 in. (167.6 x 183.5 cm); chair: 26 1/4 x 13 x 12 1/2 in. (66.7 x 33 x 31.8 cm). Norton Simon Museum; Gift of Dr. and Mrs. Harry Zlotnick.

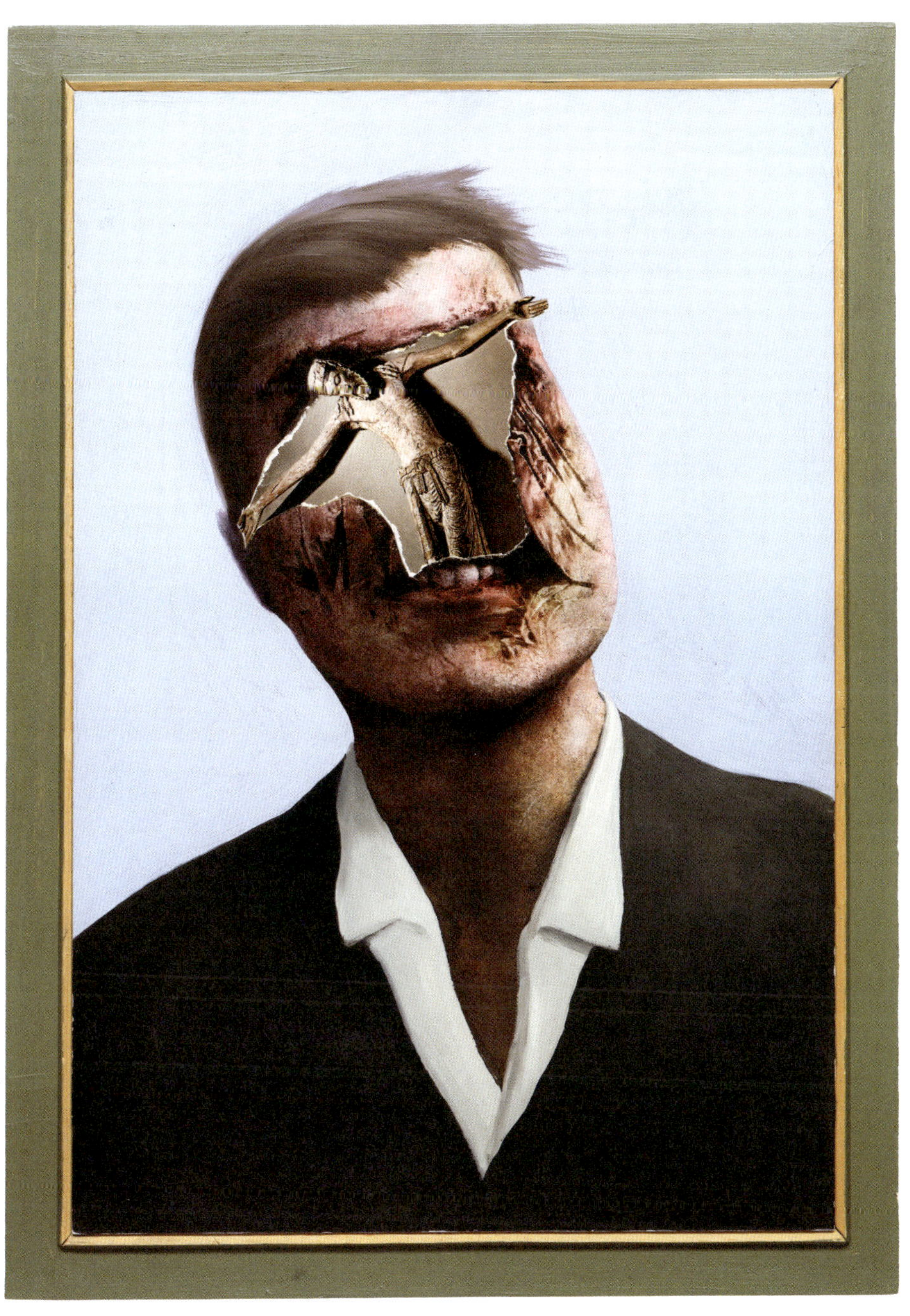

The Crucifixion, 1985. Mixed media. 29 x 21 in. (73.7 x 53.3 cm). Hammer Museum, Los Angeles; Purchase with funds provided in part by Jean Stein.

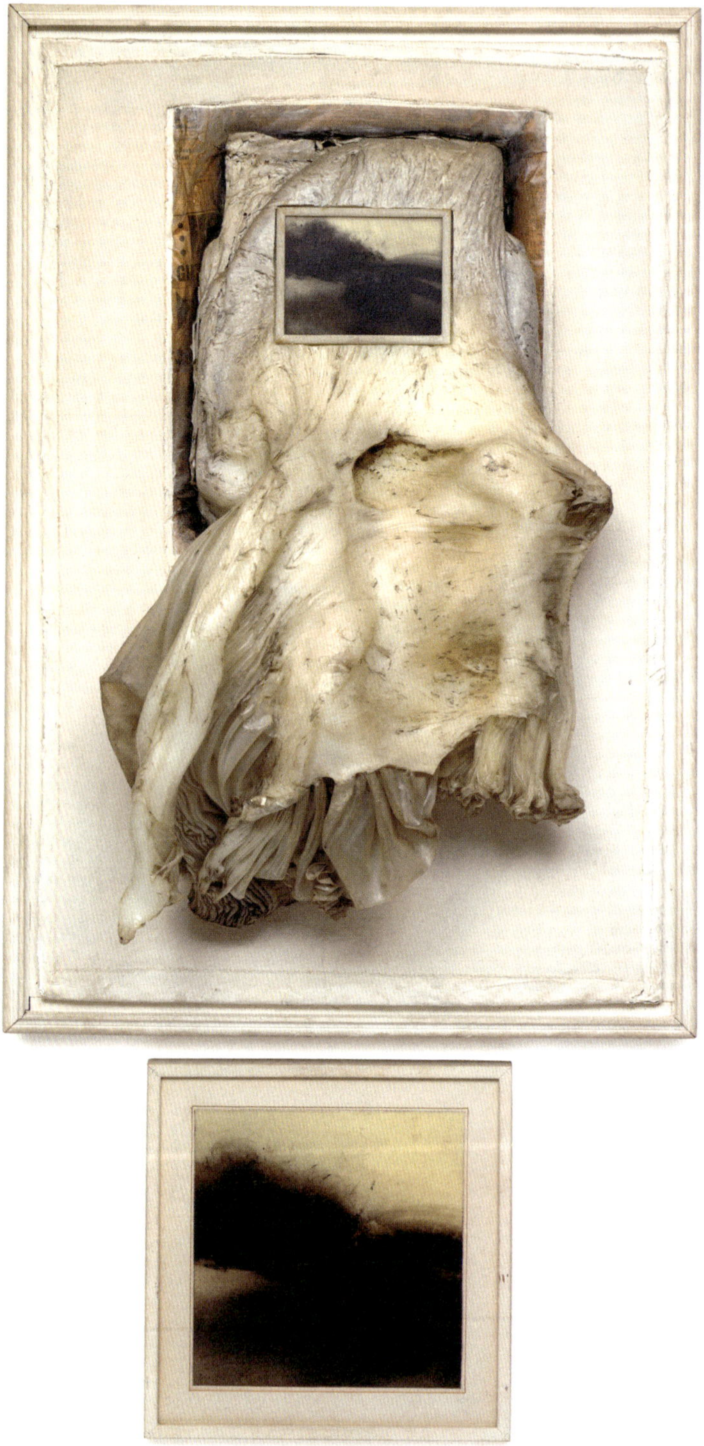

Flanders, 1961–62. Mixed media. Top part: 54 x 36 x 14 in. (137.2 x 91.4 x 35.6 cm); bottom part: 16 x 15 3/4 in. (40.6 x 40 cm). Collection of Ernest and Eunice White.

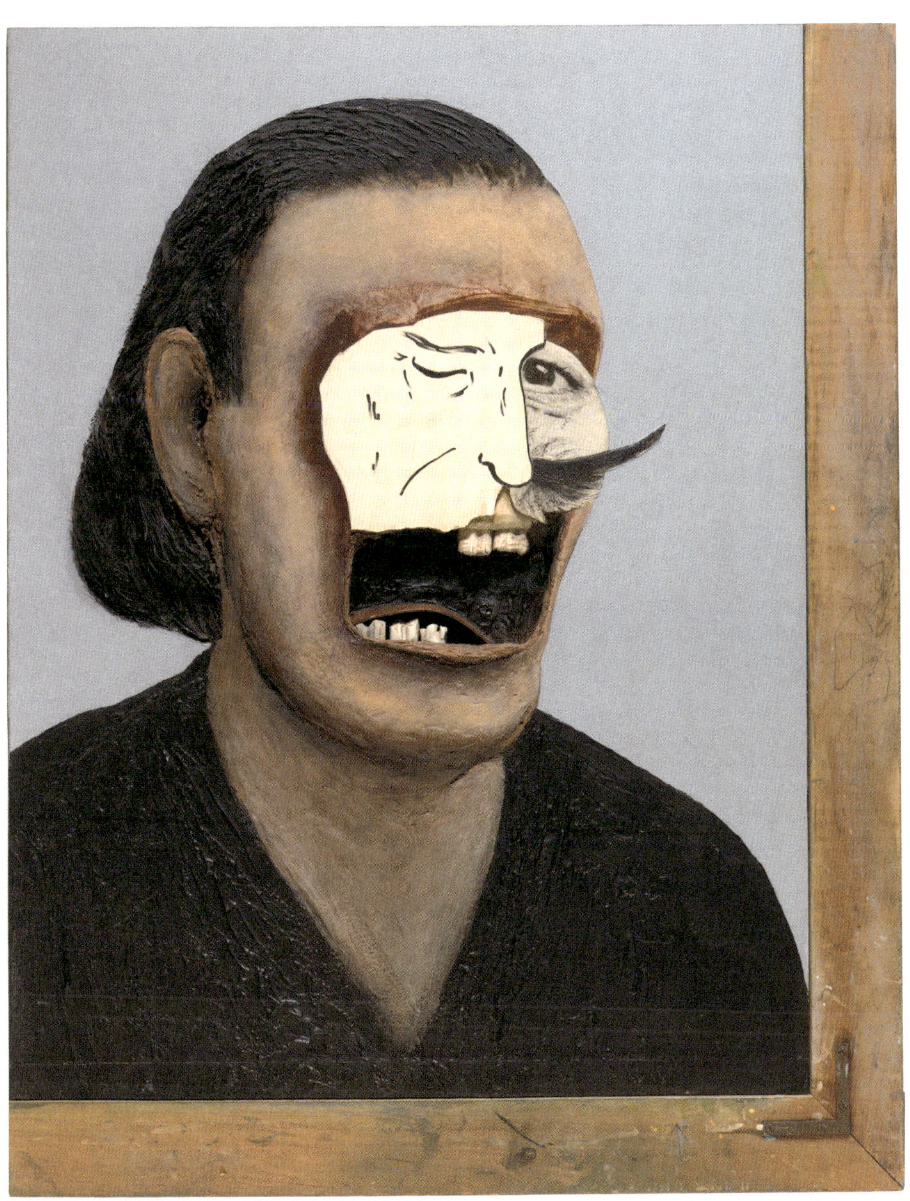

Dali and Me, 2006. Mixed media. 33 x 26 in. (83.8 x 66 cm). The Collection of Patrick and Soo Jin Jeong-Painter.

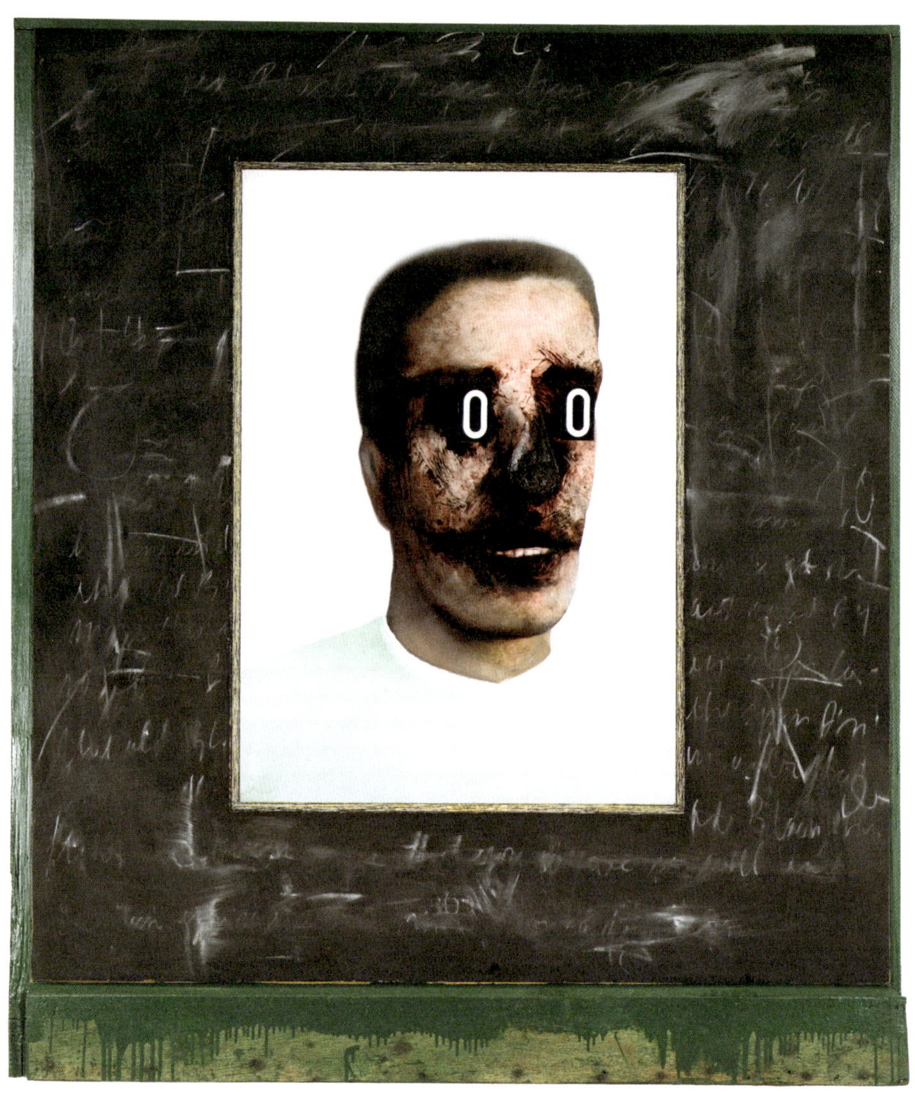

That Old Black Magic, 1985. Mixed media on board. 67 x 57 in. (170.2 x 144.8 cm). Laguna Art Museum Collection; Gift of Ruth and Murray Gribin.

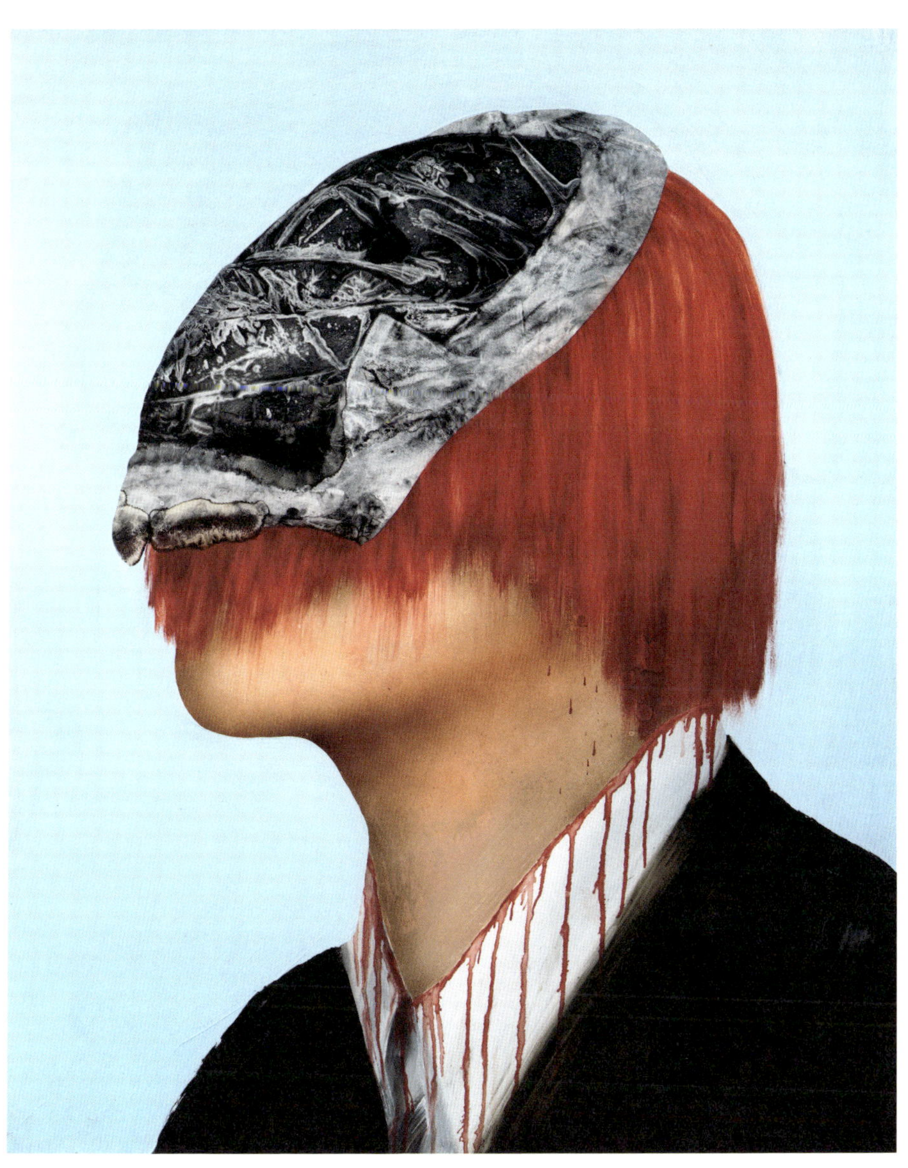

Who's on Third? 1971–73. Oil on canvas. 60 x 50 in. (152.4 x 127 cm). Jones/Faulkner Collection, Chicago; courtesy the artist and Kent Gallery, New York.

Julie Becker

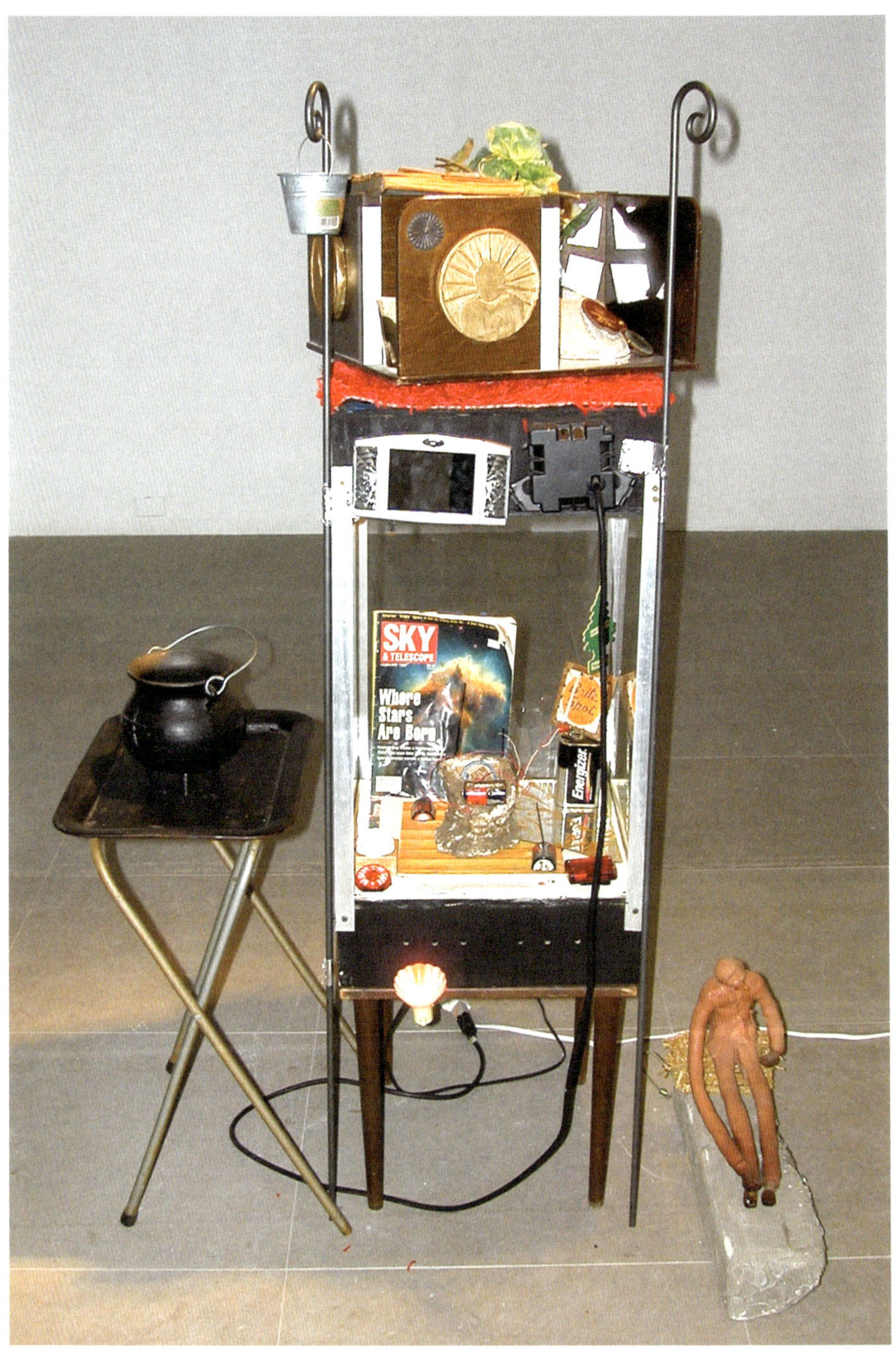

Homemade Microphone, 2004. Mixed media. 60 x 45 x 28 in. (152.4 x 114.3 x 71.1 cm). Courtesy Tim Nye, New York.

If she wasn't an artist, Julie Becker might have been an astronaut. She combines a sense of magical wonder with a capacity for complete absorption, and she focuses on a project or idea as if it's a mission to the moon. Her drawings, sculptures, installations, films, and photographs testify to her rare ability to evoke in people the desire to transcend their circumstances and step into another dimension. She soaks up all the solitude and unrivaled focus that come from working in the same room day after day, watching the same thing over and over, and spins it into a fragile paradise.

Becker concocts elaborate scenarios populated by odd and engaging characters, the types of characters that come only to the minds of those who carefully watch and digest other people's habits, tendencies, and actions. She is extraordinarily sensitive to the people and environments she encounters. Her work reflects her belief that "the history of recent art could be told as the transformation of the artist's presence from belonging to a community with shared assumptions to one of idiosyncrasy (or even obsession, serious obsession) and a sense of quirkiness, ranging along a scale from hilarity to deep depression."[1]

For her massive installation *Researchers, Residents, a Place to Rest* (1993–96), Becker invented mysterious fictional characters and then imagined intimate details, habitats, and histories for them. The installation, which was also her graduate thesis project, includes a full-scale version and a model-size version of several connected rooms and apartments. She was "looking for structure in all of that open (and closed) space.... It kept growing from there."[2] Each of the various environments and interiors in *Researchers* is devised to fit a specific character—except the waiting room, which could belong to a psychiatrist, a real estate agent, or a concierge (a variety of desk plates allow for the designation to change). The doubling that occurs with the two versions (model and life-size) adds to the confusion and disorientation of the work. She explains: "In my work I try to mimic the process of how we think and how we integrate ourselves into the world so that we can see without impediments. Locations taken out of books and movies, characters abstracted from real life, all of them interact within these walls and invite the viewer to travel with them. I hope that my work moves people—from one place to another! The viewer, by way of being in the installation, becomes a character too."[3]

Becker weaves stories of lives lived in a parallel world, offering escape fantasies and dreams and hope and a tinge of horror if you go down the wrong path. *Leda and the Swan* (1993/2000), a video she made in collaboration with her father (who provides the narration), features an angelic young girl wandering through a forest. A narrator reads a text compiled from the writings of Vladimir Nabokov and other sources. She recalls "being very interested in creating new ways of using preexisting films out there, editing them into something extremely far from their origins, allowing for new ways of presenting dialogue." The video continues from the forest to other dreamlike worlds, again illustrating the artist's interest in journeys of the mind and body.

Like a modern-day shaman, Becker leads us by the hand through her own heavenly (or hellish) world. She refers to the artist's imagination as a disease, as if it's something she's been cursed with. Or maybe it's something she just can't shut off. For the installation piece *Golden Force Field* (1999), she imagined a "force field" of creativity with protective properties not unlike those of the sun. The space in which the force field is active is designated by gold decals placed on the four walls of the room. The piece, which also includes written instructions, calls for a considerable amount of faith on the part of the viewer. Becker hopes that "the need for the 'truth' will overwhelm [viewers] and challenge the very existence of the 'golden force field' altogether."[4] If it works, viewers will see the force field spanning the room. In all her work, Becker aims to "transport viewers outside of themselves, to recognize a larger, more complex world."

Becker's interest in the life of the previous tenant of her apartment and his discarded possessions initiated the *(w)hole* project, which started in 2000 and includes a film, photographs, collages and drawings, models, and sculptures. She spent several years digging through the remnants of the man's belongings, which were abandoned in the apartment building's basement after his death: "No one ever came to collect [his] things. It's like he mattered to no one. He was about as invisible as a person could be. I guess I wanted to bring him to life again and ask him some questions... as well as honor him just for making it through life as long as he did." She makes abstract connections between this mysterious man's life and possessions and her own ambitions, ideas, and fantasies.

The film that is part of the *(w)hole* project, *Bank Building with Music* (2002), is a raw depiction of the bank building across the street from Becker's apartment building, which she stared at daily. The film depicts a downward journey through a vertical tunnel. For a while she wanted to make a tunnel from a hole in her building's basement to the bank across the street. The film (and the tunnel plan) evokes the desire to hermit away and isolate oneself that comes from living in such a disparate, decentered city.

Another side effect of Becker's seclusion in the apartment building was a project that she referred to as "sky forecasting." She used to awaken before dawn and look out the window, trying to predict what color the sky would be each day: "I was hoping this could then be used as a tool if artists of all sorts needed the color of the sky to be particular.... I wasn't really thinking about what Photoshop could do—that would be cheating. I needed to know if it was even possible to predict this for real. I got it down to a pretty interesting science, though."

With its extended focus on a specific view, *Bank Building with Music* has that magic touch that Becker brings to everything she does. Even her simplest drawings are imbued with something fantastical, surreal, and mysterious. "I wasn't sure it was possible, but I remember standing in front of my window looking out at the city around five in the morning when I became transfixed by the connections of elements all round me. I challenged myself to create this experience. Now it's in bits and pieces and scattered all about. I didn't have enough to keep going, and it all came tumbling down." The *(w)hole* project consumed her life in almost every way, and at a certain point she became practically paralyzed and was unable to move forward with the work or begin a new project: "I entered a delirium of digression."[5] But it's out of such moments of frustration or stasis that new inspiration and revelation emerge, and Becker no doubt has much more magic to put out into the world in the future.

NOTES

1. Peter Wollen, "Julie Becker," *Afterall*, no. 2 (2000): 23.
2. Unless otherwise noted, all quotations from the artist are from conversations or e-mail correspondence with the author.
3. Bernhard Burgi, "Researchers, Residents, a Place to Rest: An Interview with Julie Becker," in *Researchers, Residents, a Place to Rest* (Zurich: Kunsthalle Zurich, 1997), 11–35.
4. Julie Becker, "Personal Notes for *Golden Force Field*," in *Peace* (Zurich: Migros Museum, 1999), 83.
5. Wollen, "Julie Becker," 26.

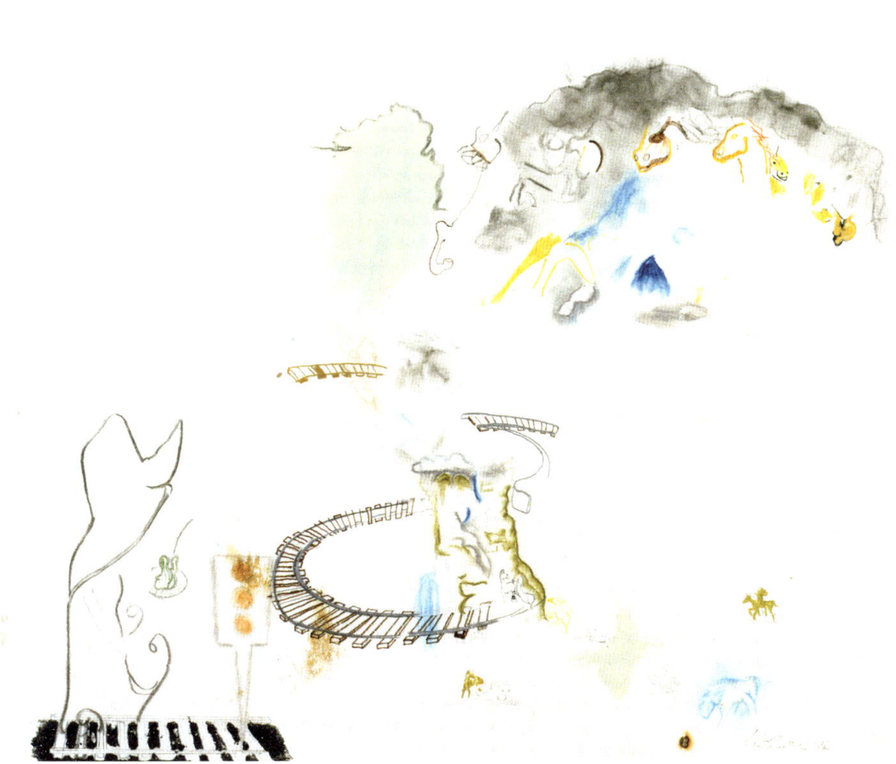

Untitled (Whole Series) (Apocalypse), 2001. Mixed media on paper. 17 3/4 x 23 1/4 in. (45.1 x 59.1 cm).
Courtesy Foundation 2021/Nyehaus, New York.

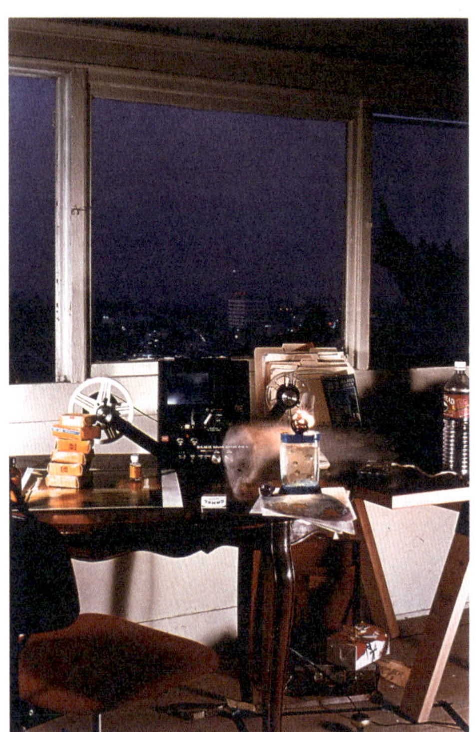

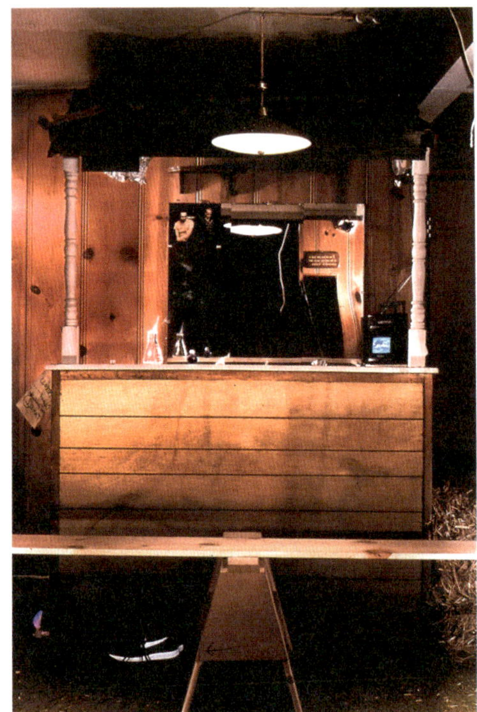

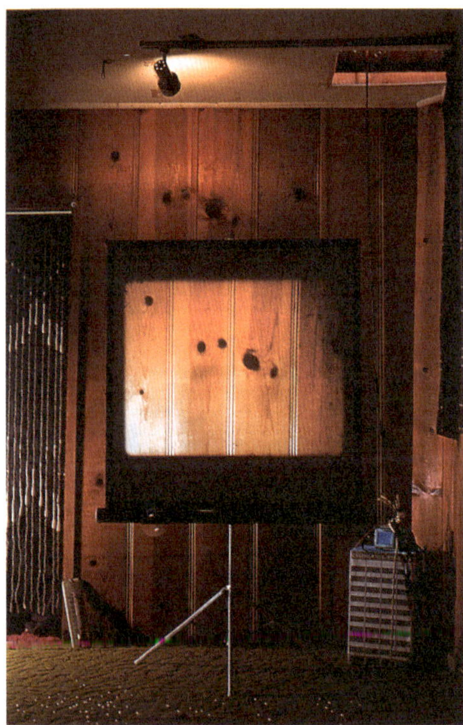

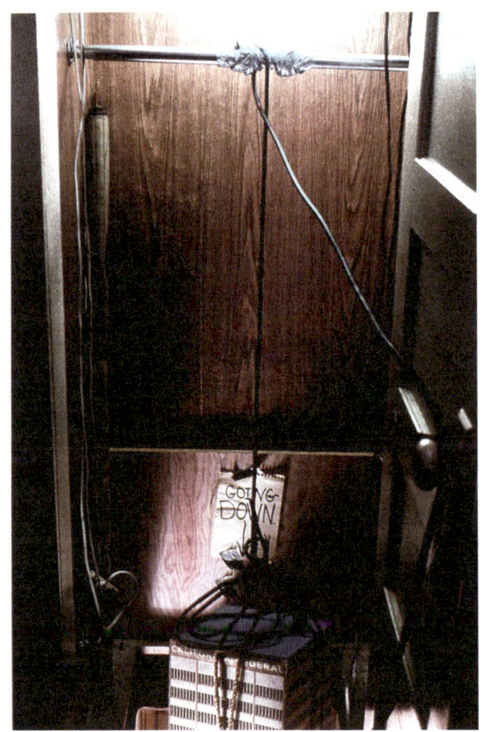

Left to right, top to bottom:
Whole (Projector), 1999. C-print on aluminum. 50 3/4 x 33 3/4 in. (128.9 x 85.7 cm). Courtesy Greene Naftali Gallery, New York.
Whole (Bar), 1999. C-print on aluminum. 50 3/4 x 33 3/4 in. (128.9 x 85.7 cm). Courtesy Greene Naftali Gallery, New York.
Whole (Screen), 1999. C-print on aluminum. 50 3/4 x 33 3/4 in. (128.9 x 85.7 cm). Courtesy Greene Naftali Gallery, New York.
Whole (Going Down), 1999. C-print on aluminum. 50 3/4 x 33 3/4 in. (128.9 x 85.7 cm). Courtesy Greene Naftali Gallery, New York.

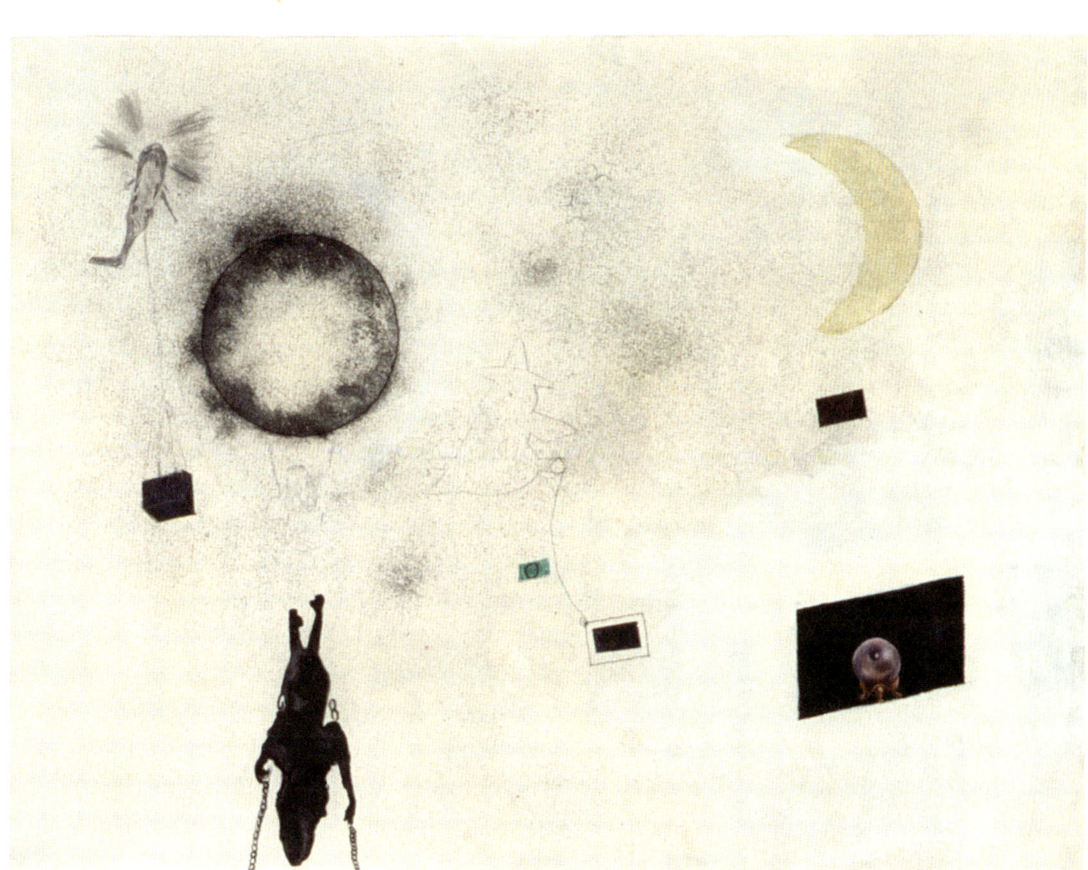

Untitled (Moon), 2003. Mixed media on paper. 17 x 23 in. (43.2 x 58.4 cm). Private collection, New York.

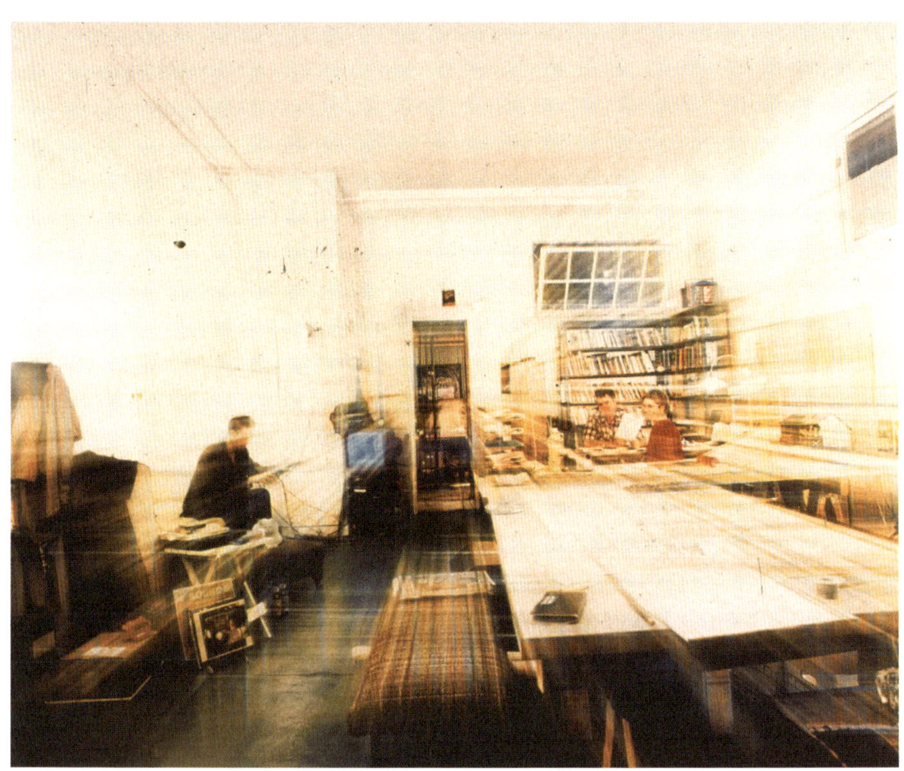

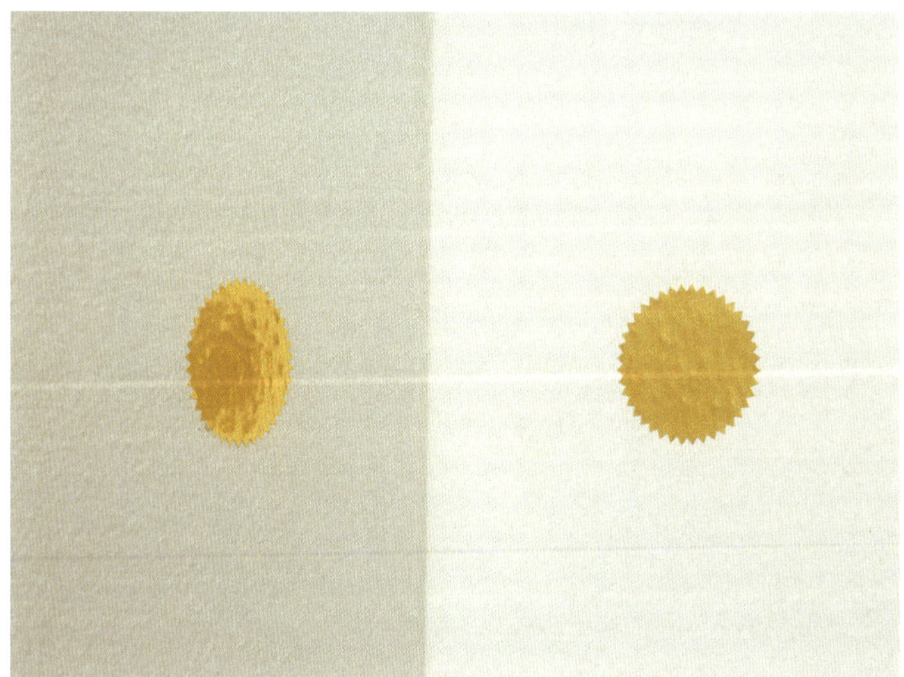

Top: *Golden Force Field*, 1999. C-print. 50 x 60 in. (127 x 152.4 cm). Courtesy the artist and Greene Naftali Gallery, New York.
Bottom: *Golden Force Field*, 1999 (detail). Installation view from the exhibition *Peace* at the Migros Museum für Gegenwartskunst, Zurich, 1999. Courtesy Greene Naftali Gallery, New York, and Migros Museum für Gegenwartskunst.

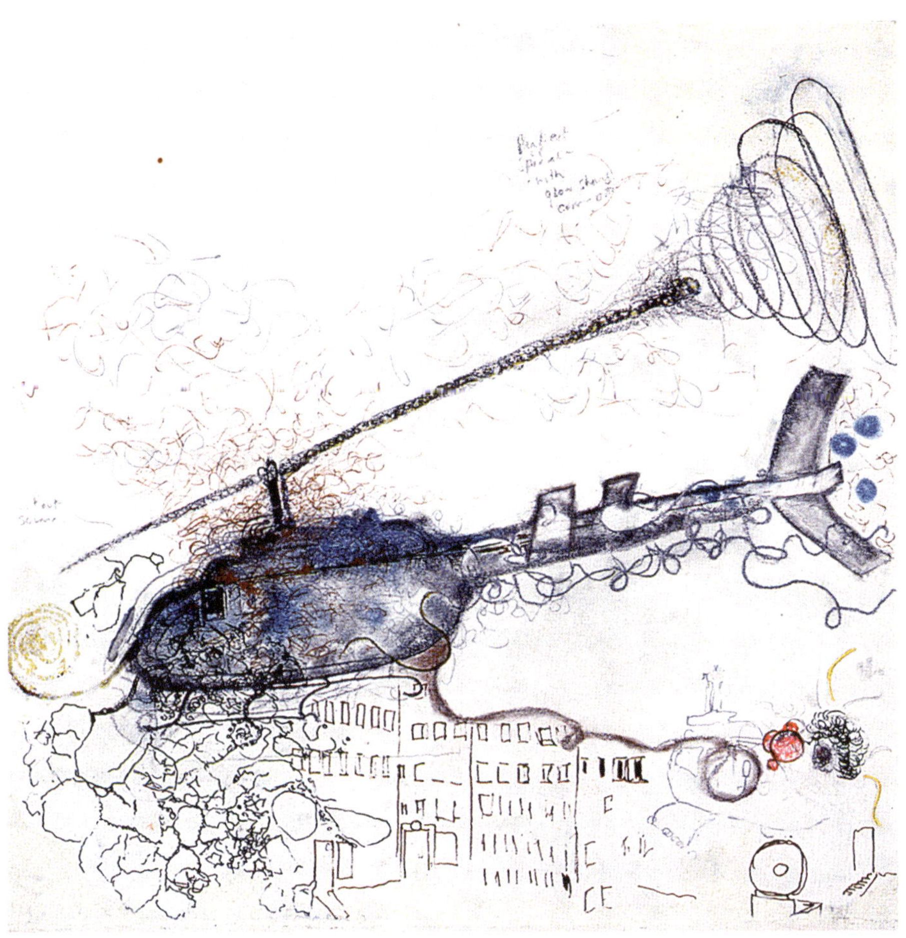

Helicopter, 1999. Ink, pencil, and mixed media on paper. 12 x 12 in. (30.5 x 30.5 cm). Courtesy Greene Naftali Gallery, New York.

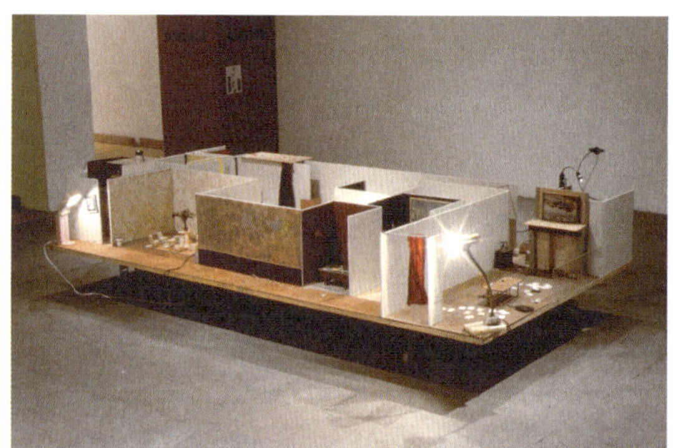

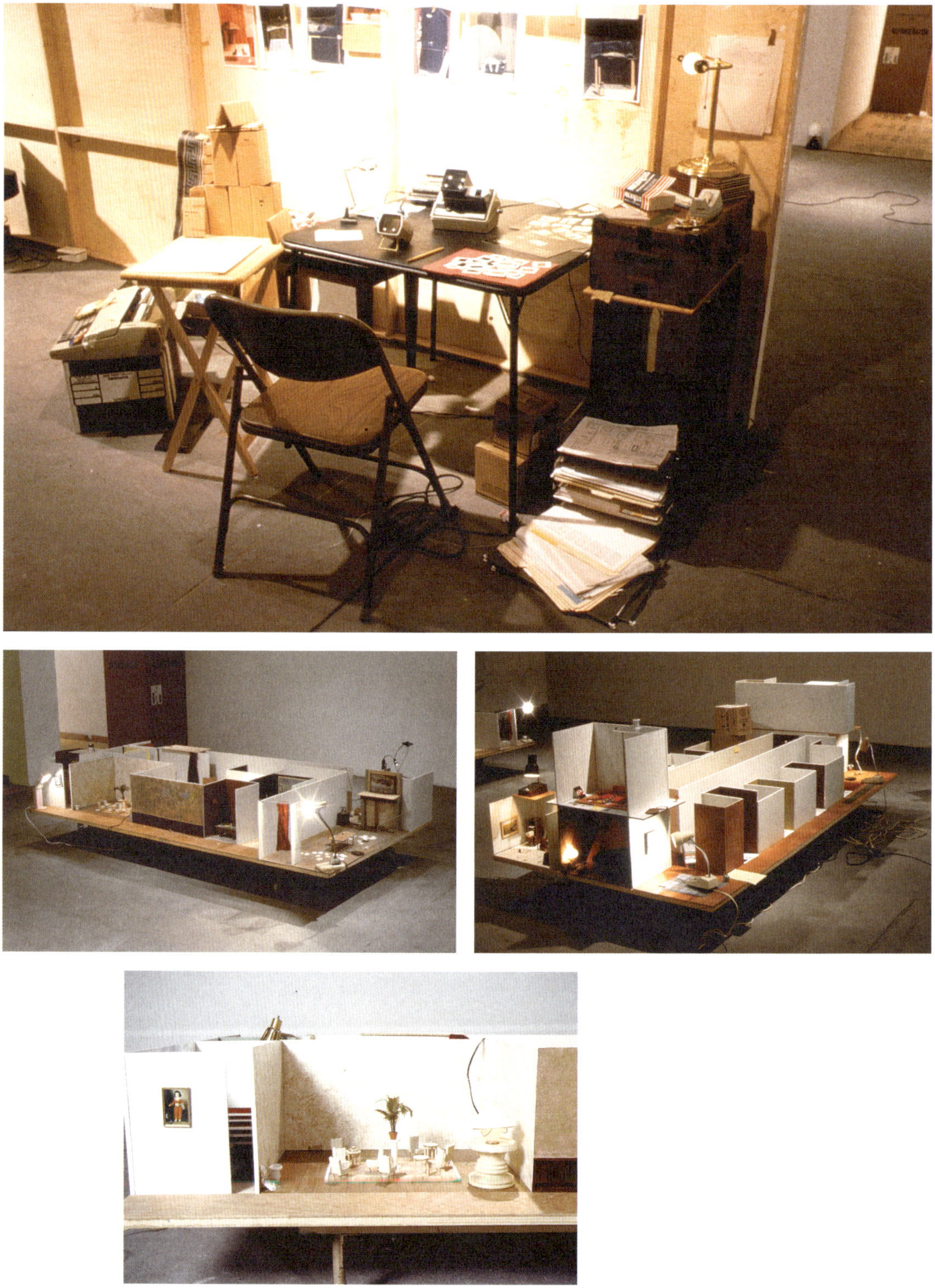

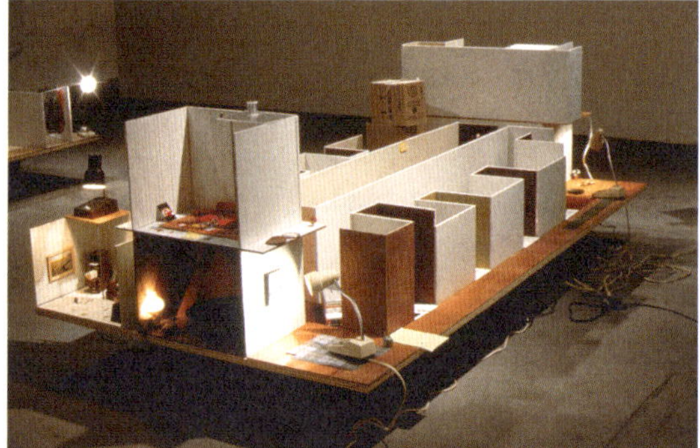

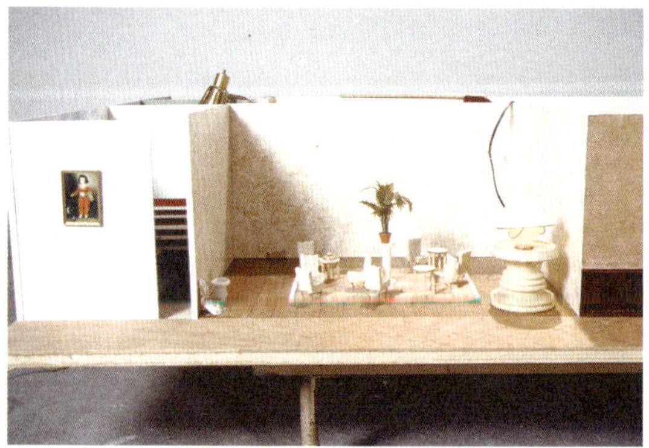

Researchers, Residents, a Place to Rest, 1993–96. Mixed-media installation. Dimensions variable. The Museum of Contemporary Art, Los Angeles; Gift of the Carol and Arthur Goldberg Collection in honor of, and kind affection for, Stuart Regen and Shaun Caley Regen. Installation view of life-size (top) and miniature (bottom) models, Kunsthalle Zürich, 1997.

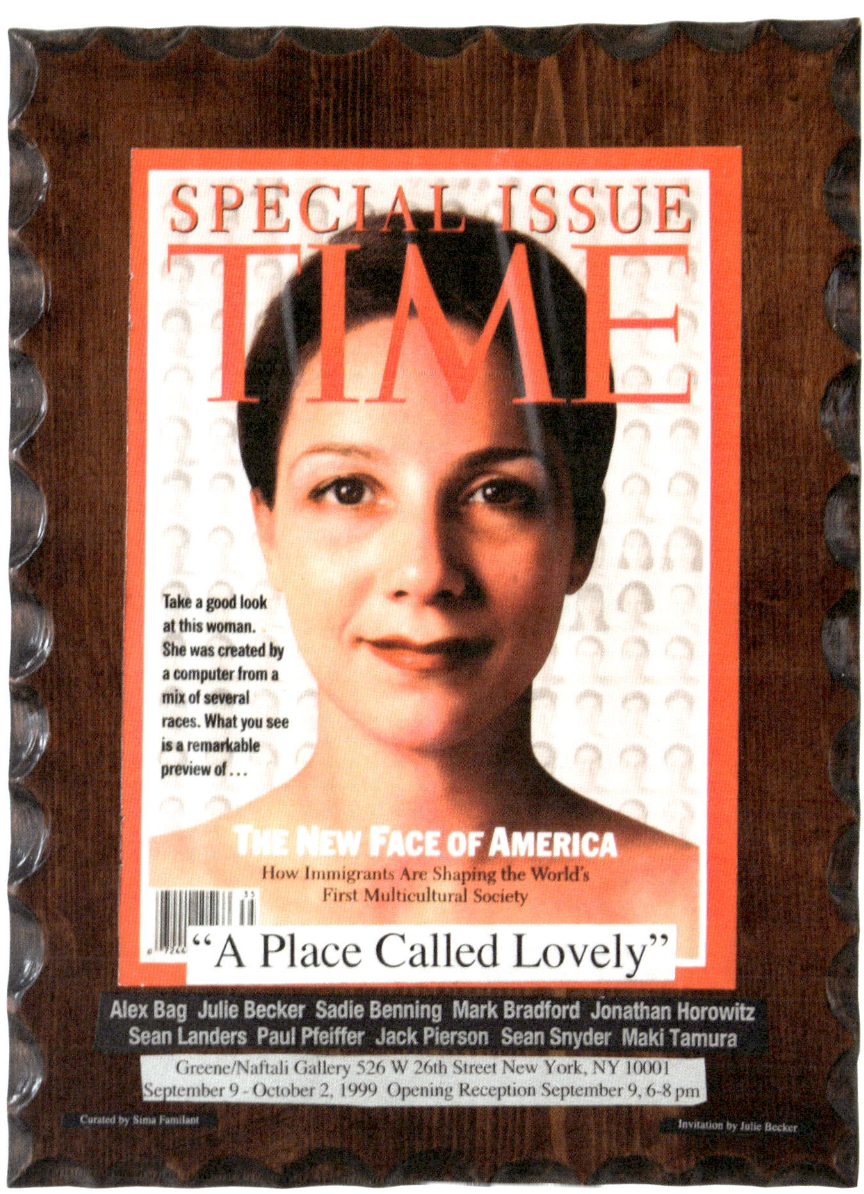

A Place Called Lovely, 1999. Mixed media. 15 x 11 in. (38.1 x 27.9 cm). Courtesy the artist and Greene Naftali Gallery, New York.

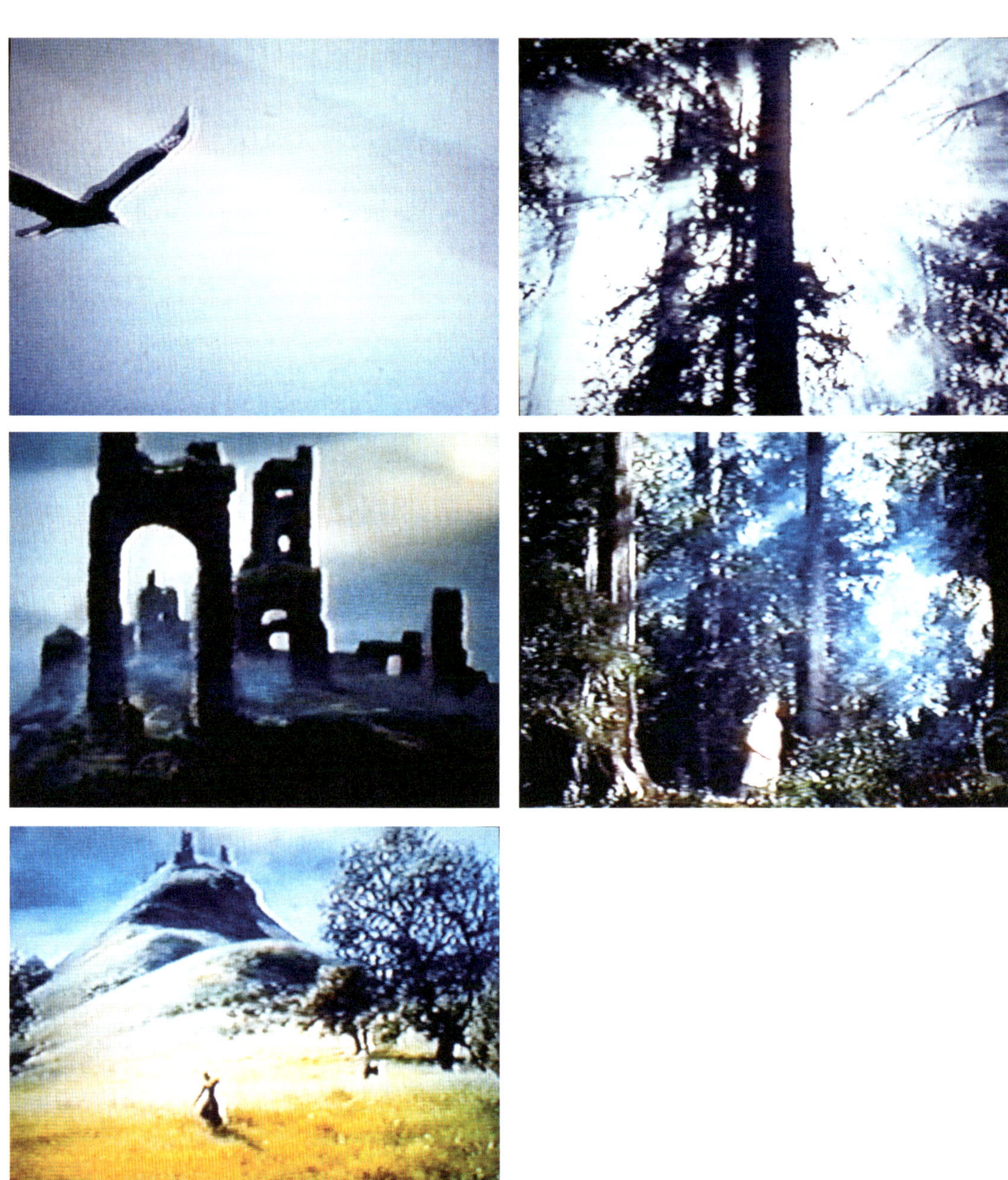

 Stills from *Leda and the Swan*, 1993/2000. Video, color, sound. 4:36 min. Courtesy Greene Naftali Gallery, New York.

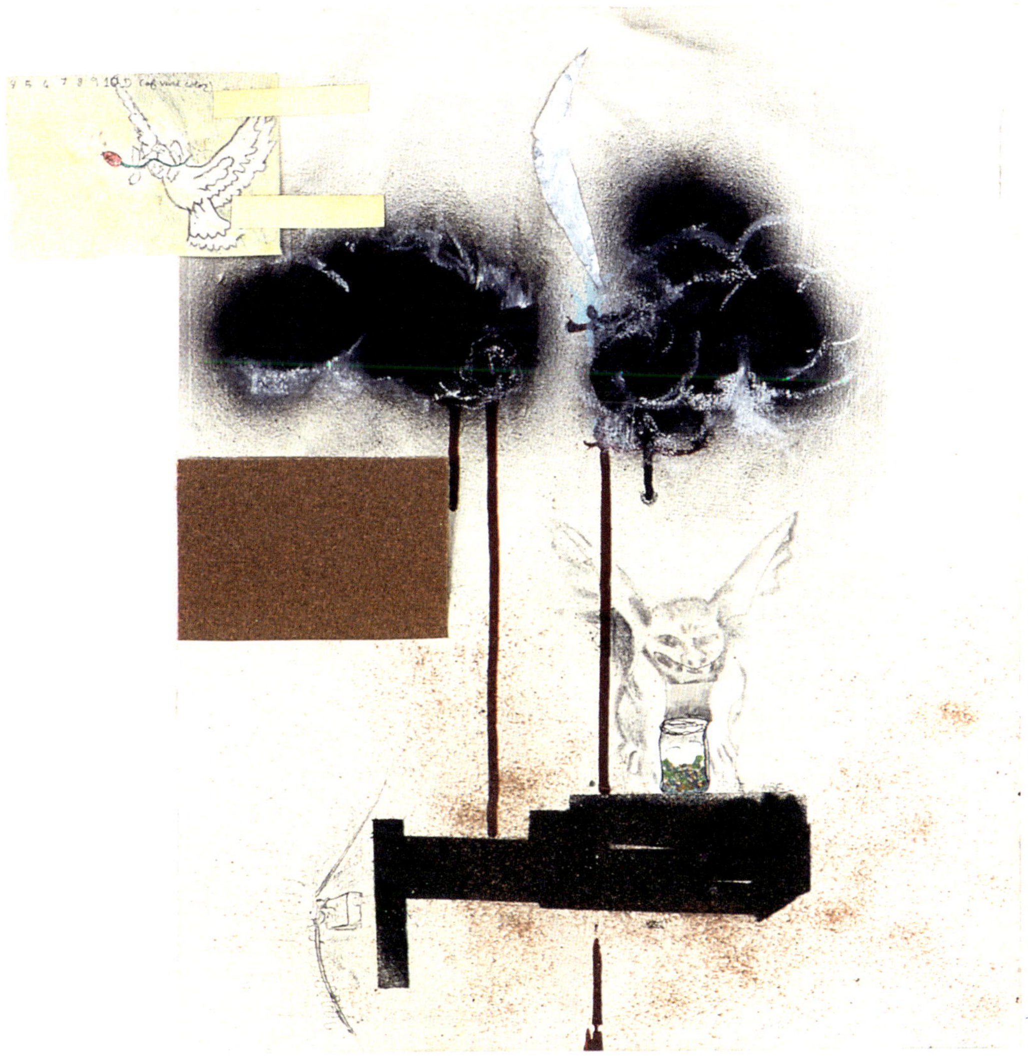

Money Changer, 2002. Mixed media on paper. 17 x 16 3/4 in. (43.1 x 42.6 cm). Private collection, New York.

Hirsch Perlman

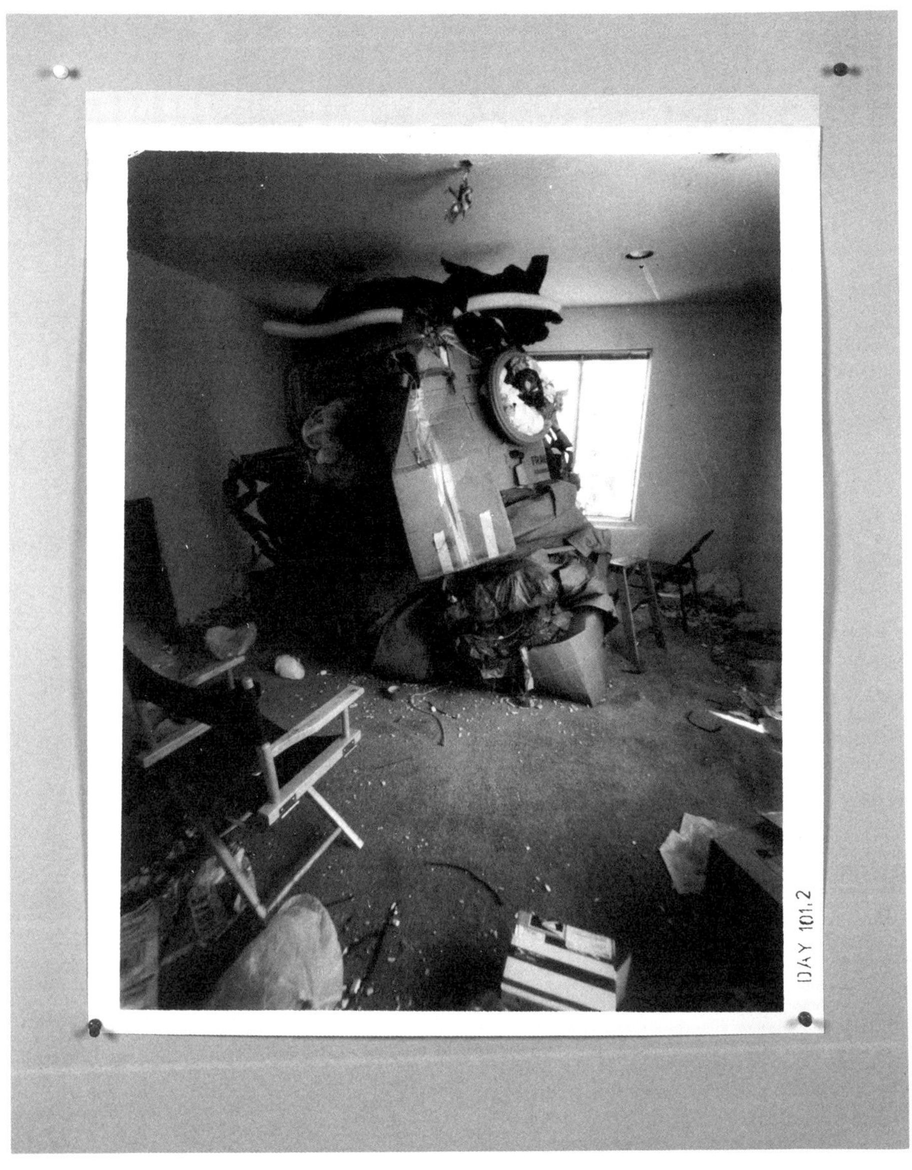

Day 101.2, 1998–2001. Gelatin silver print, vinyl, tape, pushpins, paint. 30 x 24 in. (76.2 x 61 cm). Courtesy the artist and Blum & Poe, Los Angeles.

I don't think the impulse to concoct meaning comes from the subject of the picture as much as it does from the affect of the picture. It's the affect that brings you back.

—Hirsch Perlman[1]

In his photographs, videos, text pieces, and other projects, Hirsch Perlman combines melancholy with what might be called optimistic confusion. The work is enigmatic, funny, and confounding all at once. "Something that seems to be more or less consistent in my work, at least since writing 'The Layman's Guide to Interrogation Techniques and Practices' in 1991, is a blurry threshold between whether I'm being serious and melancholy or absurd and cartoony.... I'm excited when I can't decide myself." Straddling that line between haunting and silly, his photographs capture mysterious landscapes, strange experiments, odd characters, and unexplained phenomena. They are documents of something that might have occurred yesterday or a century ago or tomorrow—it's the confusion or gray area that makes the work so compelling. He relies on the viewer's willingness to go along with him, to enter his world and let go of any preconceptions.

When Perlman moved to Los Angeles in the 1990s, he turned an extra room in his apartment into a make-believe world that nobody else was allowed to enter. He constructed a pinhole camera from discarded cardboard and began to use trash he had around his small carpeted studio—leftovers from delivery boxes, with V8 juice cans used as adornments—to build figures that eventually engulfed the entire room. These became "images of confinement, escape, impending doom, sexual curiosity, sadness, solitude, chaos, violence, intense silliness, being at the end of one's rope."[2] With the pinhole camera, he documented the robotlike cardboard figures' growth each day, creating a diary of the studio life, the time spent inventing and compiling and organizing imagination into object (the individual photos are titled by the days, e.g., *Day 71.6*, 1999–2000) until eventually he destroyed the creatures, reducing them to a compressed pile of garbage.

Perlman later moved out of his studio and began working on the rooftop of his building, making what were ostensibly drawings with a flashlight and long exposures, watching the night sky, waiting for the moon, a shooting star, or a friendly Martian. They look like amateurs' pictures documenting unexplained phenomena or UFOs (each photograph in the two series, titled Sketches and My Reproof, is numbered). The later variations of 2003–4, titled Apparatum Armorum Ineptum, feature what appear to be rockets landing and/or taking off and bizarre cosmic explosions made using more amateur light tricks. These dark and enigmatic (almost entirely black and white) pictures quite accurately reflect the isolating life of an artist spending day after day alone in the studio, trying to create something out of nothing.

The romantic and melancholic aspect makes its way into all of Perlman's work. His 2003 series Operation Idiocracy features isolated explosions, almost as if he'd gone from his rooftop deeper into the night sky, right into outer space. The images recall Harold Edgerton's iconic photographs of nuclear detonations but clearly are homemade, handcrafted, and somewhat absurd. Since the rooftop experiments Perlman has made a series of photographs on the beach that look almost like images of Mars or the moon or postnuclear devastation (Ergo Despero, 2007), and he drew a series of cats, which he then made into a series of pseudo-3D silk screens called Schrödinger Cats (2007, numbered), inspired by the experiments of the Austrian physicist who used a cat to illustrate the paradoxical nature of quantum mechanics. He also recently presented for sale in two gallery exhibitions unlimited copies of the U.S. Army's *Counterinsurgency Manual*. The proceeds went to both National Popular Vote (a campaign to dismantle the Electoral College) and the Center for Constitutional Rights (an organization fighting for the rights of the Guantánamo Bay prisoners to contest their detentions). He's concocted a universe of UFOs, atom bomb explosions, trash robots, and cats. Like a lone child building castles in the sand, Perlman keeps tinkering with photographic devices and whatever material makes it into his studio, creating a disturbing and paranoid yet contained, focused, silent, and contemplative universe of his own.

In 2000 Perlman was commissioned to make a series of pictures of cats and dogs for the Maria Fareri Children's Hospital in Westchester County, New York, and for the Cleveland Clinic. He aimed to "make pictures that are empathetic to the fear and anxiety hospitals induce. I wanted images that communicate repose and a meditative, sympathetic affect. These pictures sought personal, private relationships—a partnership with the viewer/patient." He produced the prints in an unlimited edition, and patients were able to choose an image to take back to their rooms and eventually to take home. This project and its healing aspect provided the artist with a sense of relief in its honesty, as opposed to the slipperiness of the contemporary art context of galleries and museums. While the practice of photographing cats and dogs for the hospital led to his current series of photographs of his cat, the more recent images "are of a different animal nature: nervous, fidgety. They're a parallel universe where we don't matter and aren't welcome."

So what drew him to start making portraits of his own cat? "Given the amount of cat memes, let alone pet photography in general, it strikes me as utterly absurd to be taking pictures of my cat. Still, I have to confess to seeing ancient Egyptian cat idols in some pictures, Muybridge in others, or Louis Wain in others—an odd constellation." Wain is one of Perlman's favorite artists. He was a turn-of-the-twentieth-century British illustrator who gained fame for his anthropomorphized cats, featured largely in children's books, and also suffered from schizophrenia. Wain made paintings as well, and as his disease advanced, his paintings and drawings become increasingly psychedelic—and further distanced from his book illustrations. It's these fantastical cat pictures that have stuck with Perlman and piqued his interest in depicting felines.

Perlman's cat portraits began slowly as he puttered about in his backyard with his 4x5 camera and a vague idea of somehow making use of the yard. "Oddly, I kept imagining Abraham Lincoln either glooming around a fire in the evenings or playing horseshoes in the shade of palm trees and California oaks. I started mulling over the space through photos, and of course the cat was showing up in them. Invoking Lincoln was starting to feel corny, and every time I'd try to imagine Lincoln in the picture, there was the cat instead. Her need for adoration won out over Lincoln's."

For Perlman, the cat pictures are "a cautionary tale about being out of our depth, in trouble, in the wrong place at the wrong time, and with an ever-dimming light at the end of the tunnel, and very little to no agency left, on the brink, but still at a turning point." Hence the underlying thread of melancholy throughout his oeuvre. The new photographs featured in this show turn the household feline into a regal portrait subject. The large (around six by nine feet) black-and-white pictures are studies of movement, stillness, and the art of capturing your subject. They portray the cat motionless like a king in one shot, or about to flee in another, looking more like a technical defect than an actual breathing figure. She's staring at you, alive and intimidating, and then we see her innocently hanging around. In a couple of the photographs, Perlman inverted the pictures, making the black background white, so the cat's ghostly figure becomes a blurry gray abstraction. These icons of the absurd provide a quick glimpse inside the artist's head and the curious world he's emerged from.

NOTES

1. Unless otherwise noted, all quotations from the artist are from conversations or e-mail correspondence with the author.
2. Benjamin Weissman, "Hirsch Perlman Saved from Avalanche," *Frieze*, no. 74 (April 2003): 74.

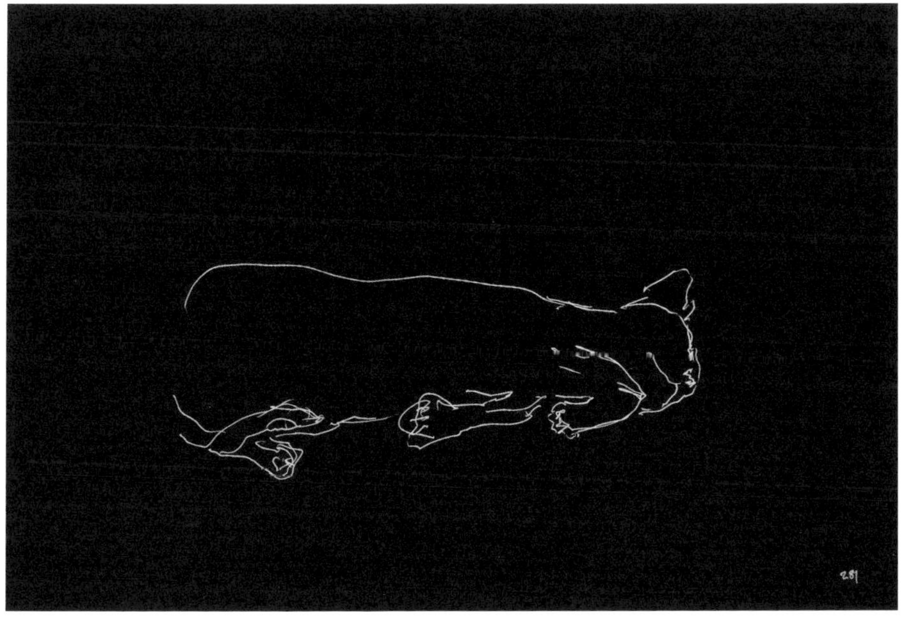

Not a Schrödinger Cat #281, 2007. Silk screen. 57 3/4 x 75 3/4 in. (146.7 x 192.4 cm). Courtesy the artist and Blum & Poe, Los Angeles.

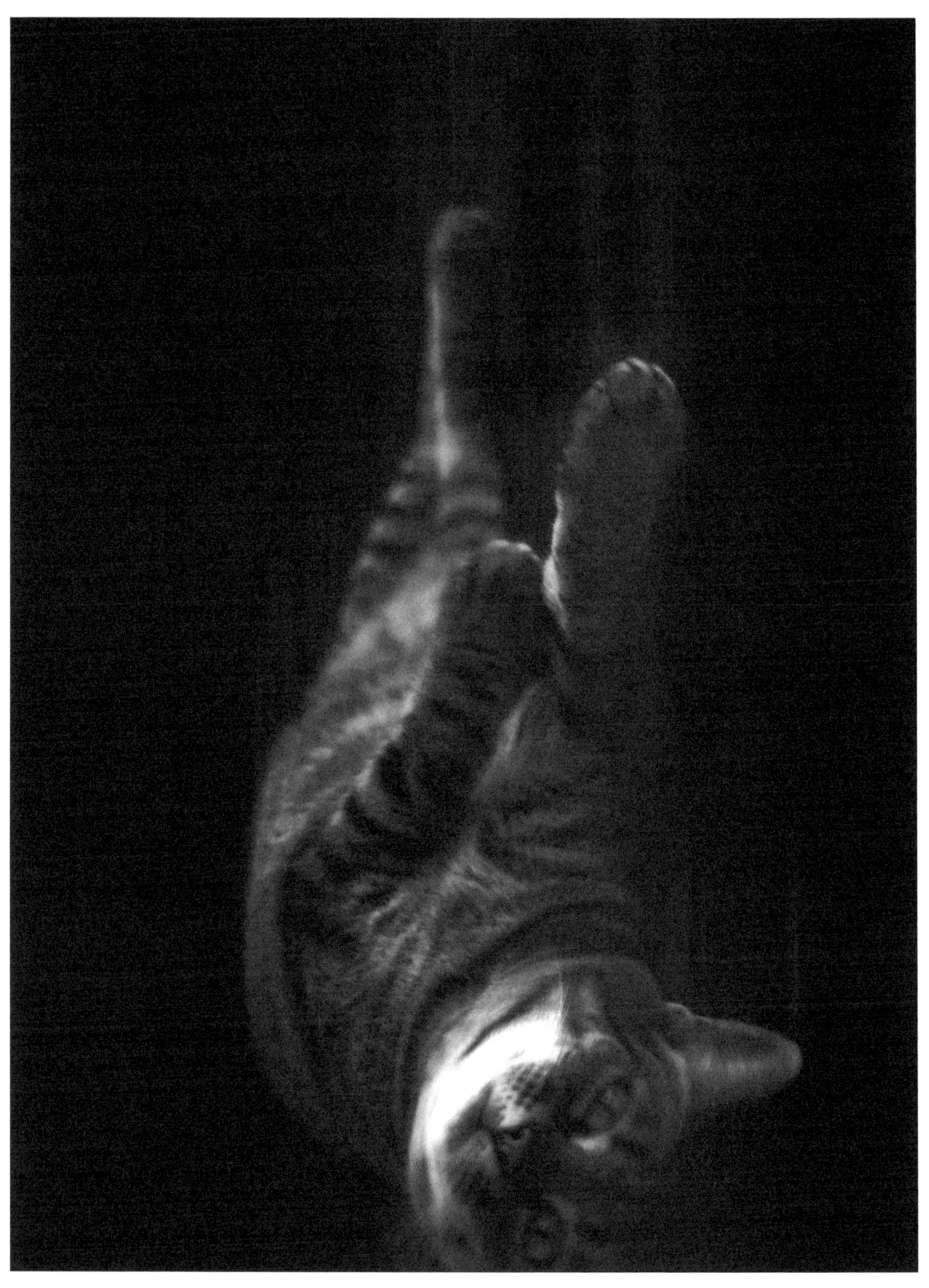

An Animus Cat Apostate, 2008. Chromogenic print. 97 x 72 in. (246.4 x 182.9 cm). Courtesy the artist and Blum & Poe, Los Angeles.

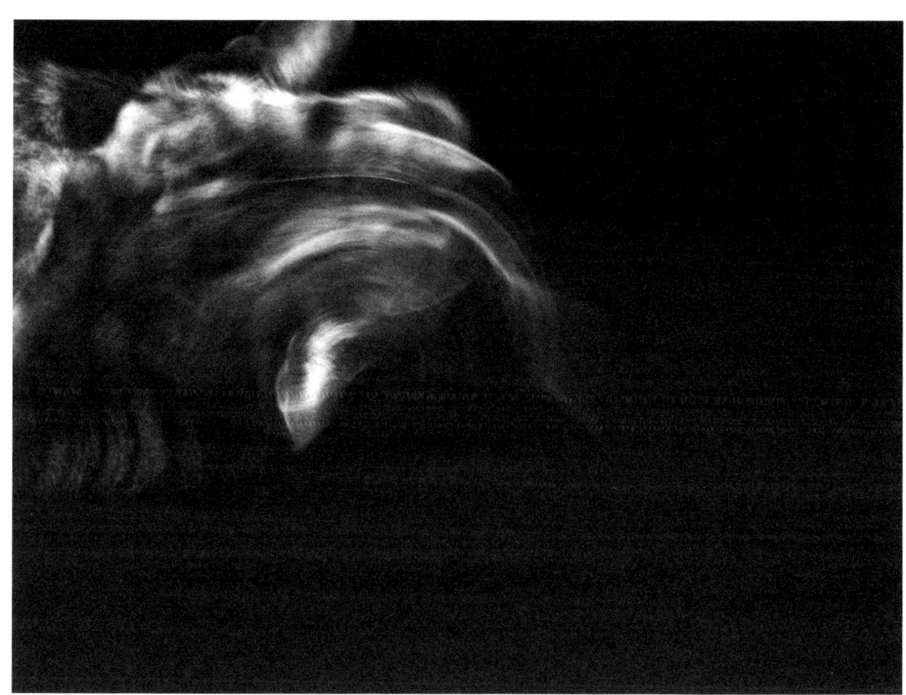

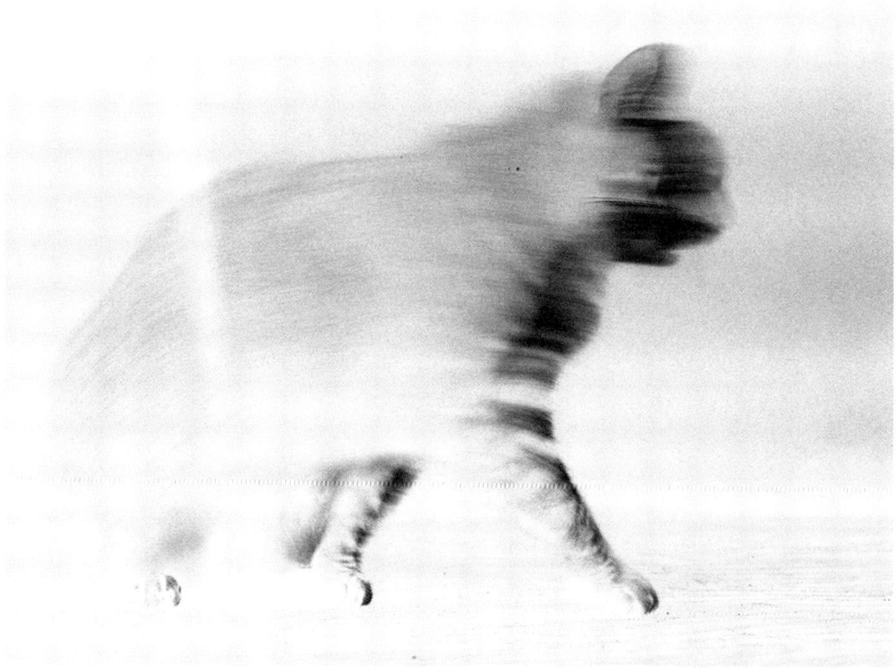

Top: *An Animus Cat Amok & Asunder*, 2008. Chromogenic print. 72 x 97 in. (182.9 x 246.4 cm). Courtesy the artist and Blum & Poe, Los Angeles.
Bottom: *An Animus Cat Antagonist*, 2008. 72 x 97 in. (182.9 x 246.4 cm). Chromogenic print. Courtesy the artist and Blum & Poe, Los Angeles.

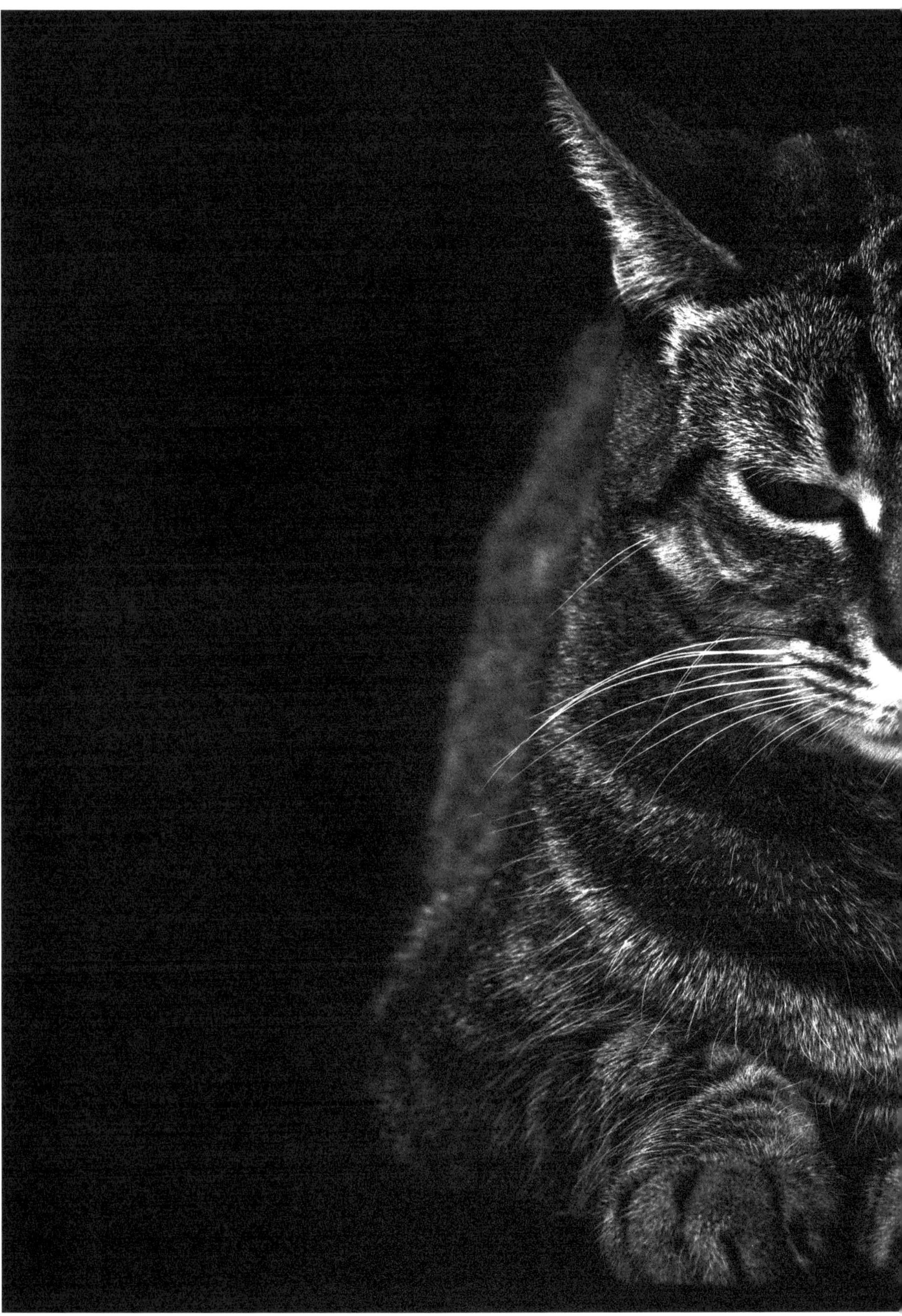

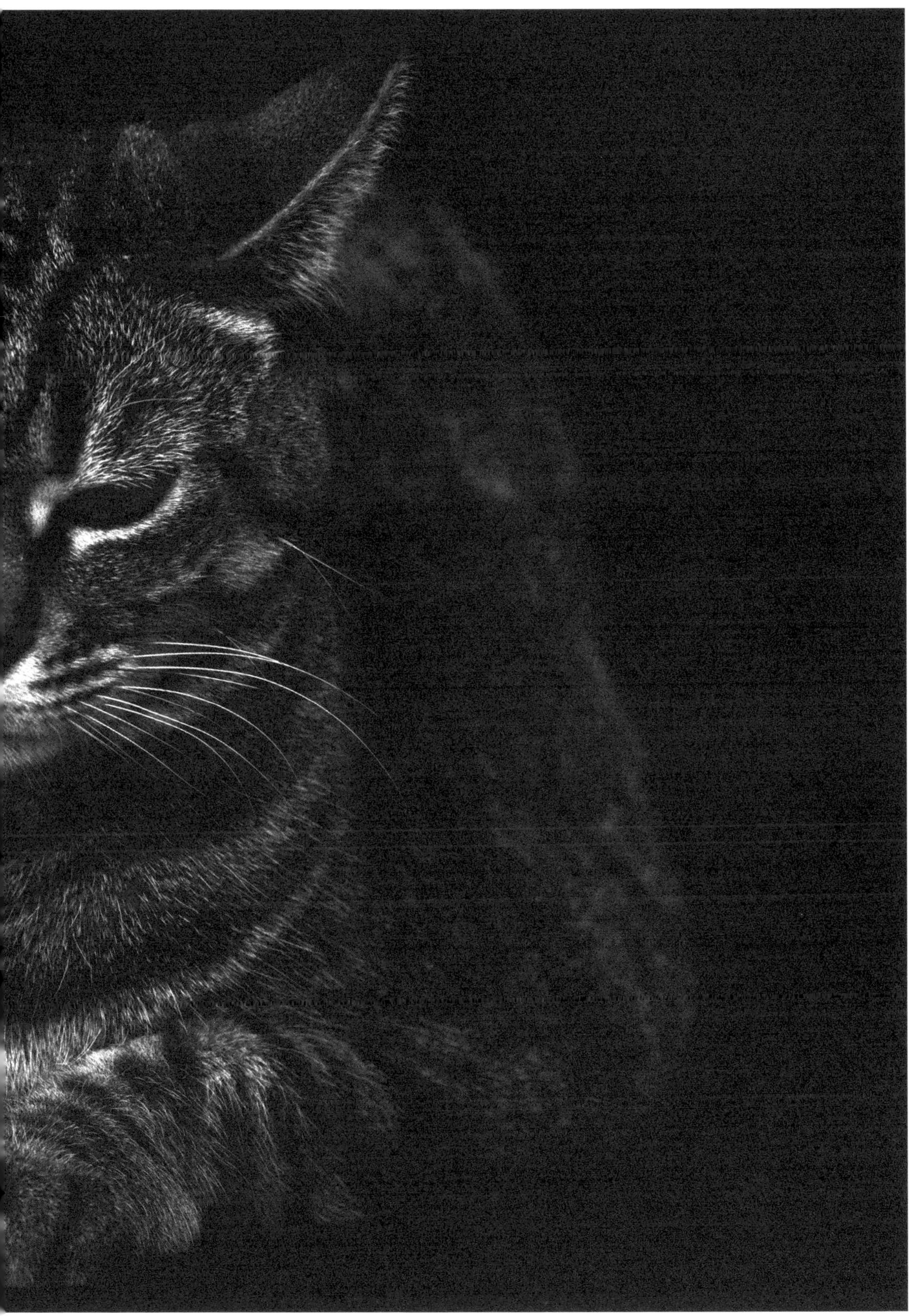

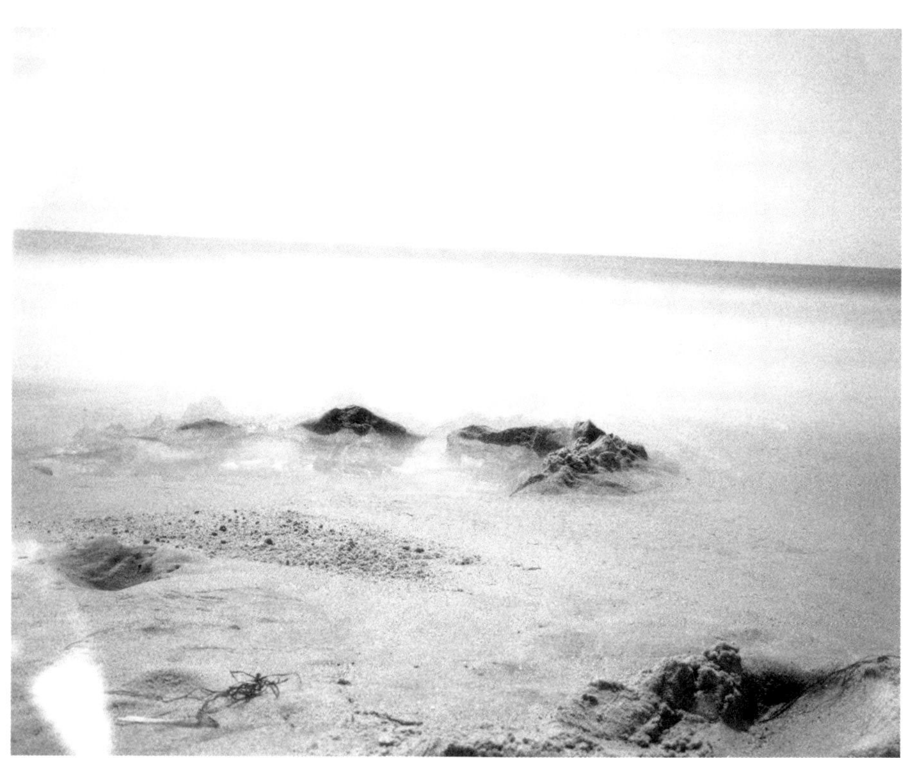

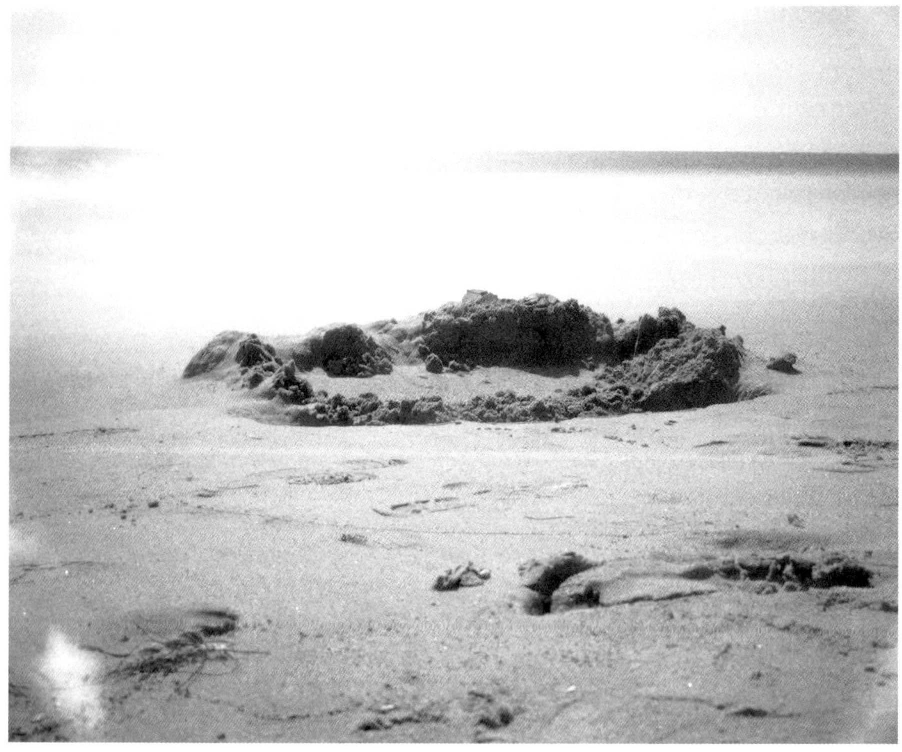

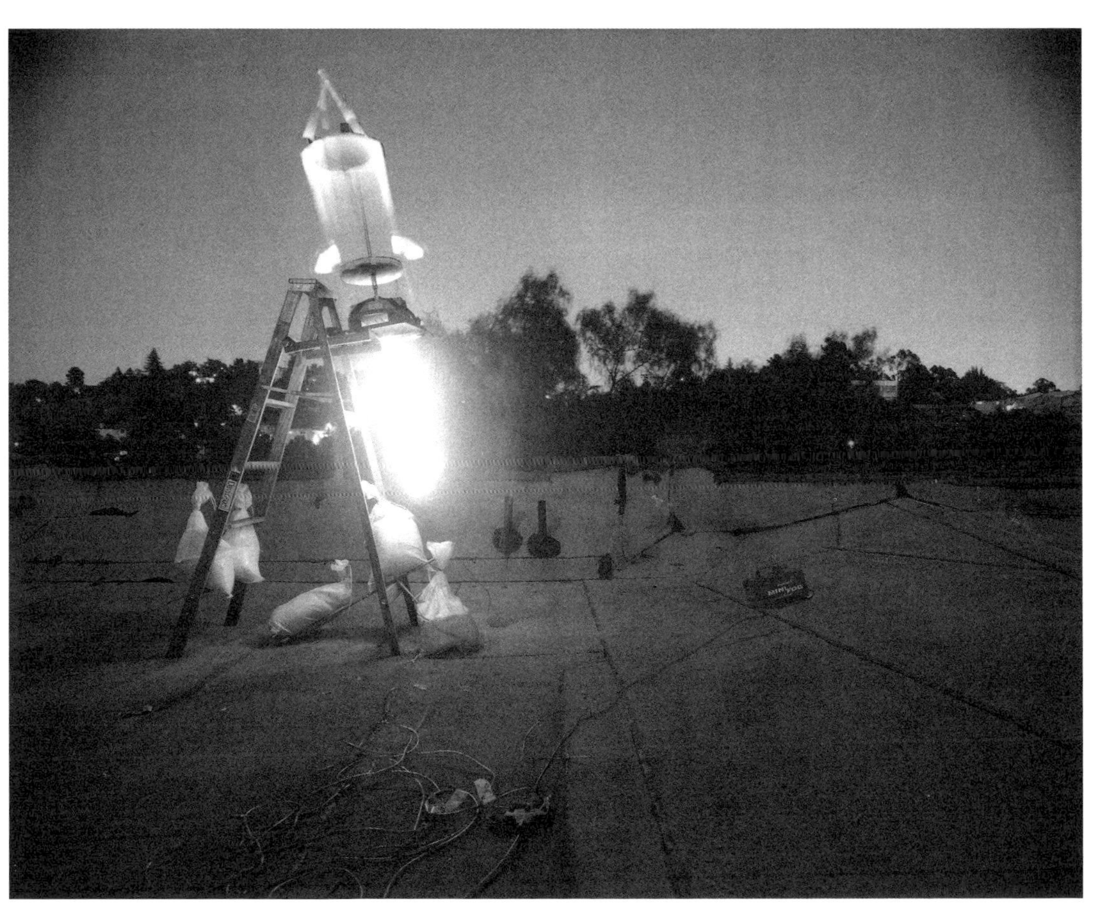

Previous spread: *Animus Cat* (detail), 2008. Chromogenic print. 72 x 97 in. (182.9 x 246.4 cm). Courtesy the artist and Blum & Poe, Los Angeles.
Opposite, top: *Ergo Despero #332*, 2007. Gelatin silver print. 47 x 52 x 1 1/2 in. (119.4 x 132.1 x 3.8 cm). Courtesy the artist and Blum & Poe, Los Angeles.
Opposite, bottom: *Ergo Despero #333*, 2007. Gelatin silver print. 47 x 52 x 1 1/2 in. (119.4 x 132.1 x 3.8 cm). Courtesy the artist and Blum & Poe, Los Angeles.
Above: *Apparatum Armorum Ineptum #9*, 2003–4. Gelatin silver print. 37 x 41 3/4 in. (94 x 106 cm). Courtesy the artist and Blum & Poe, Los Angeles.

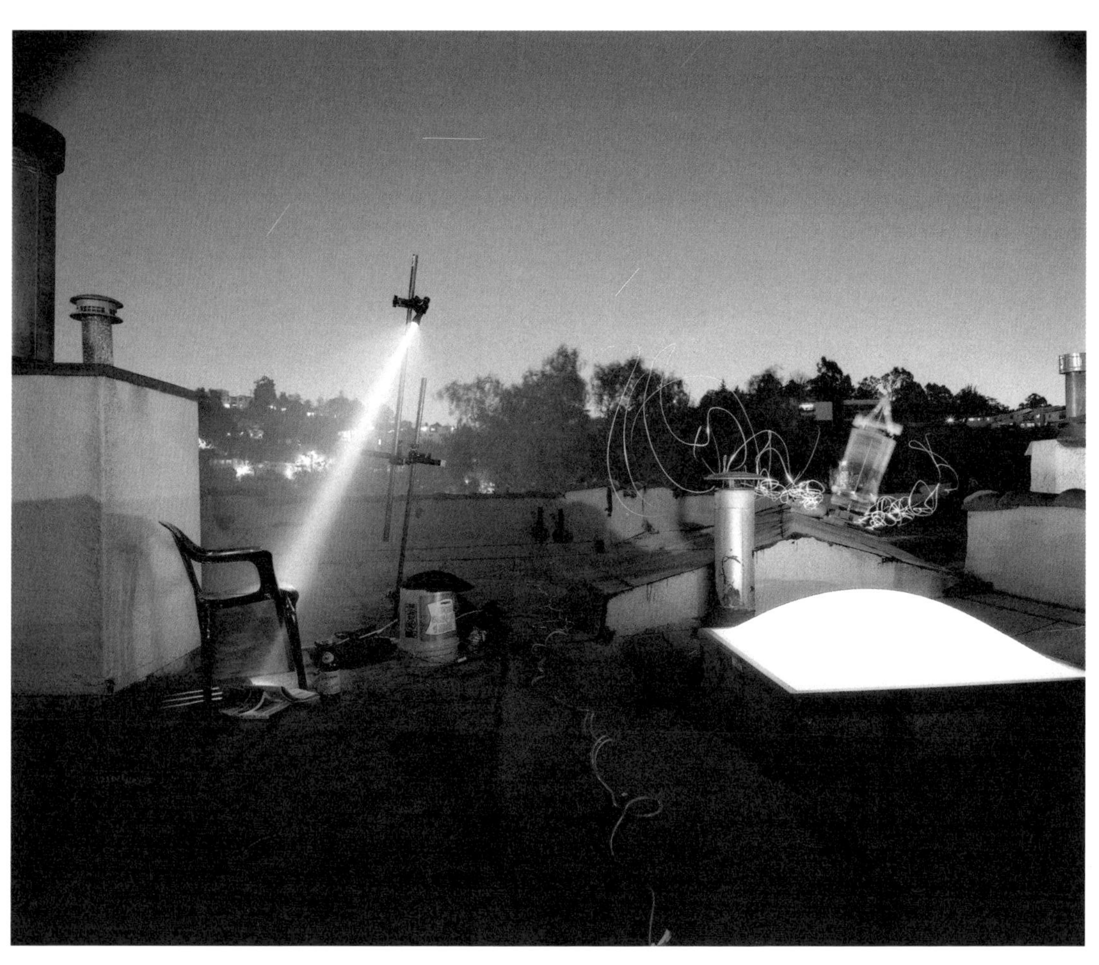

Above: *My Reproof #7 (January)*, 2003. Black-and-white fiber photo. 16 x 20 in. (40.6 x 50.8 cm). Courtesy the artist and Blum & Poe, Los Angeles.
Opposite, top: *Operation Idiocracy, Roll #17, Frame 16/17*, 2003–4. Gelatin silver print. 20 x 24 in. (50.8 x 61 cm). Courtesy the artist and Blum & Poe, Los Angeles.
Opposite, bottom: *Operation Idiocracy, Roll #3, Frame 3/4*, 2007. Chromogenic print. 31 1/4 x 40 in. (79.4 x 101.6 cm). Hammer Museum, Los Angeles, Purchase.

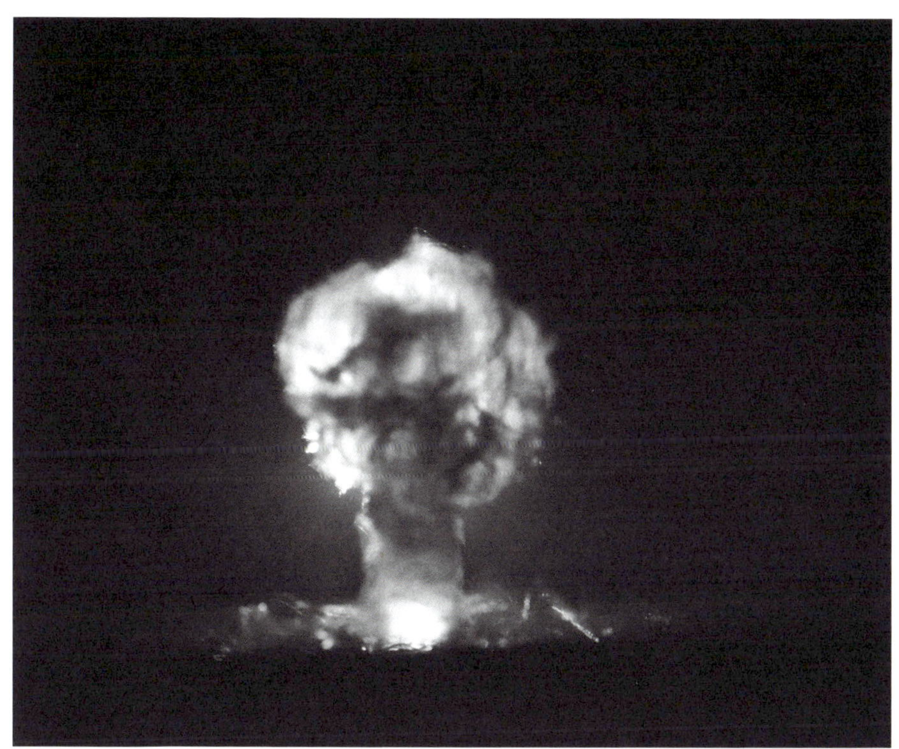

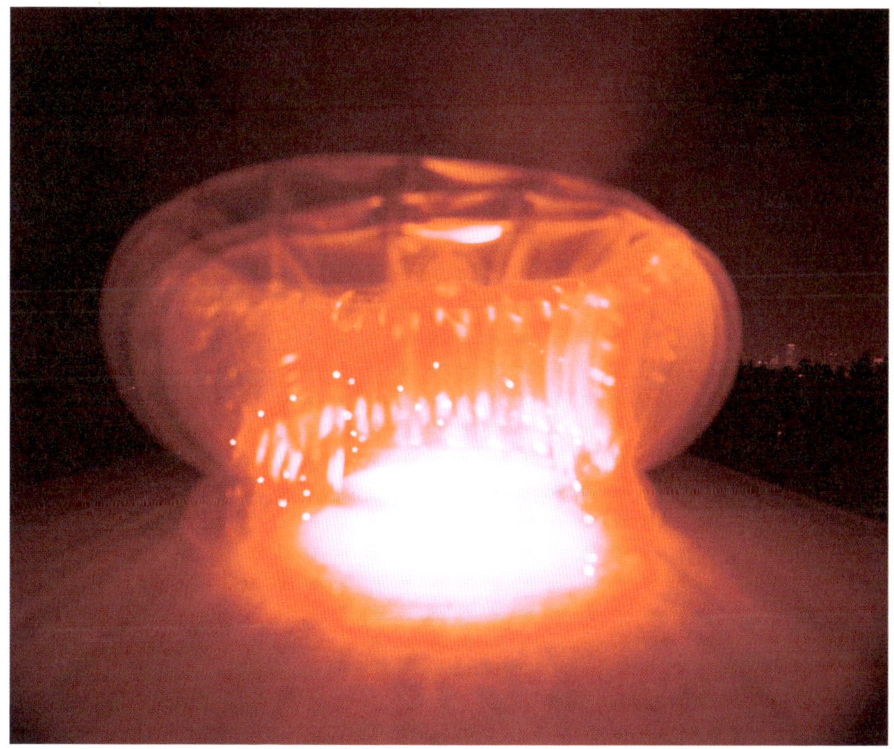

Charles Irvin

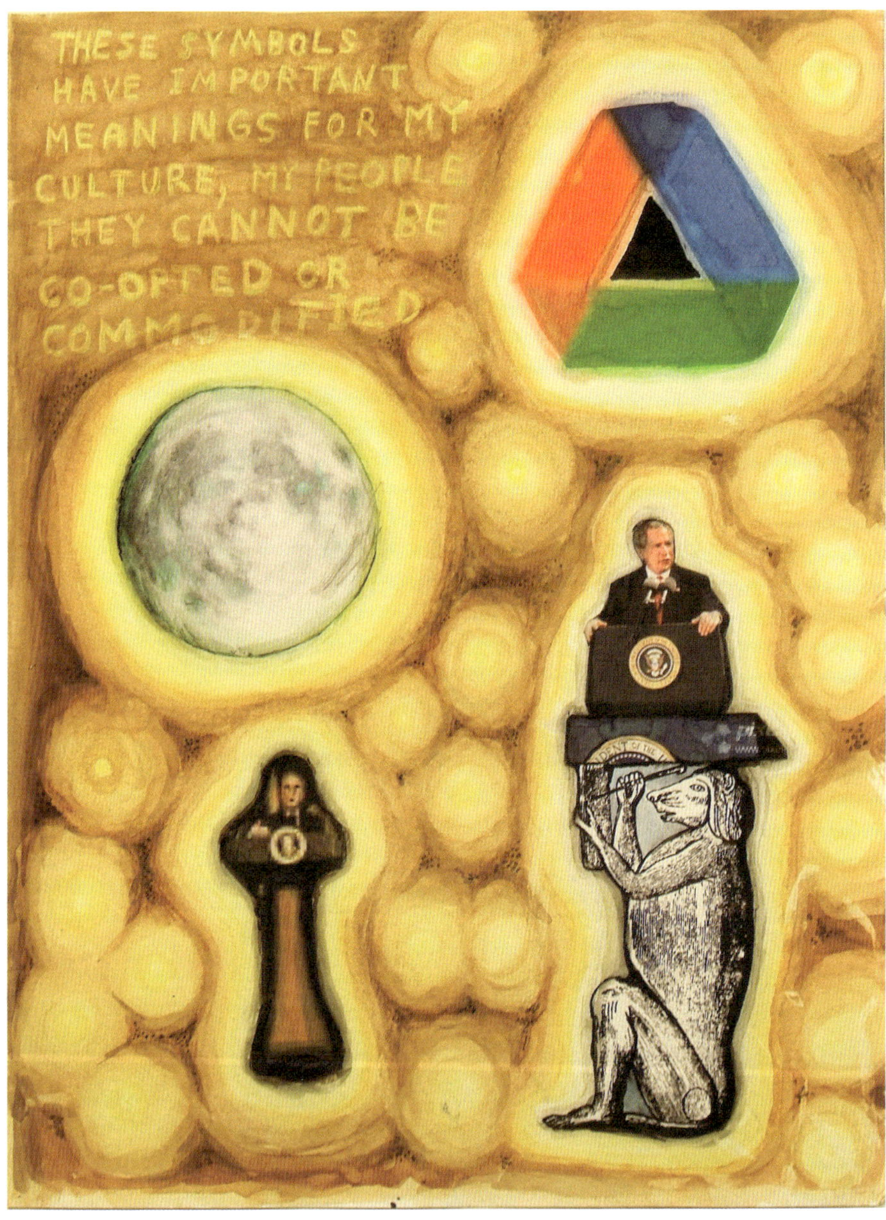

Symbolic Podium, 2007. Mixed media on paper. 24 x 18 in. (61 x 45.7 cm). Courtesy the artist.

Charles Irvin's artwork transports viewers into a new dimension or alternate reality. He makes what could be called intuitive or somewhat childlike drawings populated by zany characters: aliens, animals that act like humans, and humans who act like animals. Inspired by dreams and fantasies and heavily influenced by the work of painter Peter Saul, one of Irvin's undergraduate teachers, the characters seem to emanate from the subconscious. An untitled drawing from 2007 features a teddy bear at a podium leading a "boner conference." Irvin depicts these outcasts and creeps and animal/human/aliens in a sympathetic manner that disarms the viewer: "I think a successful artwork alters your perception of reality. It should lead you to reevaluate what art is, or even the nature of existence."[1] Many of the drawings also feature texts that combine political commentary with obscure philosophies and contain bizarre phrases that are difficult to decode. Irvin takes the surrealists' "irrational approach to art making" as inspiration for his videos, drawings, and paintings, and he envisions scenarios and characters that could come only from an unfettered imagination.

Although he was raised Catholic, Irvin has released himself from the plague of Catholic guilt. He's astonishingly unselfconscious: in a performance piece titled *Breaking Boundaries* (2003), he break-dances, wearing only a pair of athletic socks, following a routine he learned from an instructional video (the song is Kraftwerk's "Tour de France"). In graduate school he presented a video for his MFA thesis project that included a scene of him pleasuring himself with a stuffed toy bird. But this work is not about shock. In fact, it doesn't even seem to occur to him that this might be inappropriate or disturbing for his friends and family, not to mention strangers, to watch. He's continuing the tradition of John Waters, Pee-wee Herman, Mike Kelley, and Paul McCarthy, introducing us to a mad world in which outlandish characters and actions represent the ordinary and paranoia is mixed with a strange sort of optimism. Irvin doesn't even appear to be trying to violate taboos—when you enter his work, it's as if taboos never existed.

Irvin's paintings and drawings may look like the work of a madman, but he's not crazy. He's actually engaged in extensive, ongoing research and often gets consumed in exploring strange phenomena and theories. And his work communicates this research, providing bits and pieces of the information that he's digested and processed. His perception of reality comes off as especially unfiltered and untainted, which nurtures an extremely vivid and wild imagination.

As his drawings and paintings reveal, Irvin is especially fascinated by conspiracy theories and unconventional psychology. His ongoing amateur research led him to the book *Psychic Dictatorship in the U.S.A.* by Alex Constantine, which introduced him to the False Memory Syndrome Foundation (FMSF). The FMSF became the stimulus for a new video mixing live action with animation and digital special effects, which is tentatively titled *Membrane Lane*. "It was a case of truth being stranger than fiction, and I read everything I could find about the FMSF." The FMSF is an advocacy group started for parents of children suffering from "false memory syndrome," which, according to the foundation, results when a therapist convinces a patient to believe, falsely, that he or she has repressed memories of sexual, physical, or mental abuse. This somewhat dubious foundation and its defenders shared some of the same qualities with the "conspiracy theory" documentaries that Irvin had been watching, such as *Loose Change* and *Zeitgeist*, which are distributed mainly via the Internet. These types of videos became especially popular for promoting 9/11 conspiracy theories. The videos prey on people's fears and lack of understanding of politics and unexplained phenomena, which parallels in many ways the controversy surrounding the FMSF and its legitimacy. Irvin saw something he wanted to emulate in the formal aspects of this genre of videos, though he wanted a subject more modest in scope. The story of the FMSF, which has been well documented and verified, was an easy story for him to tell given his interest in the mistreatment of the powerless, which has been a recurring theme in his work.

In the video, Irvin uses this pseudo-documentary/conspiracy-theory style with cut-ins of his stand-up comedy routine and other odd characters. One of the characters is a militiaman who frames the journalistic, documentary aspects of the work while critiquing Irvin's personal motives for taking on such controversial subject matter. Irvin explains: "The militiaman was inspired by Susan Faludi's book *Stiffed: The Betrayal of the American Man*. In it Faludi talks about the militia movement from the 1990s and how it was mobilized by the federal government's attack on the Branch Davidian compound in Waco, Texas. A year or so after that, the militiamen had a memorial for the survivors, but the child survivors were terrified because the militiamen were wearing camouflage just like the ATF officers who raided their compound!" In Irvin's world, as in this anecdote, it's never clear who the good guys are, who the bad ones are, or whether everyone is both.

Irvin's cut-and-paste approach of moving in and out of scenarios with characters and events that are constantly questioning or contradicting one another keeps everything slightly off balance. He lets his curiosity guide him, and his works are continually being remade, reworked, and expanded. For the new video he brought in footage from his older video works and began to combine these different elements. At times he felt "like he was building Frankenstein's monster in tackling such a difficult, painful subject."

Irvin is a rare breed of artist who soaks up the culture around him like a sponge—everything from tabloid trash to PBS politics and the blogosphere, and many of his references aren't on the mainstream cultural radar. He eats it all up and expels bits and pieces in his work, leaving a trail of confusion, mistrust, ecstasy, bewilderment, and awe. He's at once hilarious and scary and provocative and annoying and bizarre and otherworldly and prophetic and sad and inspiring and disturbing. He's an artist's artist whose complexity may be unappreciated by the general public but whose boundless imagination and energy have earned him the admiration of his peers. His true impact has barely begun to take hold.

NOTES

1. All quotations from the artist are from conversations or e-mail correspondence with the author.

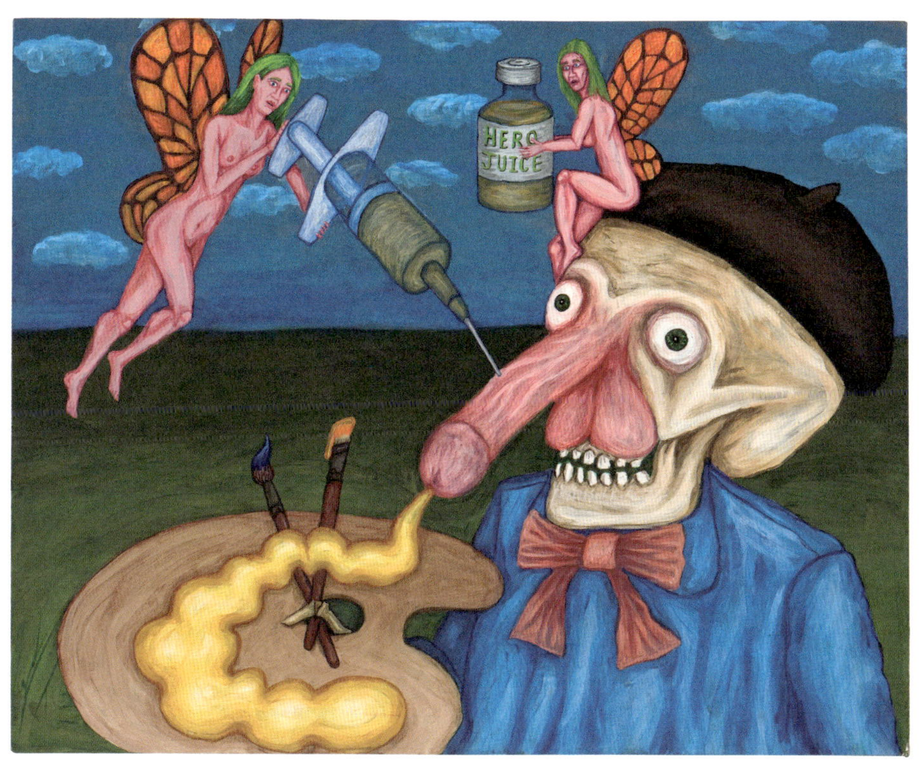

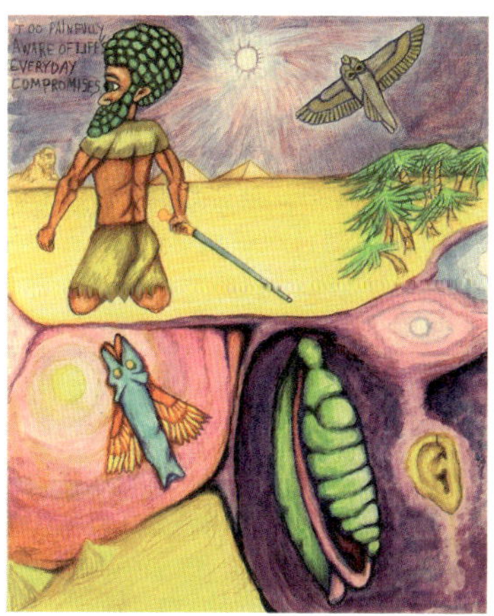

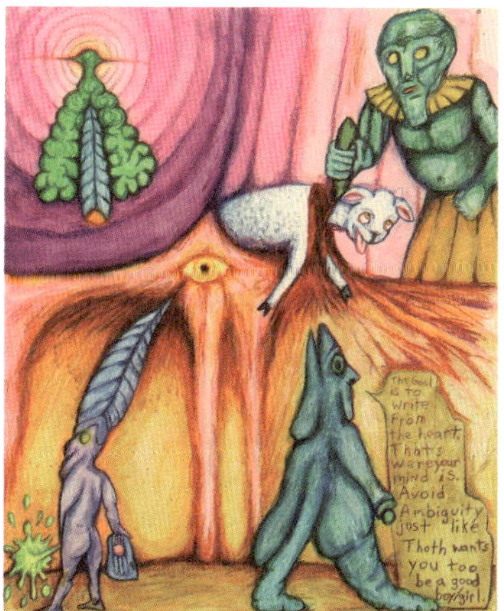

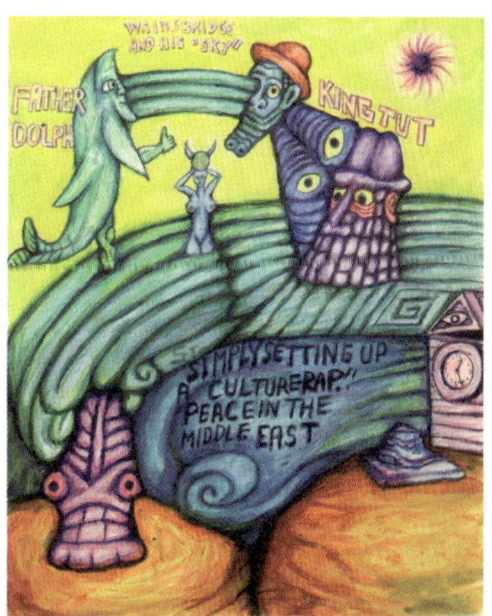

Top: *Self-Portrait*, 2006. Acrylic on canvas. 24 x 30 in. (61 x 76.2 cm). Courtesy the artist.
Bottom: *Egyptian Triptych*, 2007. Mixed media on paper. 17 x 14 in. (43.2 x 35.6 cm) each. Courtesy the artist.

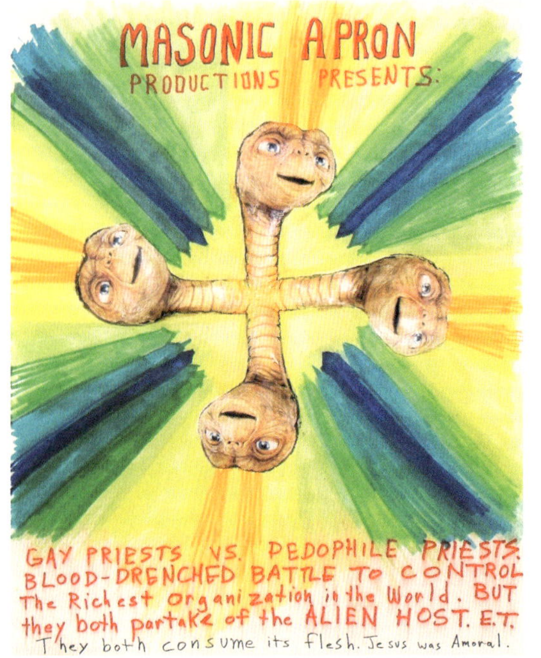

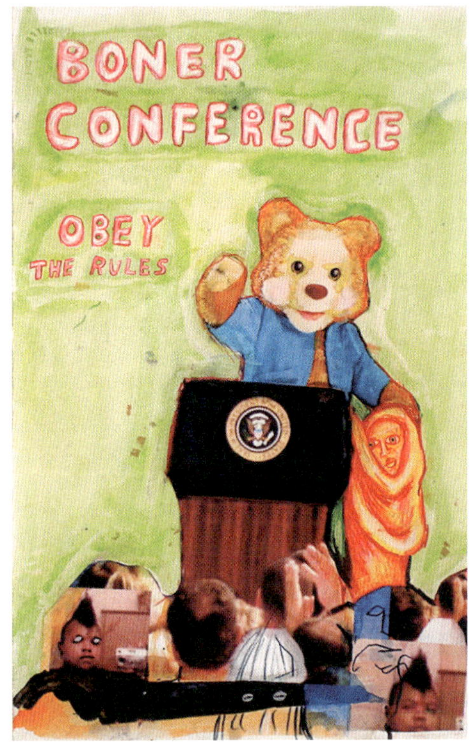

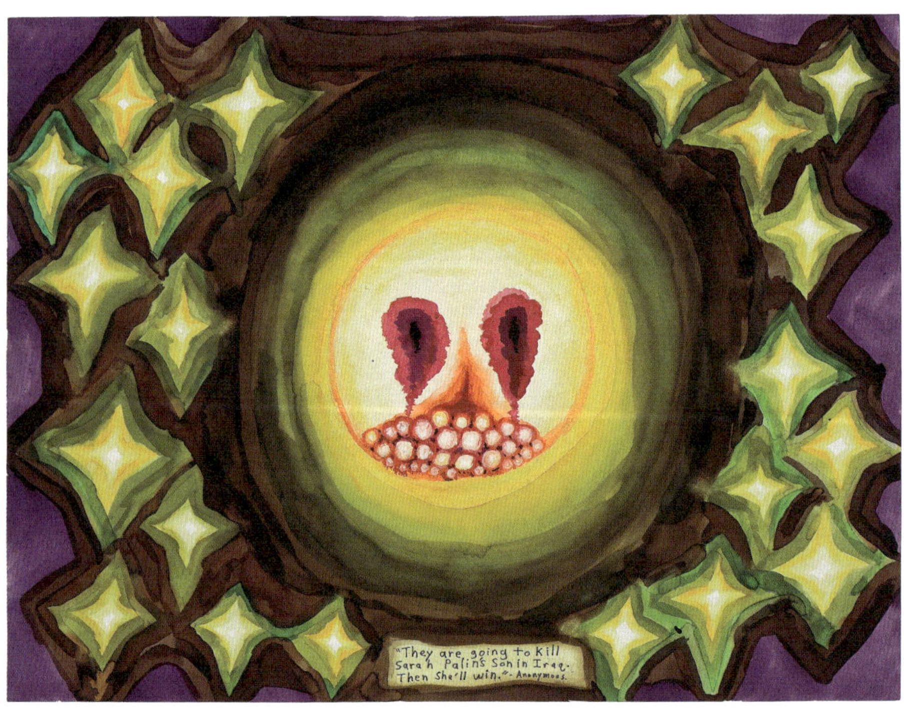

Top left: *Untitled (Masonic Apron)*, 2007. Mixed media on paper. 14 x 11 in. (35.6 x 27.9 cm). Courtesy the artist.
Top right: Untitled, 2007. Mixed media. 19 x 13 in. (48.3 x 33 cm). Courtesy the artist.
Bottom: Untitled, 2008. Ink and acrylic on paper. 18 x 24 in. (45.7 X 61 cm). Courtesy the artist.

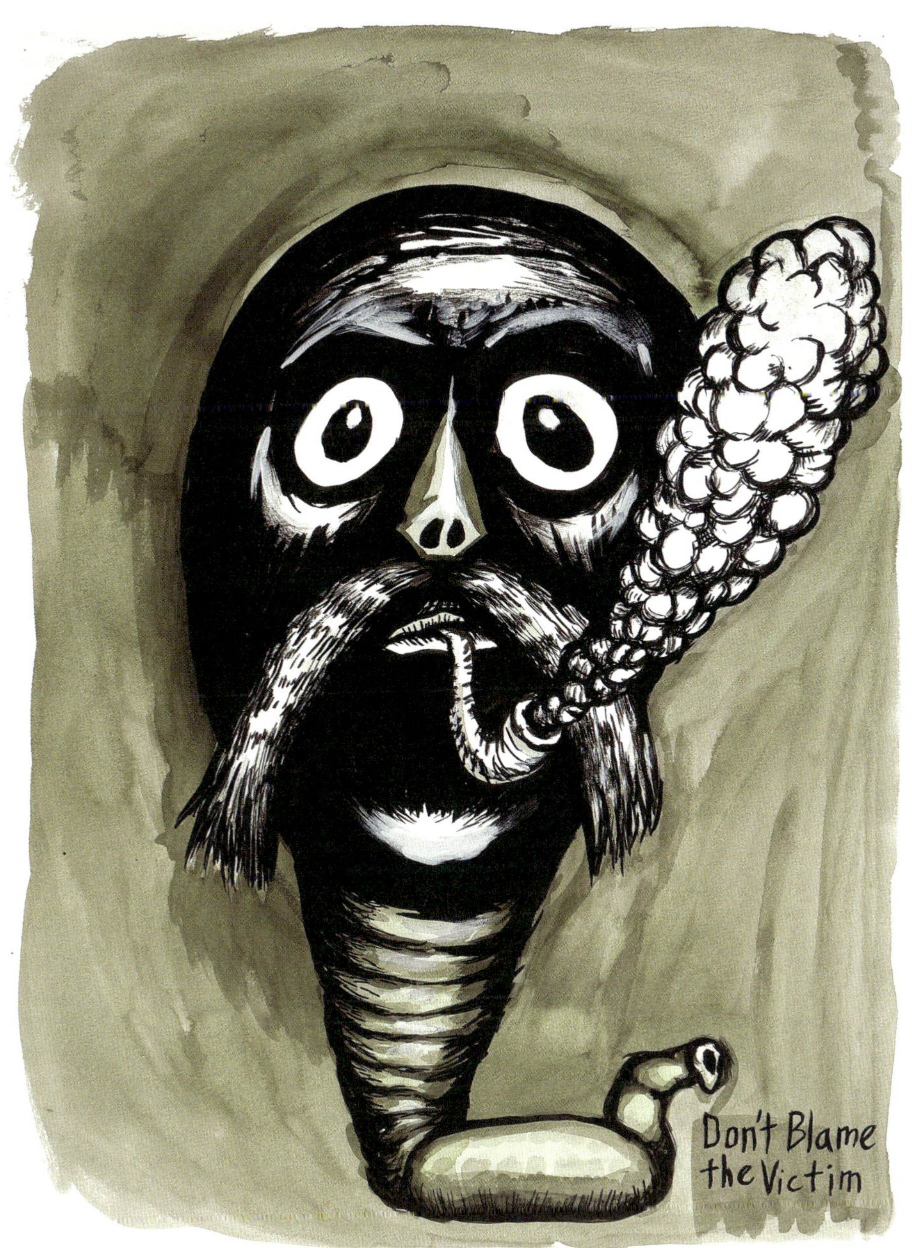

Untitled, 2008. Ink and acrylic on paper. 24 x 18 in. (61 x 45.7 cm). Courtesy the artist.

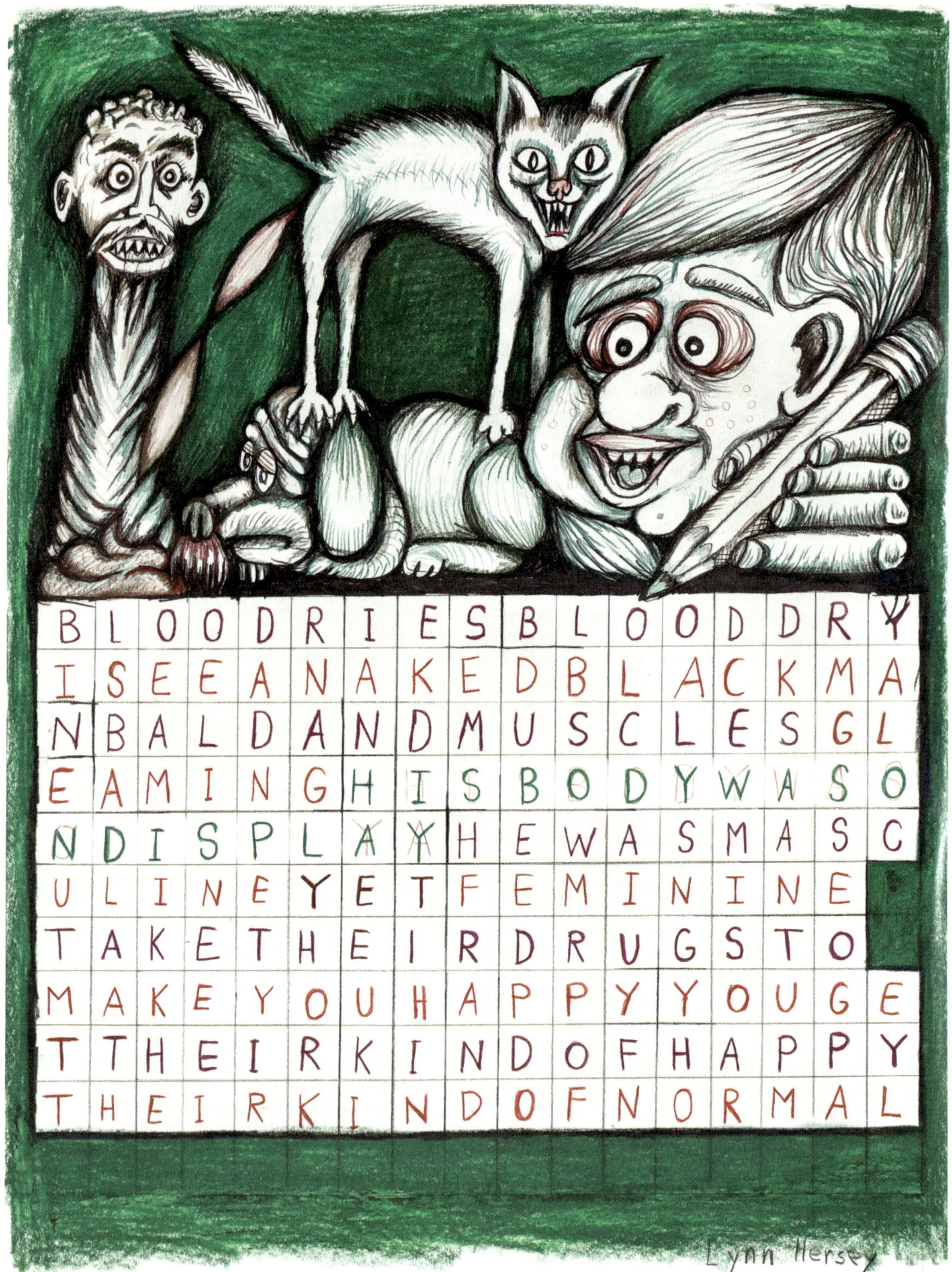

Puzzle, 2008. Prismacolor pencil on paper. 24 x 18 in. (61 x 45.7 cm). Courtesy the artist.

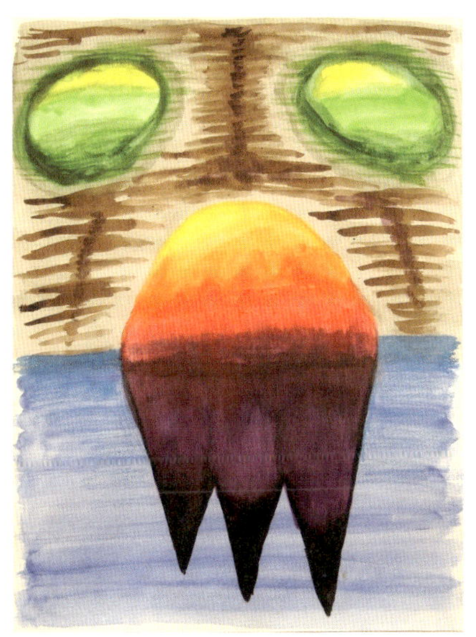

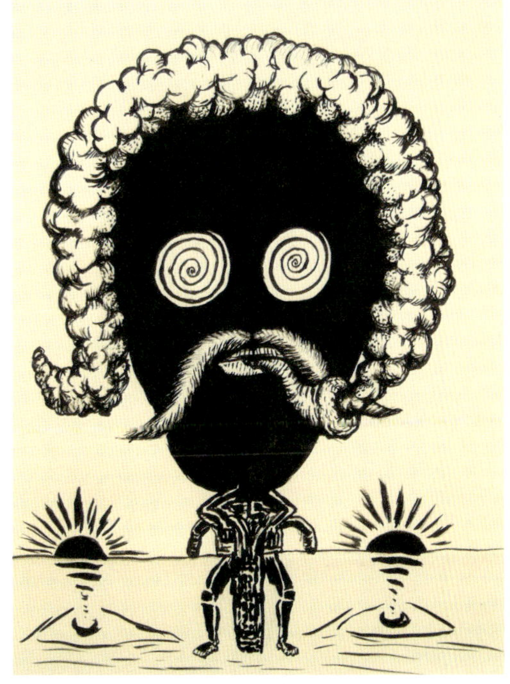

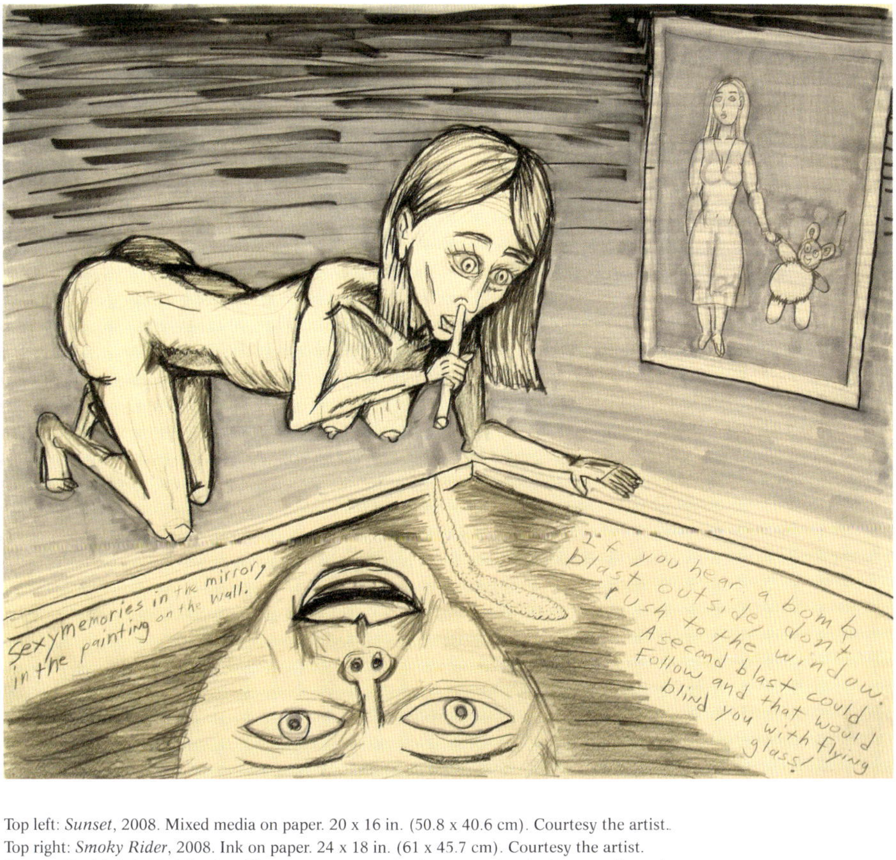

Top left: *Sunset*, 2008. Mixed media on paper. 20 x 16 in. (50.8 x 40.6 cm). Courtesy the artist.
Top right: *Smoky Rider*, 2008. Ink on paper. 24 x 18 in. (61 x 45.7 cm). Courtesy the artist.
Bottom: Untitled, 2008. Mixed media on paper. 14 x 17 in. (35.6 x 43.2 cm). Courtesy the artist.

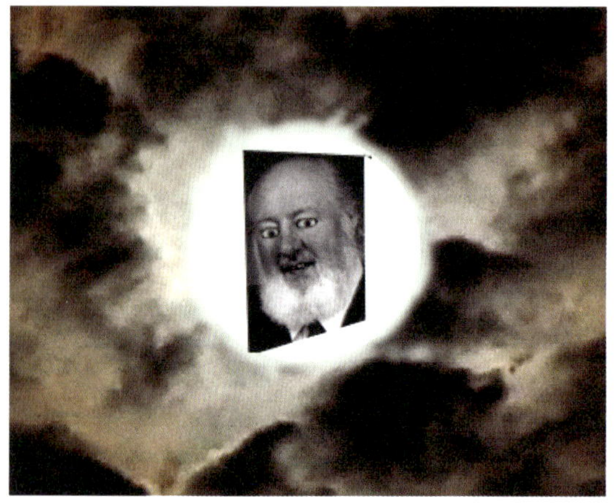
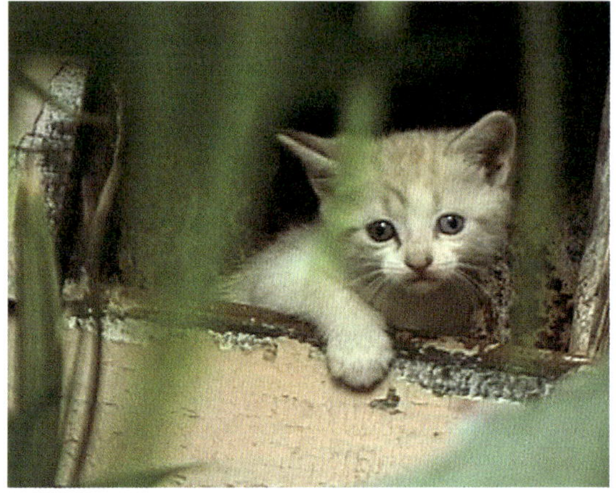
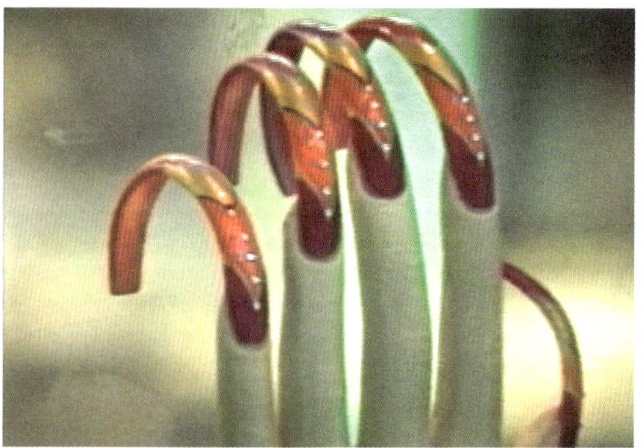
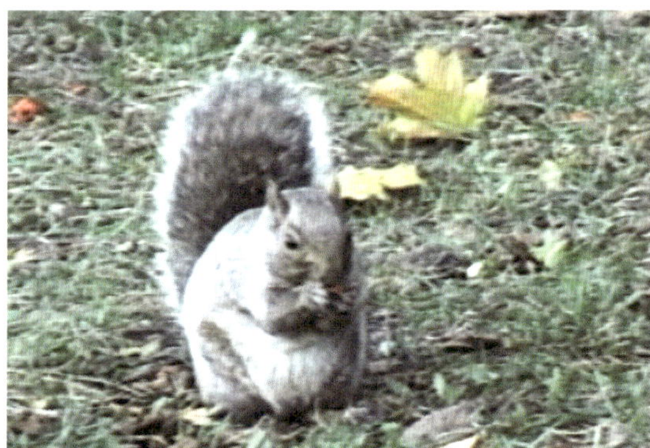
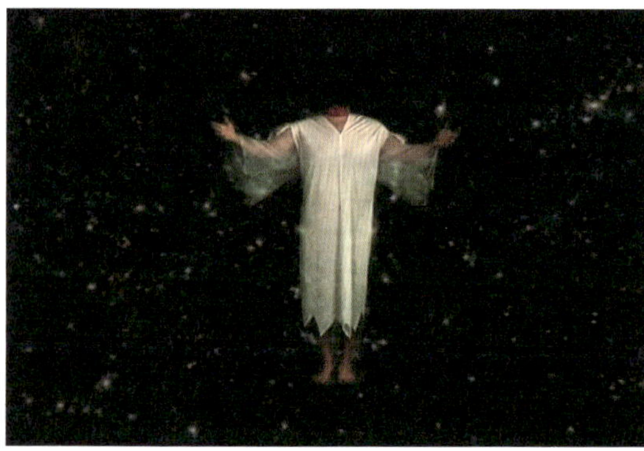
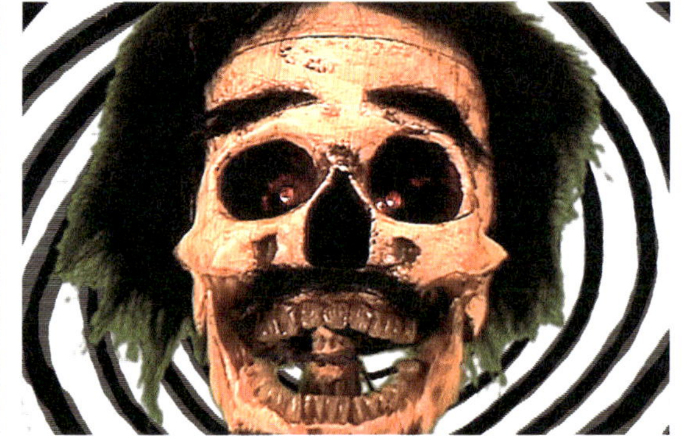

Top: Stills from *Membrane Lane*, 2009. Video, color, sound. Approx. 30 min. Courtesy the artist.
Middle: Stills from *Shenanigans*, 1997. Video, color, sound. 2:30 min. Courtesy the artist.
Bottom: Stills from *Babyscapes*, 2003. Video, color, sound. 18 min. Courtesy the artist.

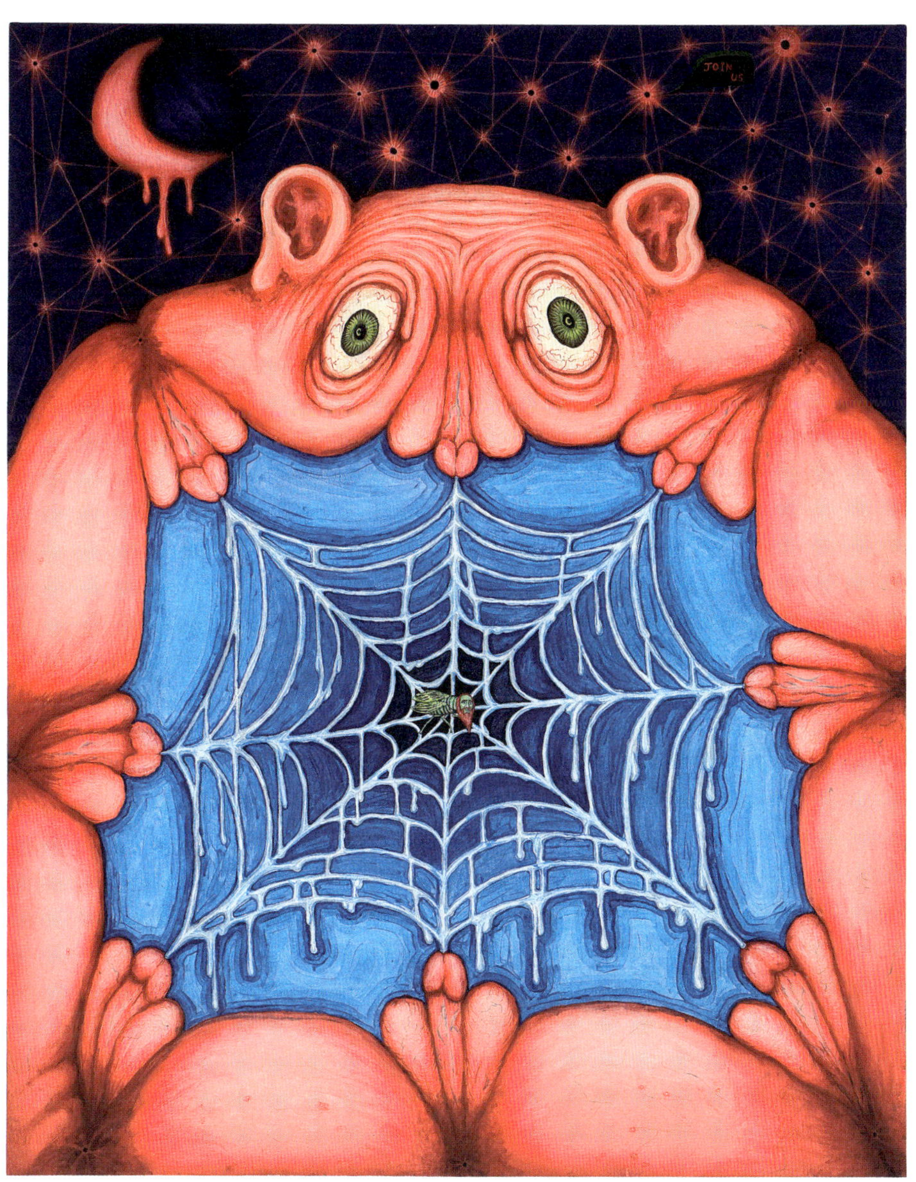

Wang Web, 2006. Acrylic on canvas. 60 x 48 in. (152.4 x 121.9 cm). Courtesy the artist.

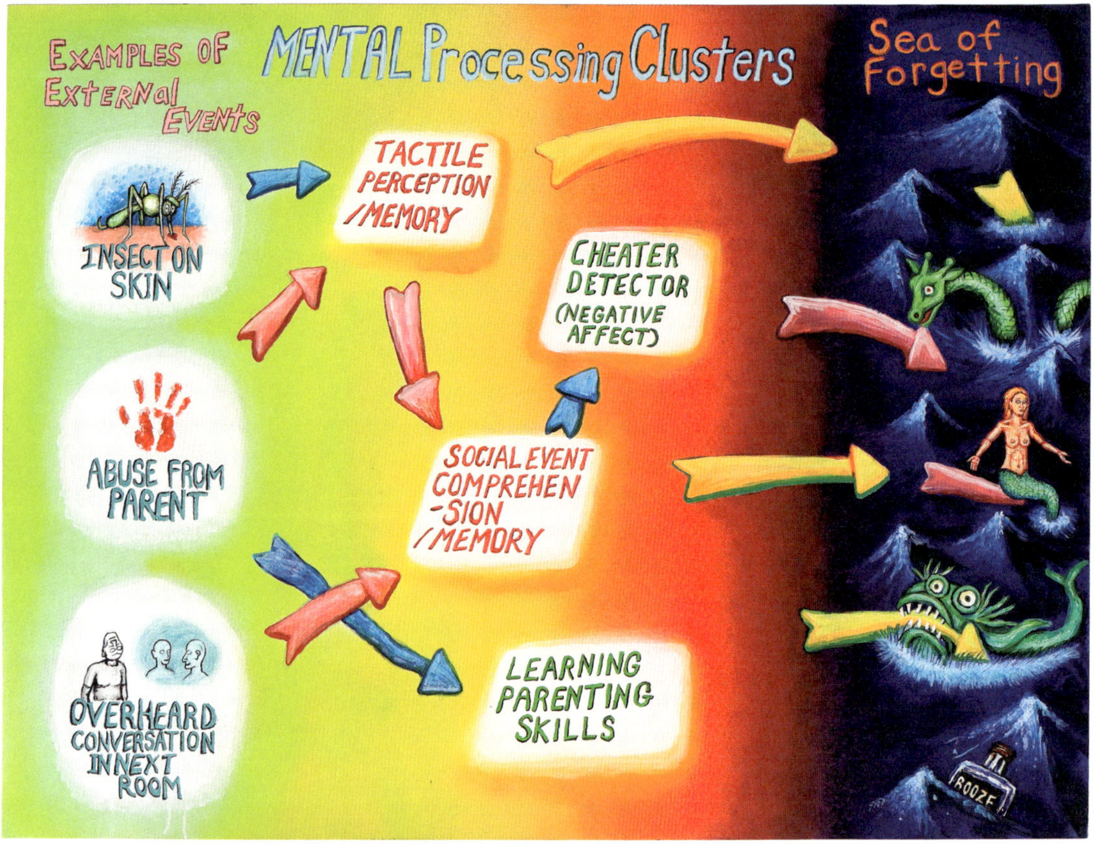

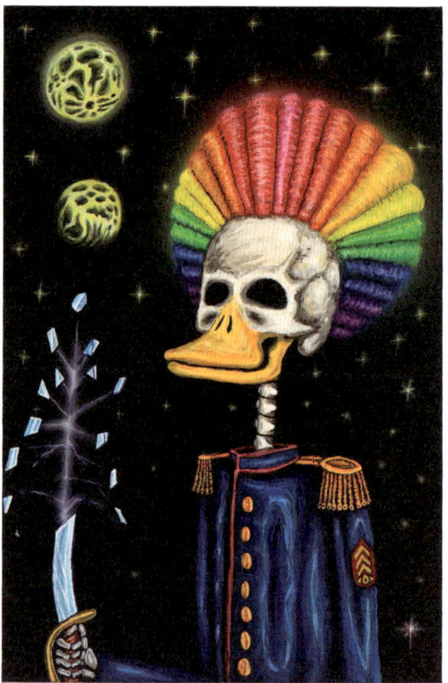

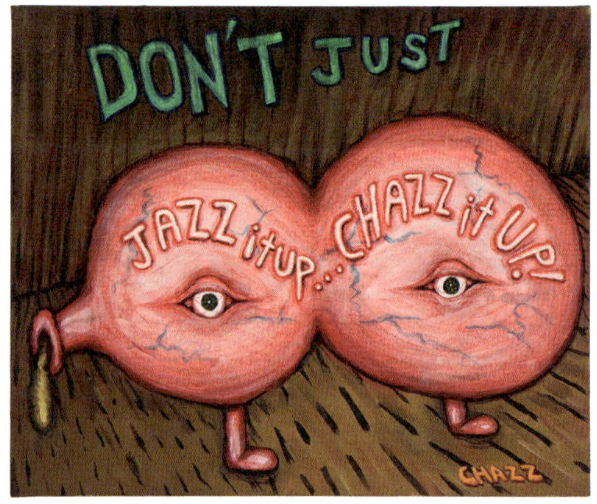

Top: *Diagram*, 2008. Acrylic on canvas. 36 x 48 in. (91.4 x 121.9 cm). Courtesy the artist.
Bottom left: *Decline of American Fun*, 2008. Acrylic on canvas. 36 x 24 in. (91.4 x 61 cm). Courtesy the artist.
Bottom right: *Chazz it up*, 2008. Acrylic on canvas. 20 x 24 in. (50.8 x 61 cm). Courtesy the artist.

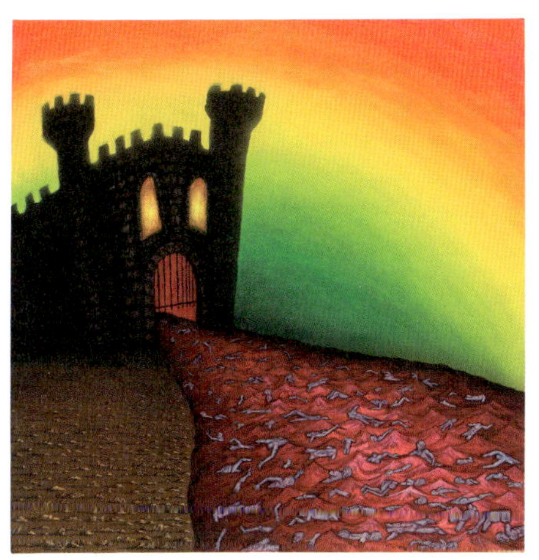

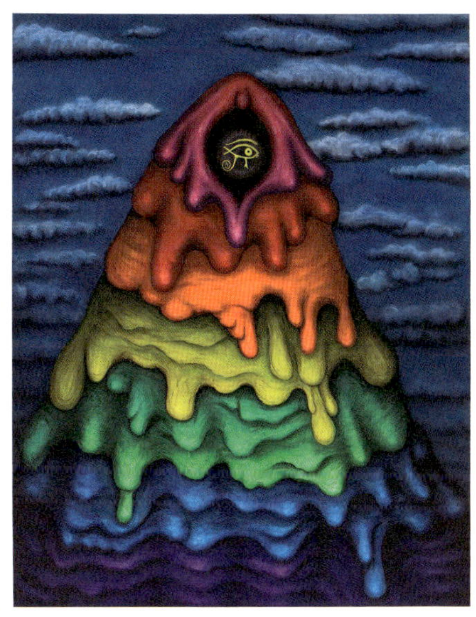

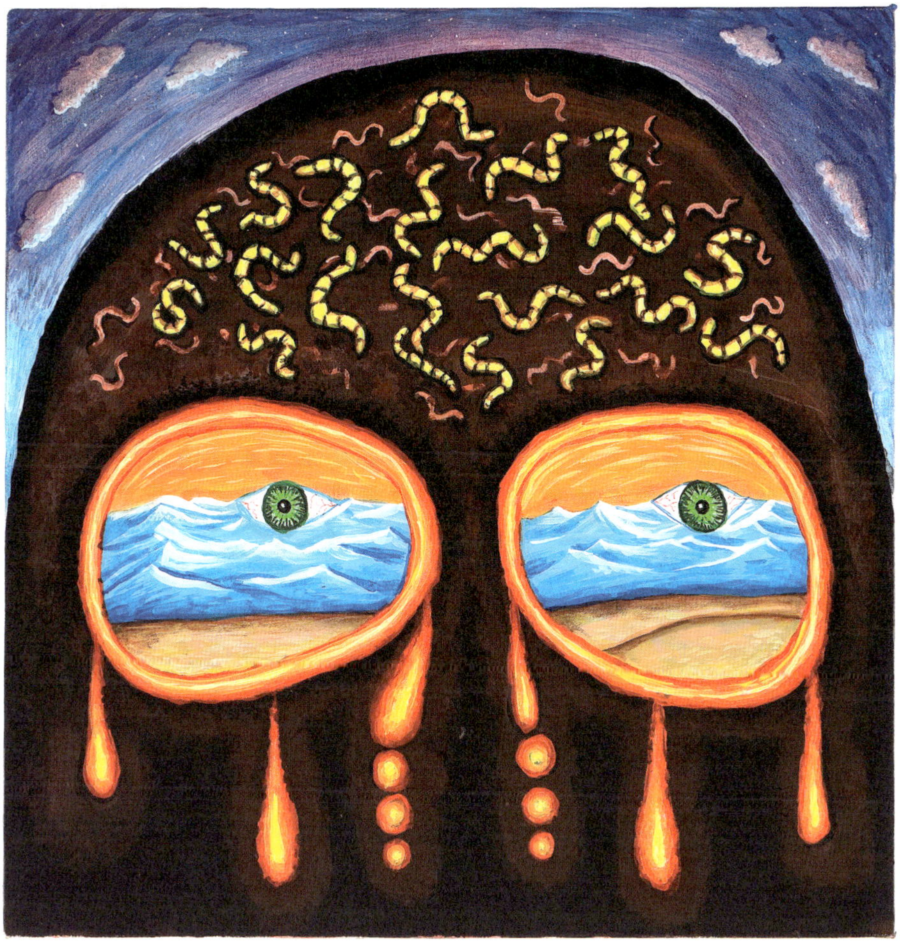

Top left: *Nasty Castle*, 2006. Acrylic on canvas. 36 x 36 in. (91.4 x 91.4 cm). Courtesy the artist.
Top right: Untitled, 2006. Acrylic on canvas. 60 x 48 in. (152.4 x 121.9 cm). Courtesy the artist.
Bottom: Untitled, 2008. Acrylic on canvas. 24 x 24 in. (61 x 61 cm). Courtesy the artist.

Victoria Reynolds

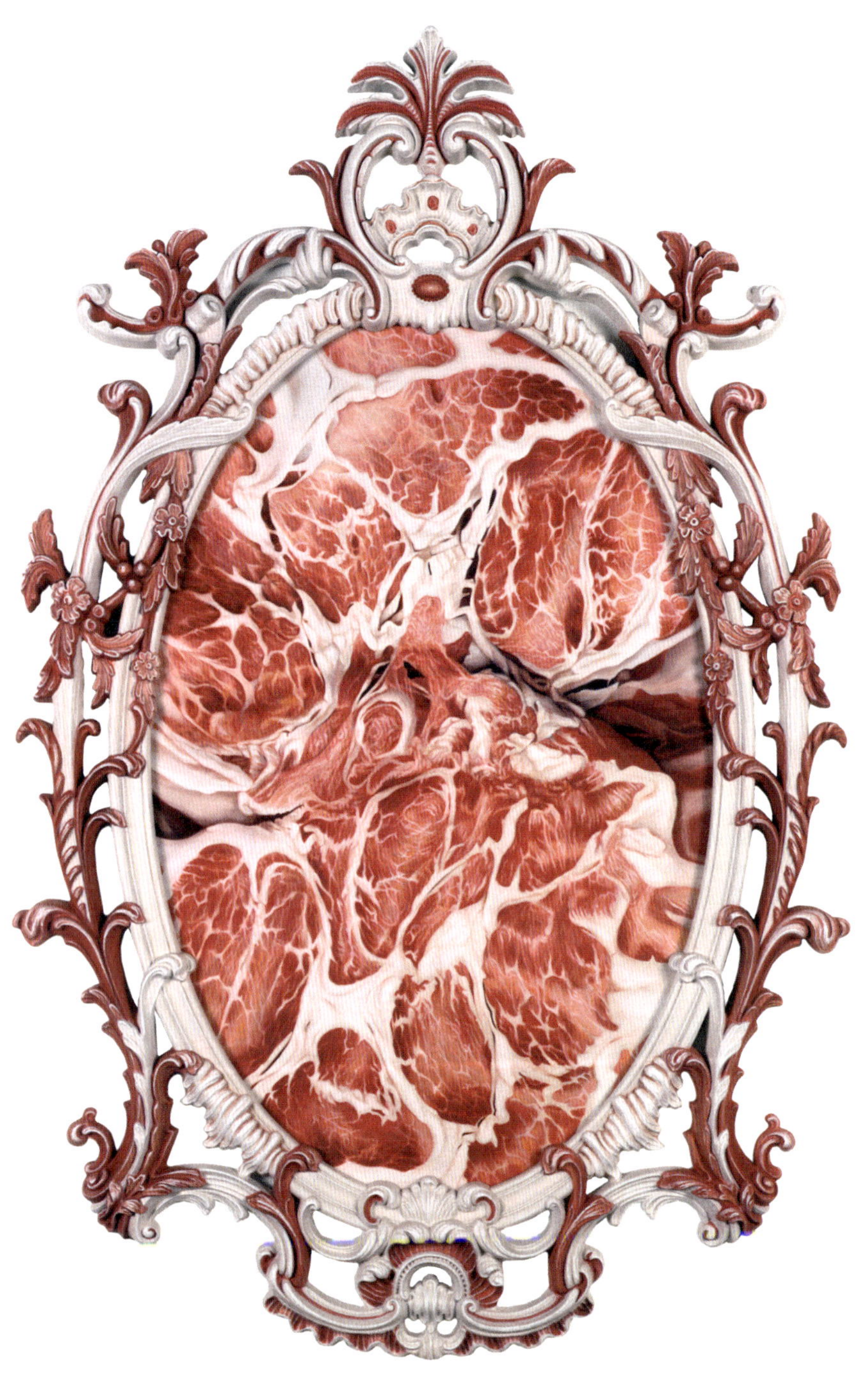

Down the Primrose Path, 2004. Oil on panel, frame. 44 x 29 in. (111.8 x 73.7 cm). Collection of Reesey Shaw.

The life is more than meat.
(Luke 12:23)

All the fat is the Lord's.
(Leviticus 3:16)

And he shall take away all the fat thereof, as the fat is taken away from off the sacrifice of peace offerings; and the priest shall burn it upon the altar for a sweet savour unto the LORD.
(Leviticus 4:31)

"We should just give our fat to God," Victoria Reynolds declares as she recalls biblical evocations of flesh and meat.[1] Her richly rendered paintings of raw meat remind us of our hedonistic desires and temptations. Her seductive images feel almost voyeuristic, and we may be ashamed by the delight we get from looking at them, but we can't make ourselves turn away. Viewers often remark, "It's beautiful—what is it?" It is only when they discover that the subject is animal flesh that revulsion may set in.

Reynolds emphasizes the beauty of meat, which is not usually a subject of aesthetic contemplation. She paints luscious, succulent, gorgeous pictures of venison, bacon strips, tripe, and reindeer meat in bold strokes, often encasing the paintings in elaborate rococo frames, which gives the meat an almost regal quality.[2] The painting *For the Carnal in Dante's Hell* (1999) depicts a side of raw, striated brisket whose curling, marbled fat is echoed by its ornate frame. Whether her subject is fresh from the butcher or ripe from the slaughter, Reynolds's depictions of meat recall Dutch portraiture and Northern Renaissance still life and *vanitas* painting. In her world, reindeer meat, chicken, pork, and other sinewy tissues and tendrils are elevated to gems, pearls, and organic, blossoming, flowerlike growths. The regal and decadent depictions of meat remind us of the transience of life. We see the fresh, ripe flesh frozen in time, on the verge of metamorphosis, knowing that in mere minutes or hours the pinks and reds will begin to rot and mold, turning gray and brown and putrid. In her paintings and drawings, Reynolds celebrates the fleeting beauty of a slab of steak or strips of bacon, and animates liver, tripe, and bung (the anus of a slaughtered animal) to look almost graceful and human. "The flesh I paint is all our flesh—made from flesh, continually being recycled from other flora and fauna."

Although Reynolds is fascinated by her subjects' sensual textures, the smell of decaying flesh is for her the worst part of being a meat painter. She chooses her subjects by seeking out the formations that are "the most attractive and have a seductive, visceral flow. I look for rhythmic undulations, wrinkles, and swells with which to make gestures on the canvas. Cuts that have intense color, varied translucence, and ruffled, ornate textures are the most beautiful." Her graphite drawings "emphasize the visceral, linear movement throughout a piece," which she compares to the "incessant beat, structure, and ornamentation of baroque music." The complex, drapery-like folds, creases, and crinkles in the drawing *Resplendent Bung* (2008) remind her of Bach's Double Violin Concerto and Bernini's *Ecstasy of Saint Theresa* (1645–52).

While living in Sweden, Reynolds attended a reindeer slaughter in the village of Åsele, in Lapland.[3] Dependent on one another for survival, the Sami have bred and herded reindeer for centuries. Just as Native Americans let no part of the buffalo go to waste, the Sami use every part of the reindeer, even putting bits in their coffee. Reynolds describes the event:

In a clearing in the snow-covered forest, a semi-trailer truck (a literal slaughterhouse on wheels) pulled up to the reindeer corral. Live reindeer pranced in one end and swung out the other as butchered carcasses on meat hooks. Near the truck, people occasionally stirred buckets of blood for making blood sausage. Dazzling lakes of red frozen reindeer blood created Pollockesque patterns on the glittering snow. Near the slaughter, a few severed reindeer heads festooned the snowy landscape like deranged Christmas decorations. Large dogs gnawed on them occasionally. Standing in the snow, I took photographs of fresh viscera and organs steaming in the arctic cold. Befriending me, a gracious Sami woman brought out organs she had always considered beautiful.

The experience of watching the reindeer slaughter led to several paintings and drawings, including *Reindeer Voluptuary* (2008), with its graceful, sinewy hunk of pink reindeer flesh that almost dances off the canvas.

Flesh fascinates Reynolds: "Flesh is infinite in its variety of textures and colors, and in its symbolic and metaphoric associations and possibilities. What's more real than flesh? It's the most relevant and literal thing, since it's where we live and what we think with. It's the ultimate, organic, watery, oily machine." Flesh is what she wants to see and make, with all its overwhelming sensations, temptations, seductions, pleasures, and pain. Oil paint was invented to render flesh realistically (or convincingly). Its slow drying time allows for blending tones and layering translucent glazes. "Like a raw, skinless spot on the canvas, paint that is still wet and blendable is said to be 'open.'" Titian's paintings, cited as the epitome of the Venetian art of painting flesh, supposedly had "thirty to forty layers of skinlike paint, with light filtering through the glazes." Reynolds's paintings serve almost as human stand-ins: "a painting's wooden stretcher can be considered a skeletal structure, with the canvas, gesso, and thin, translucent, skinlike paint layered on top like sheets of stained glass."

Before taking up meat as a subject, Reynolds depicted melting soft-serve ice cream cones as objects of desire, and messy banana splits with lacy whipped cream sprayed from a can depicted with a honeycomb, tripelike structure. "The tripe came on the ice cream's heels, and both come from the cow, who is venerated in some parts of the world." *Pillar of Fat (Edifice)* (1999) reminds Reynolds of "a pale, massive stalagmite in Carlsbad Caverns that looks like it's made of bulging, lumpy, glistening white fat." Eventually she'd like to render other dazzling things, such as human flesh, organs, and nerves; hair and fur; fleshy blossoms; cave formations; and boiling brown mud. She's had lucid dreams of being in caves that are a giant body and journeying into the mouth, throat, and lungs, and throughout the body, walking through deep forests, hills, and rivers. Clearly the body is not just a passing interest for Reynolds, and her sensitive approach to her subjects makes the work surprisingly palatable and compelling.

NOTES

1. All quotations from the artist are from conversations or e-mail correspondence with the author.
2. Reynolds feeds the leftover meat to stray cats in her neighborhood.
3. Lapland (or Sàpmi) which extends across northern Sweden, Finland, Norway, and the Kola Peninsula in Russia—is the homeland of the Sami (or Laplandic) people.

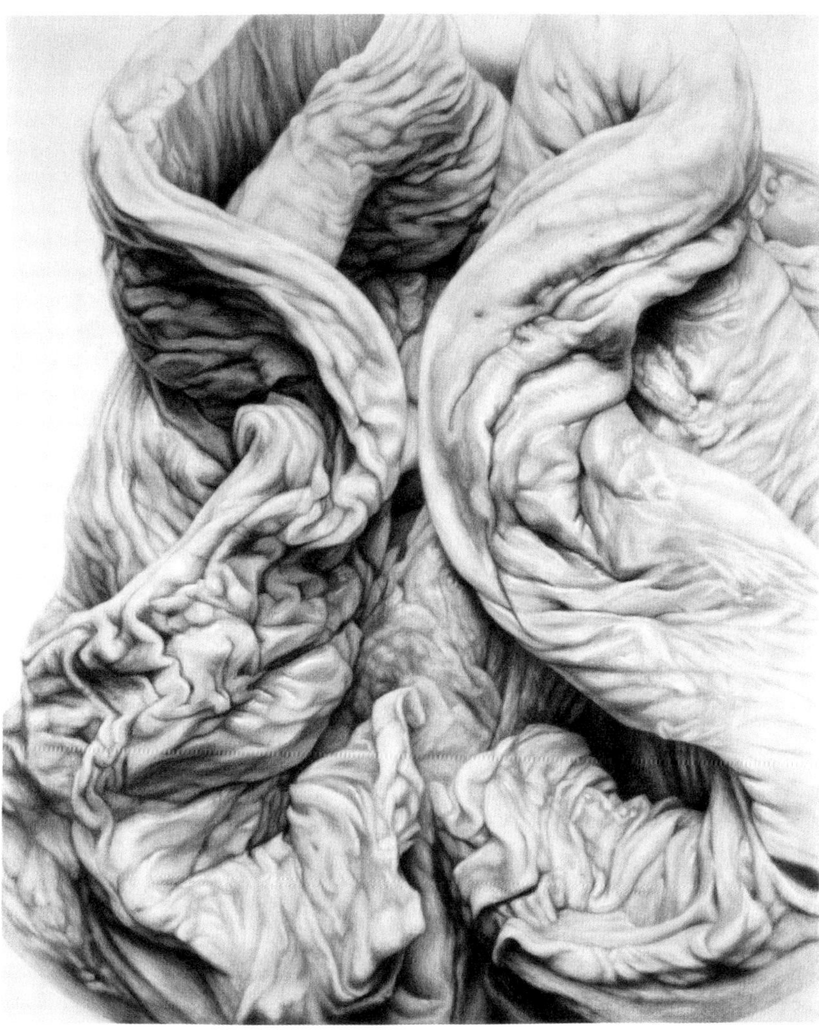

Resplendent Bung, 2008. Graphite on paper. 17 x 14 in. (43.2 x 35.6 cm). Collection of Karol Howard and George Morton.

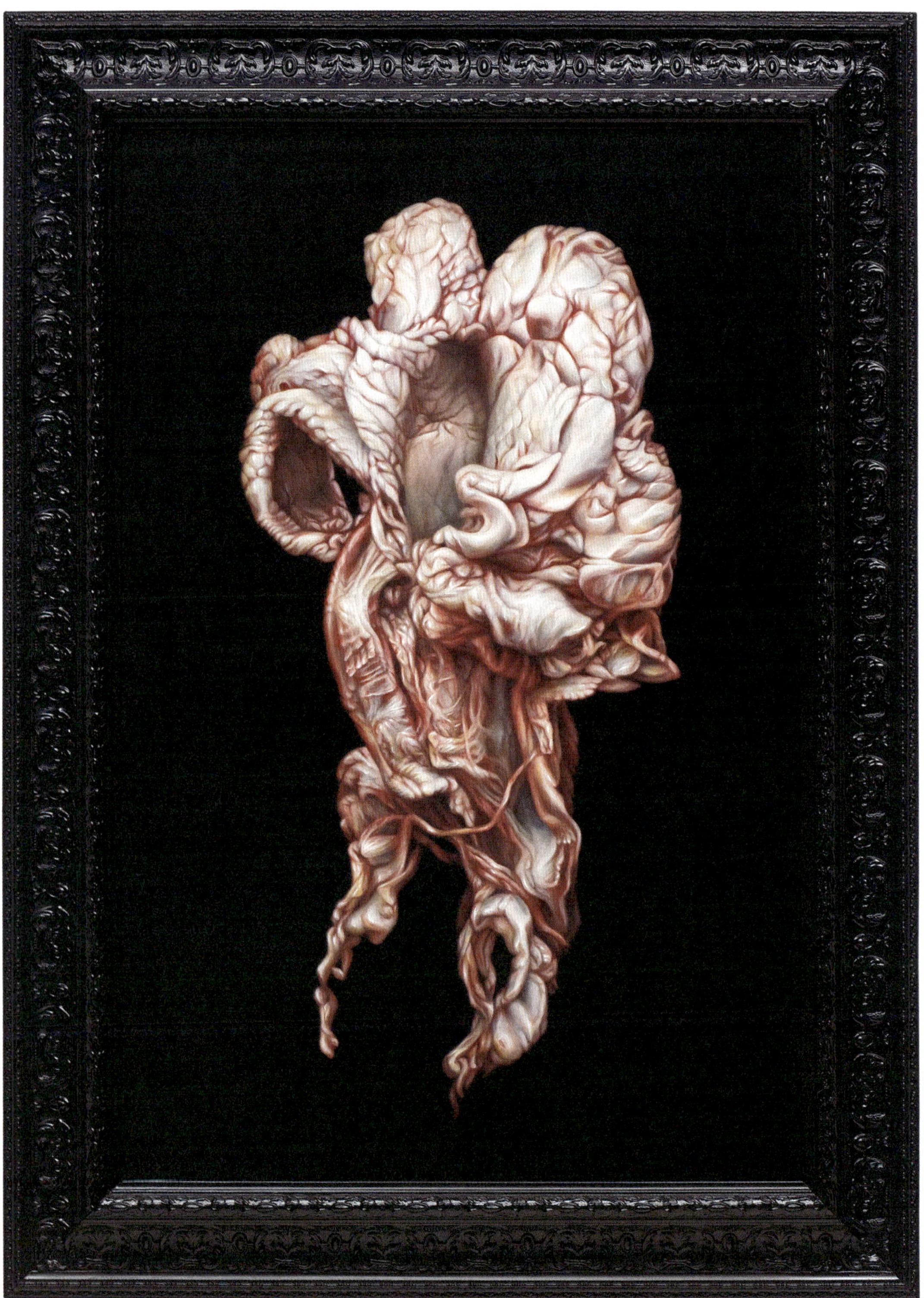

Reindeer Voluptuary, 2008. Oil on panel, frame. 44 x 32 in. (111.8 x 81.3 cm). Collection of Richard S. and Alita Rogers.

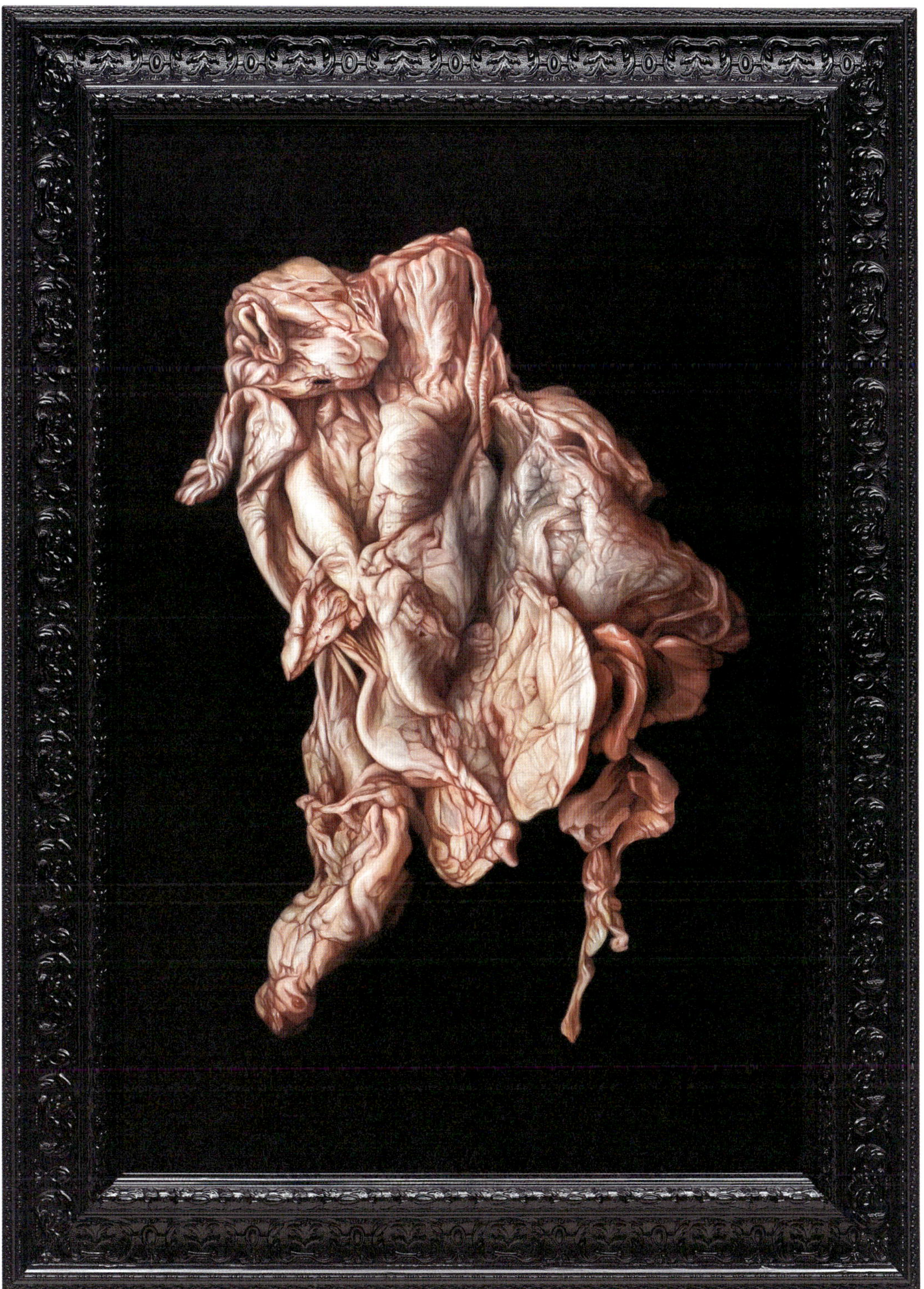

Reindeer Vision (Gievvot), 2008. Oil on panel, frame. 44 x 32 in. (111.8 x 81.3 cm). Collection of Ed Moses.

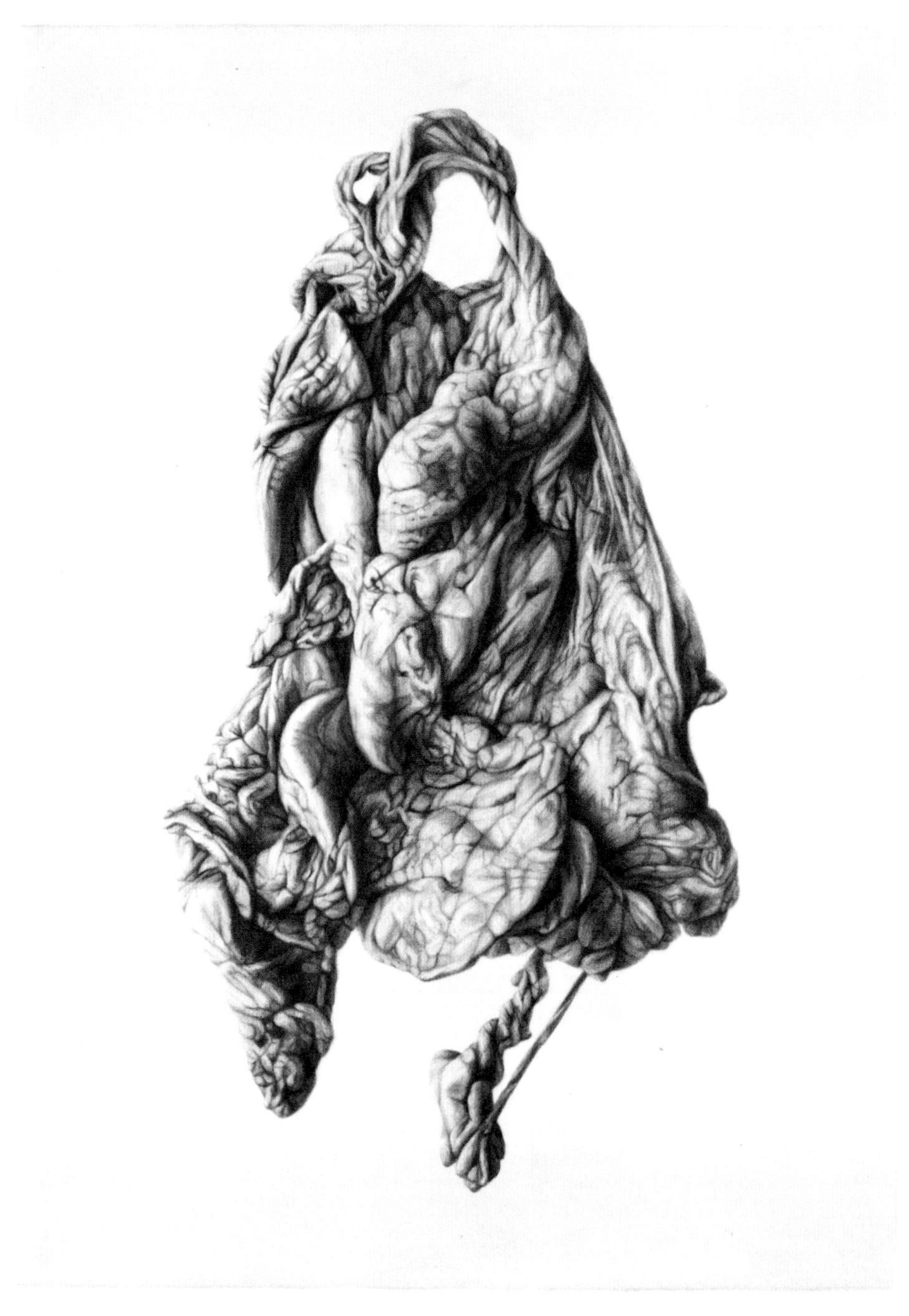

Reindeer Burka Shroud, 2008. Graphite on BFK Rives. 41 3/4 x 29 3/4 in. (106 x 75.6 cm). Hammer Museum, Los Angeles; Purchase.

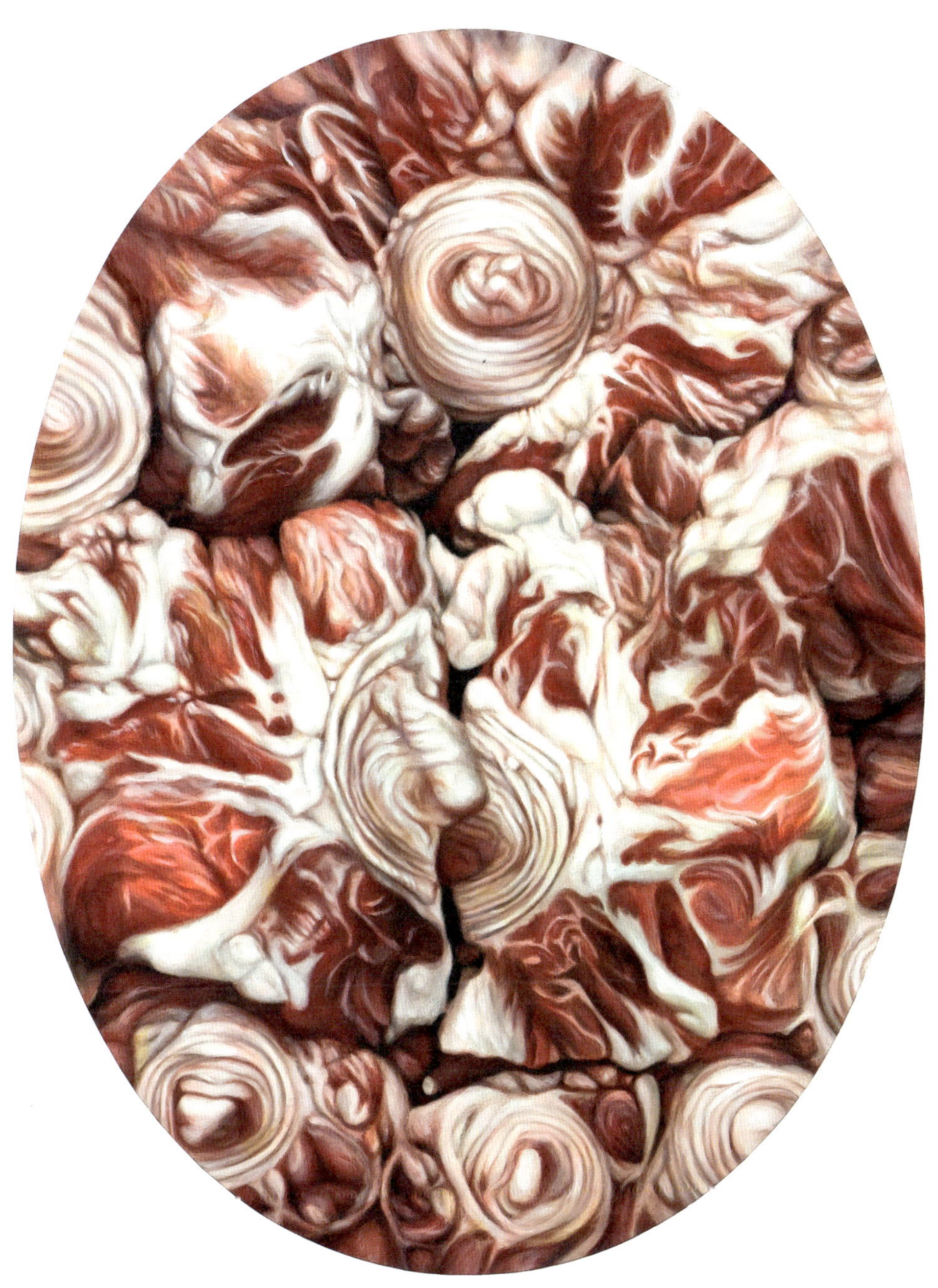

Blossoming Tail, 2008. Oil on panel. 24 x 18 in. (61 x 45.7 cm). Collection of Richard S. and Alita Rogers.

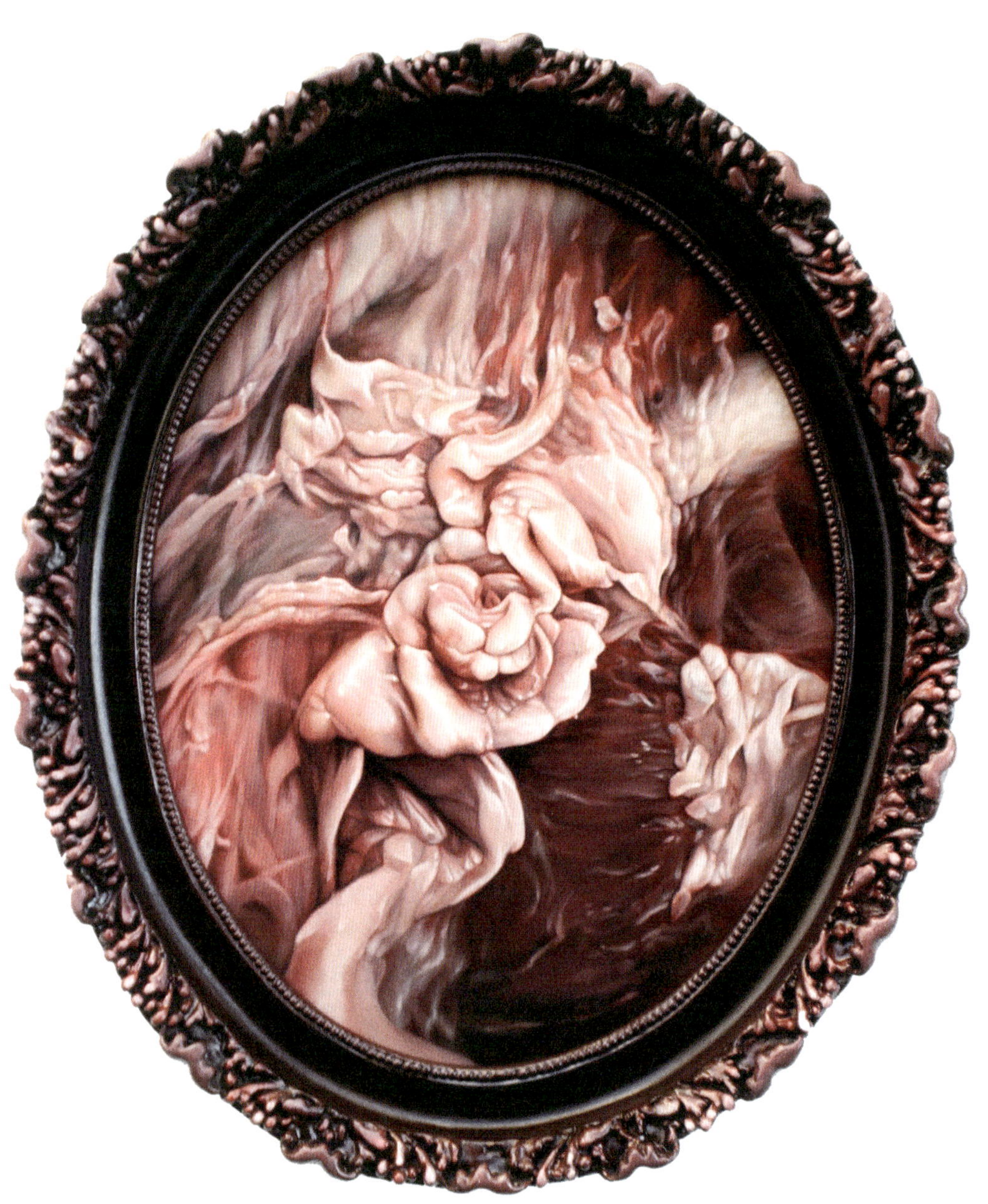

Kiss the Fat, 2004. Oil on panel, frame. 17 x 14 1/4 in. (43.2 x 36.2 cm). Richard Heller Gallery; private collection.

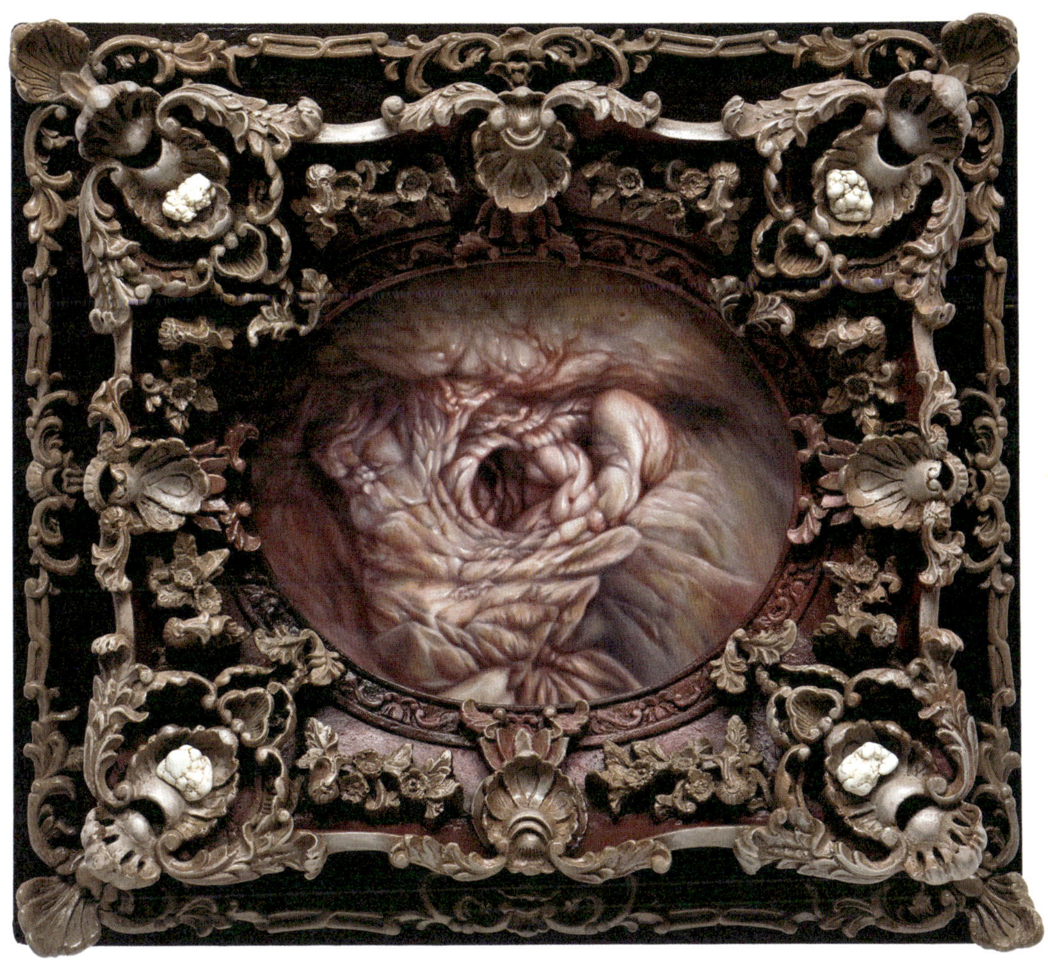

Fat Mouth, 2008. Oil on panel, frame. 16 x 18 in. (40.6 x 45.7 cm). Blaine Halvorson.

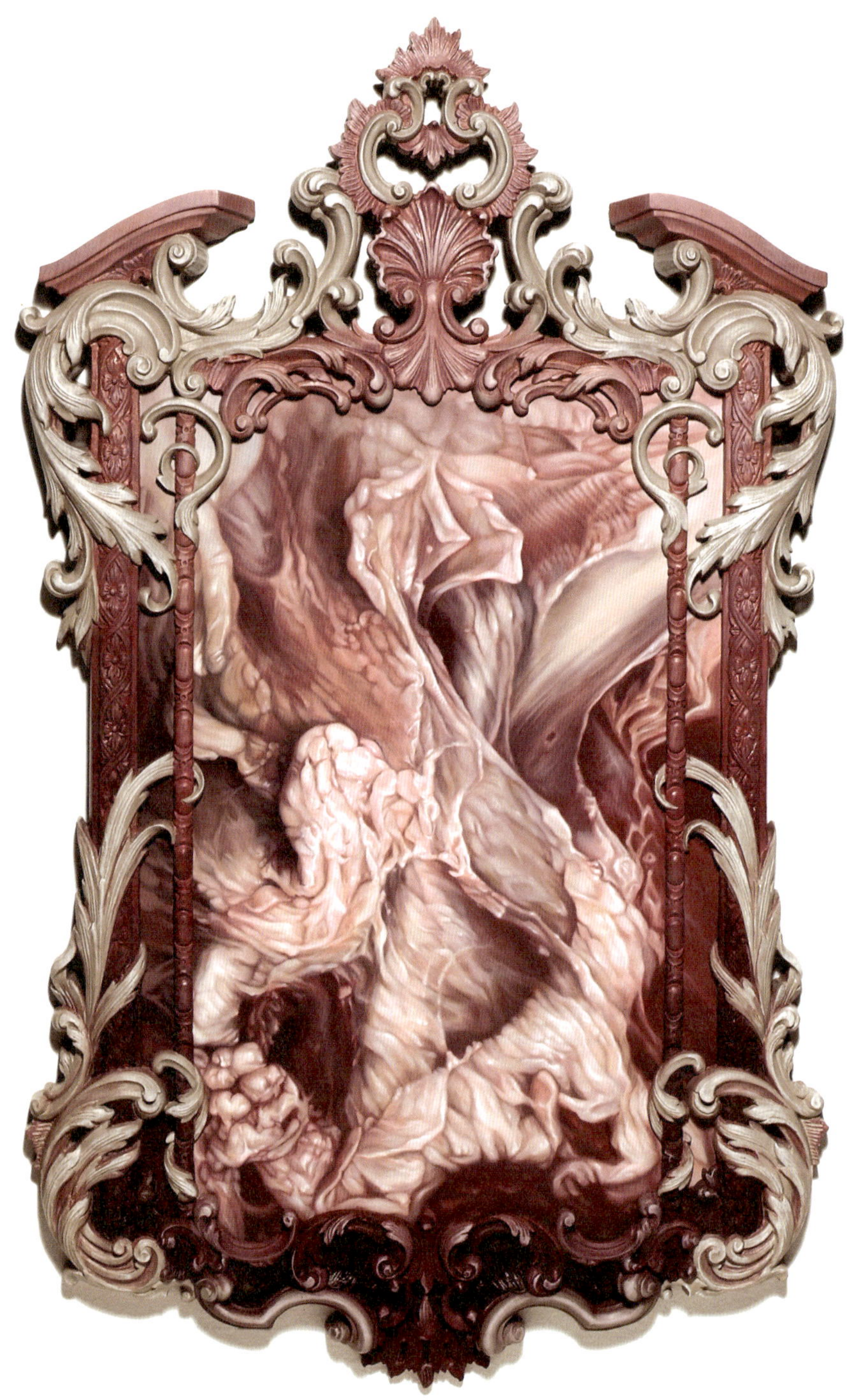

Fat of the Lamb, 2003. Oil on panel, frame. 30 x 18 1/2 in. (76.2 x 47 cm). Alan Power Collection.

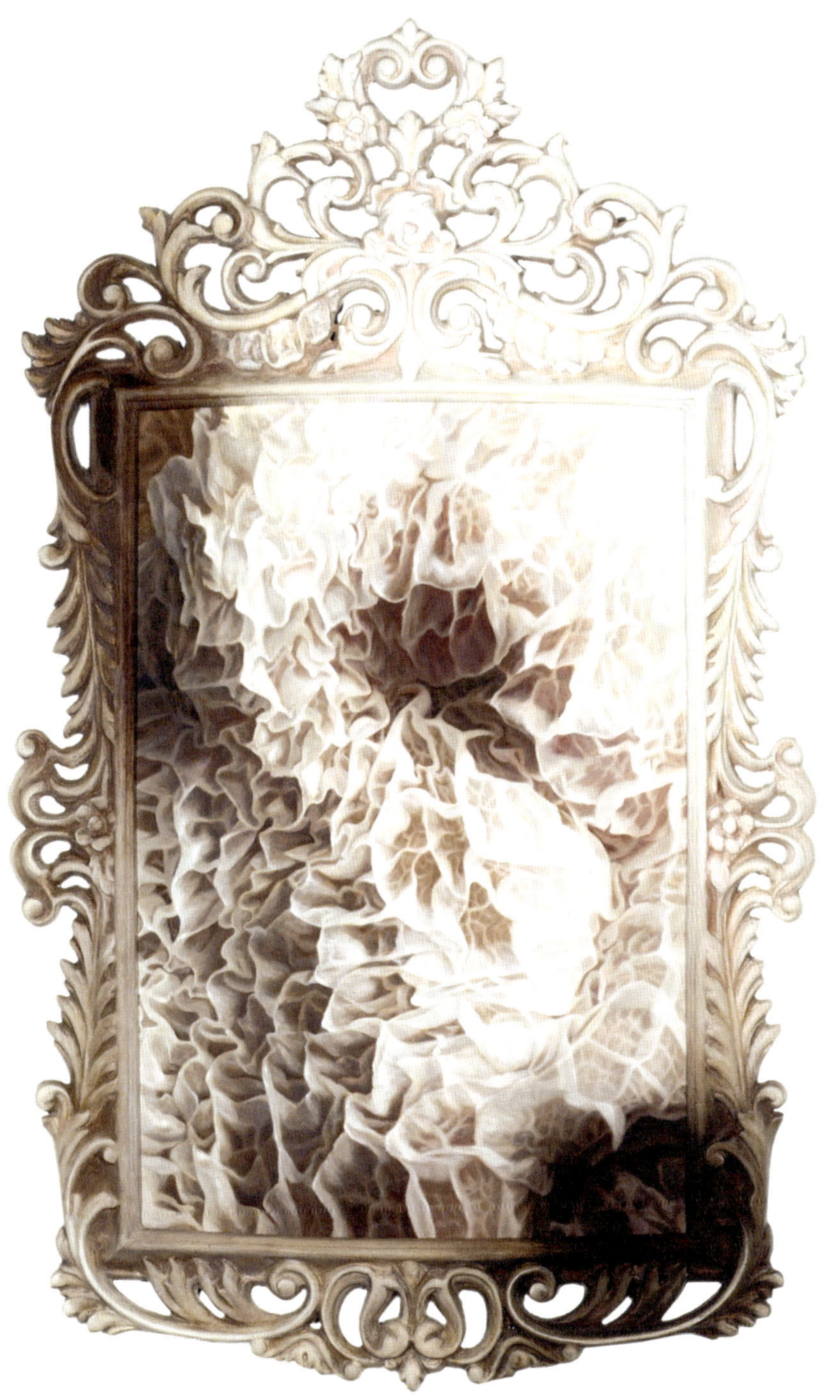

Tripe on the S-Curve, 2003. Oil on panel, frame. 29 1/8 x 17 5/8 in. (74 x 44.8 cm). Collection of Libby Lumpkin and Dave Hickey.

Kaari Upson

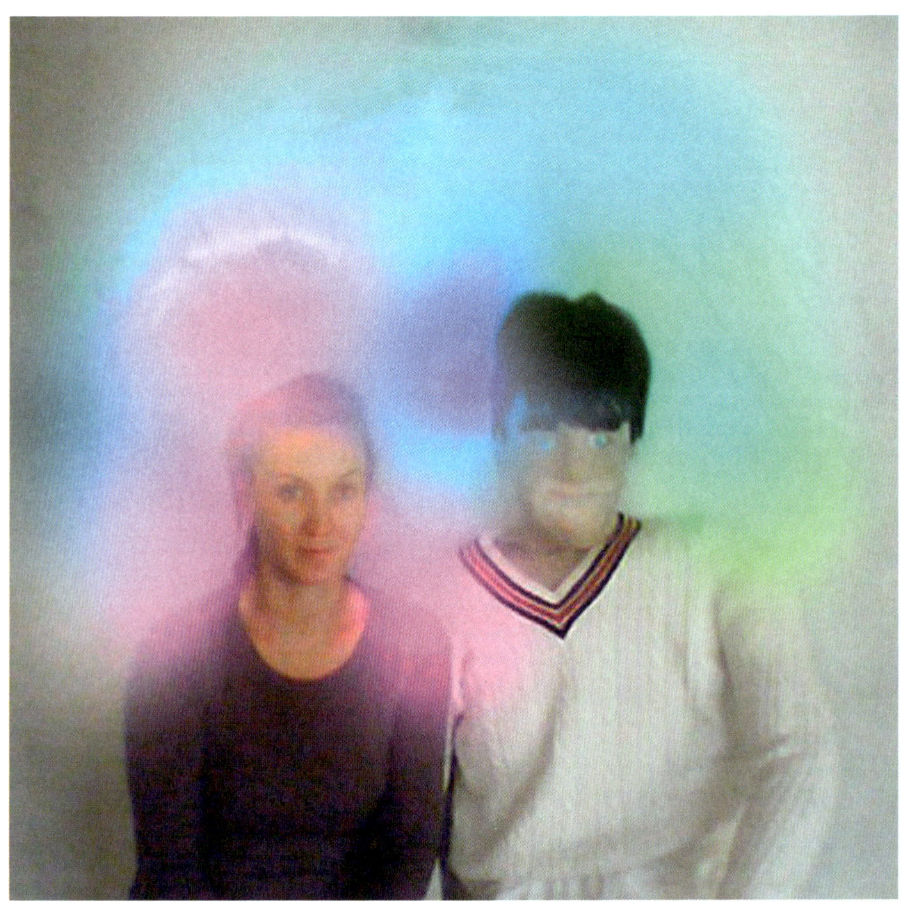

Aura Document, 2008. Ink-jet print with bleach on paper. 11 x 8 1/2 in (27.9 x 21.6 cm). Courtesy the artist and Maccarone Gallery, New York.

Kaari Upson's epic, ongoing *Larry Project* began in 2005, when she found some boxes of personal items—diaries, photo albums, a draft for a memoir, to-do lists, financial documents, letters, and more—that belonged to a man whom she had heard about but never met, and which she then used as a starting point to fill in the blanks and profile this stranger. She used both traditional investigative techniques—fingerprinting and public records searches, as well as untraditional methods like handwriting analysis and astrological compatibility reports. Her investigation quickly grew entangled with her own life, and she began to think of Larry as a stand-in for all the men in her life, using her exploration of him as a way to uncover her own issues with men: father, brother, boyfriend, husband. In fact, part of her fascination with Larry stems from his resemblance to the eighties teen idol Robby Benson (star of the 1978 movie *Ice Castles*), whom Upson both fantasized about and feared as a young girl.

Upson demolished any sense of objectivity as she further delved into this quest, making a life-size doll of the man and beginning a relationship with him that some might deem disturbing. One of the most fascinating aspects of the project is her absolute vulnerability: she's as present in the project as the mysterious Larry, and we can't consider him and his character without considering her. Upson's project grew out of reality and soon merged with fantasy, and now there is no distinction between investigator and subject, fact and fiction. In digging deeper into his life, she dug deeper into her own and implicates herself as much as, if not more than, him. When she exposes his birth certificate, she also exposes her own; when she gets his handwriting analyzed, she also has her own analyzed.

Upson has concocted a fictional narrative for the life of a man she's never actually met, and in the work she plays several roles—a mother, a lover, a sister, a seductress—which she sees as personas entirely distinct from her "real life" self. She may be using her body and her image, but she is acting out a role: "The multiplicity of these personas take *their* own shape, which is more significant to the project than I am."[1] The personas she adopts stem directly from the roles women are given in films, and for Upson, "This is a result of living in Los Angeles as an artist. The idea of reinventing oneself—of becoming one's own invention—is extremely important to this project, and it is traditionally a very Los Angeles quest. If you live out here, you are surrounded by the industry of physical, emotional, and spiritual self-improvement—navel-gazing. And it's fantastic." Upson updates the New Age, very California tradition of self-improvement by seeing herself always in relation to Larry. She's gone through est training with him and extensive self-analysis, and she has taken the Larry doll with her to see psychics, clairvoyants, and an aura photographer. "My work is driven by my interest in psychological space. The various ways in which I perceive, investigate, and metabolize the source material create a platform of intense layering in which one thing becomes an impetus for another. They also create gaps where perception fails and investigation can't reach. Most important developments take place in those gaps."

Upson has never used an actor or stand-in. Early on, she took real risks and put herself in situations where she could have met Larry but quickly realized that she had no interest in meeting the real Larry. "The project is shaped more by his absence than his presence," she notes. She does fantasize about attending his funeral—not because she wishes him dead but to gain access to the reminiscences, perceptions, and speculations of people who knew him. "The idea of what somebody means to others—that multiplicity of perspective—takes its own shape, and in this project, that shape is more significant to me than Larry is." The inevitable impact on her personal life from an immersive endeavor such as this makes it virtually impossible to keep her work and life separate. At this point, Upson says, she is "working toward ridding myself of his possession over me; loving myself before I can love another. The Honeymoon Period is over, and now I've reached a point of questioning this 'relationship.'"

Upson's interpretation of the iconic Playboy Mansion grotto (Larry has been a regular at the mansion over the last thirty or so years) is the site for this "exorcism" of sorts. She uses the structure as a set for videos that further explore the obliteration of the self that occurs when one merges with the other. She is searching for herself and at the same time analyzing her transgressions, rebellions, and personal relationships with men. As one of the chapters in *The Larry Project*, the grotto represents a decoupling of Larry and Kaari. And in building something on this scale, Upson has created a substitute or parallel world, a fantasy space composed of accumulated facts that have been filtered and physicalized. In fact, she has never actually been to the Playboy Mansion and seen the grotto firsthand. She has created several characters who are prepared to make serious attempts to get access to the mansion—they've each posed for sexy pinup pictures and sent handwritten letters to Hugh Hefner—but she has waited to see the real thing until her own grotto is completed, so that what she makes "is only a manifestation of the images, anecdotes, and mythology of the space, rather than any actual experience with it." Similarly, when she made the Larry doll in the Honeymoon Period chapter, it was based on the idea of creating an accurate representation of someone she had never met, drawing on speculation, rumor, and imagination.

Initially Upson had an overall plan for how the project would unfold in a series of chapters. The grotto was always part of the plan; she imagined it as a re-creation of Larry's desires. She questions her relationship to him in the current phase of the project. It's been more than four years since she first came upon the source material, but there was a two-year gestation period before the project began, so this "relationship" is really only two years old. In the next chapter, Larry's house (which burned down a year or so after she retrieved the boxes) will develop into another character/subject as a site of false memory. *The Larry Project* brings up numerous ethical and moral issues, but Upson has little interest in providing models of behavior or morality tales. Ultimately she's more interested in posing questions. What grew out of simple curiosity about a stranger turned into an elaborate, multilayered journey of self-exploration with no clear end in sight.

NOTES

1. All quotations from the artist are from conversations or e-mail correspondence with the author.

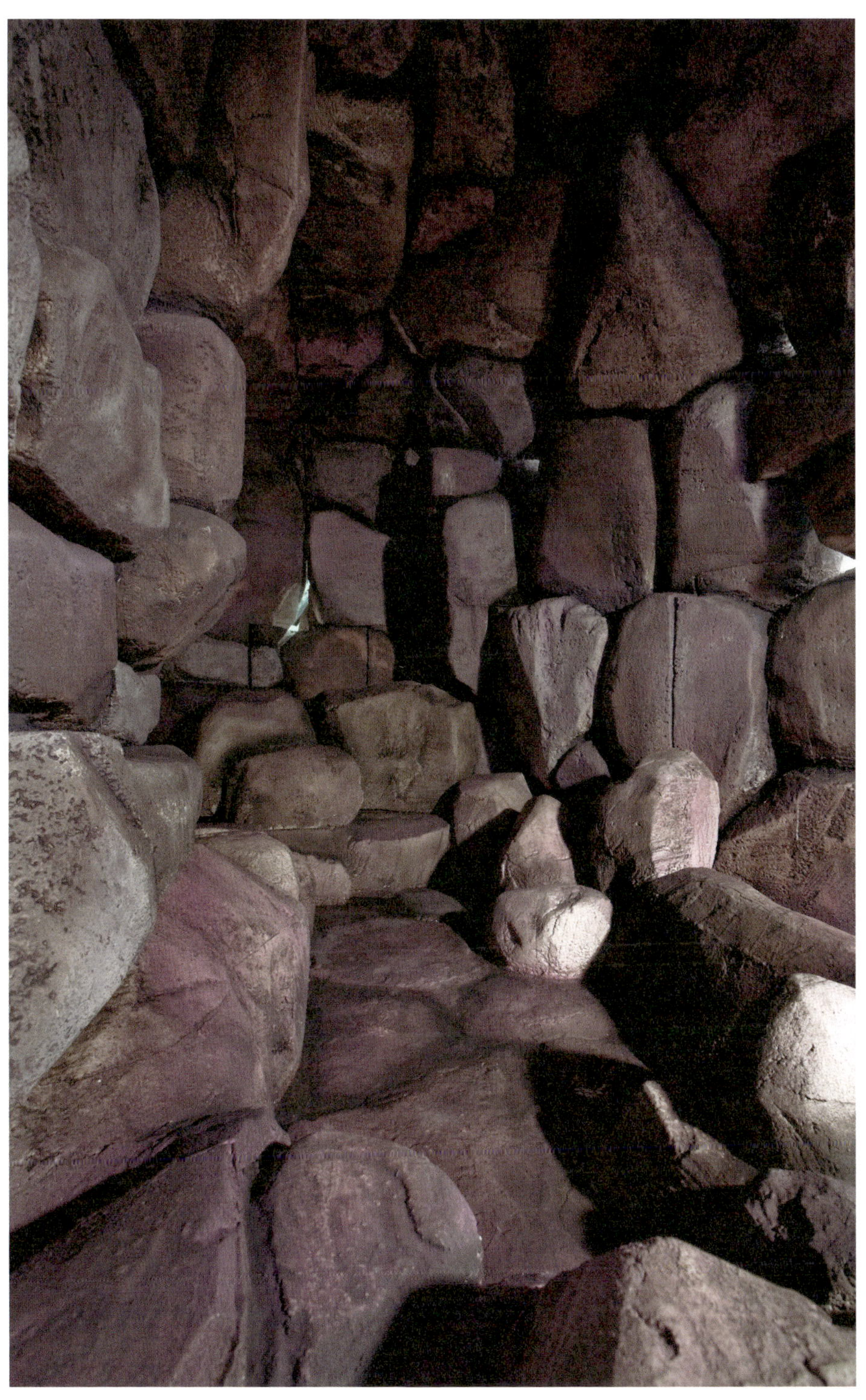

The Grotto (work in progress), 2008–9. Mixed media. Dimensions variable. Courtesy the artist and Maccarone Gallery, New York.

Mr. Hugh Hefner
10236 Charing Cross Road
Los Angeles, CA 90024

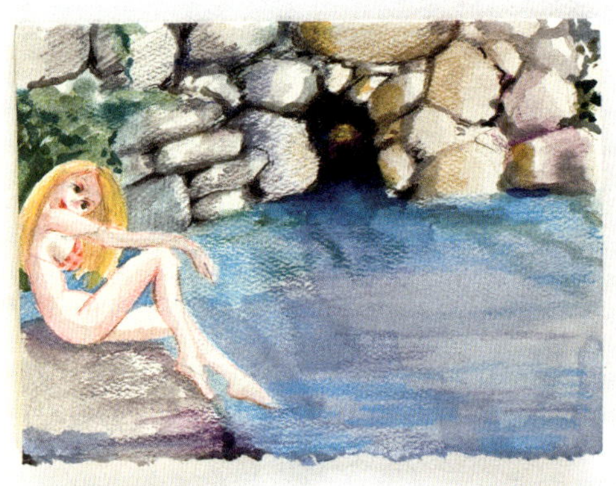

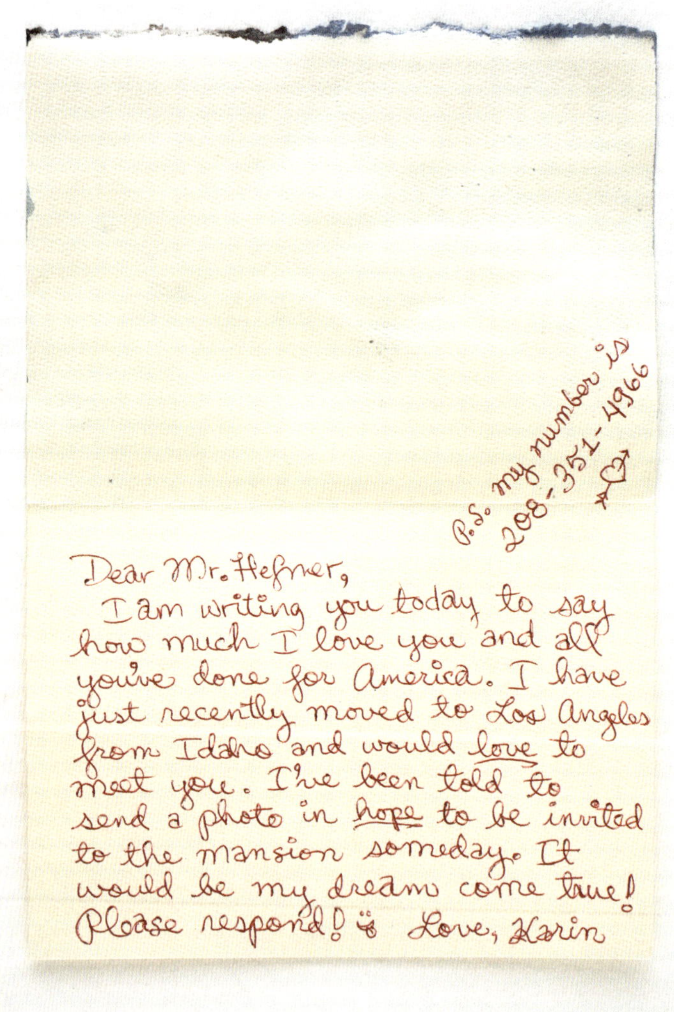

P.S. my number is
208-351-4966

Dear Mr. Hefner,
I am writing you today to say how much I love you and all you've done for America. I have just recently moved to Los Angeles from Idaho and would love to meet you. I've been told to send a photo in hope to be invited to the mansion someday. It would be my dream come true! Please respond! Love, Karin

Top: *Exterior letter 2: Idaho girl*, 2008. Watercolor on paper. Two parts, 4 x 6 in. (10.2 x 15.2 cm) each. Courtesy the artist and Maccarone Gallery, New York.

Bottom: *Letter 2: Idaho girl*, 2008. Ink on paper. 8 x 6 in. (20.3 x 15.2 cm). Courtesy the artist and Maccarone Gallery, New York.

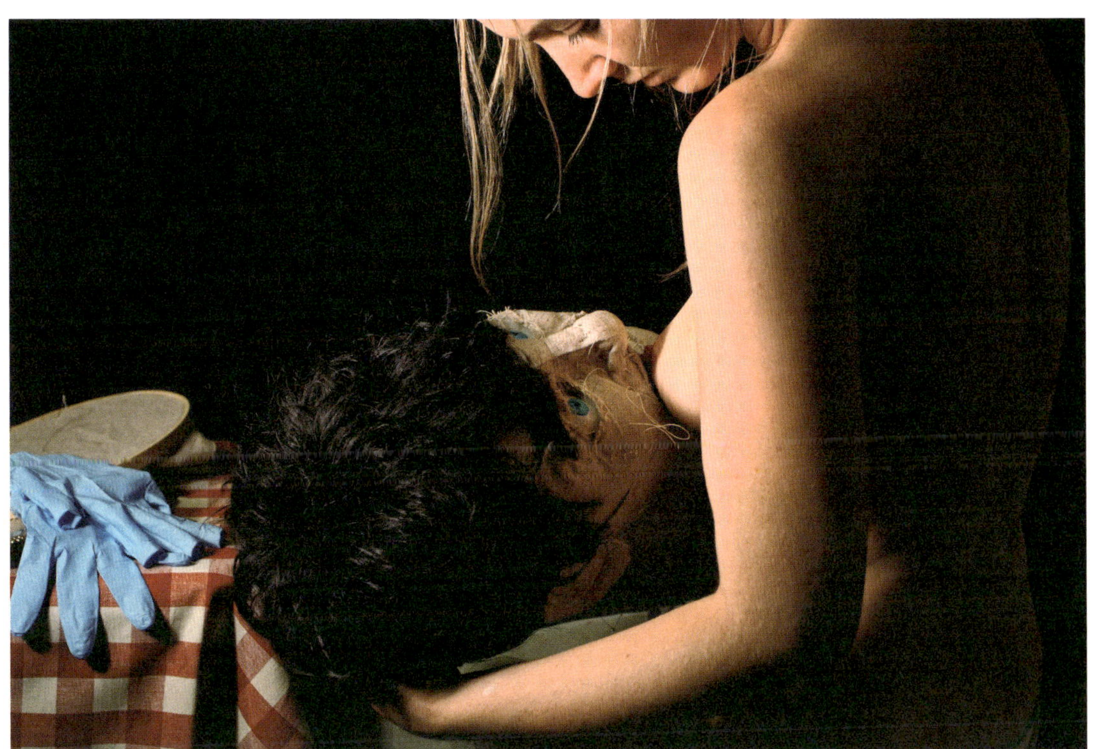

It's never enough, 2007. Photograph. 24 x 36 in. (61 x 91.4 cm). Courtesy the artist and Maccarone Gallery, New York.

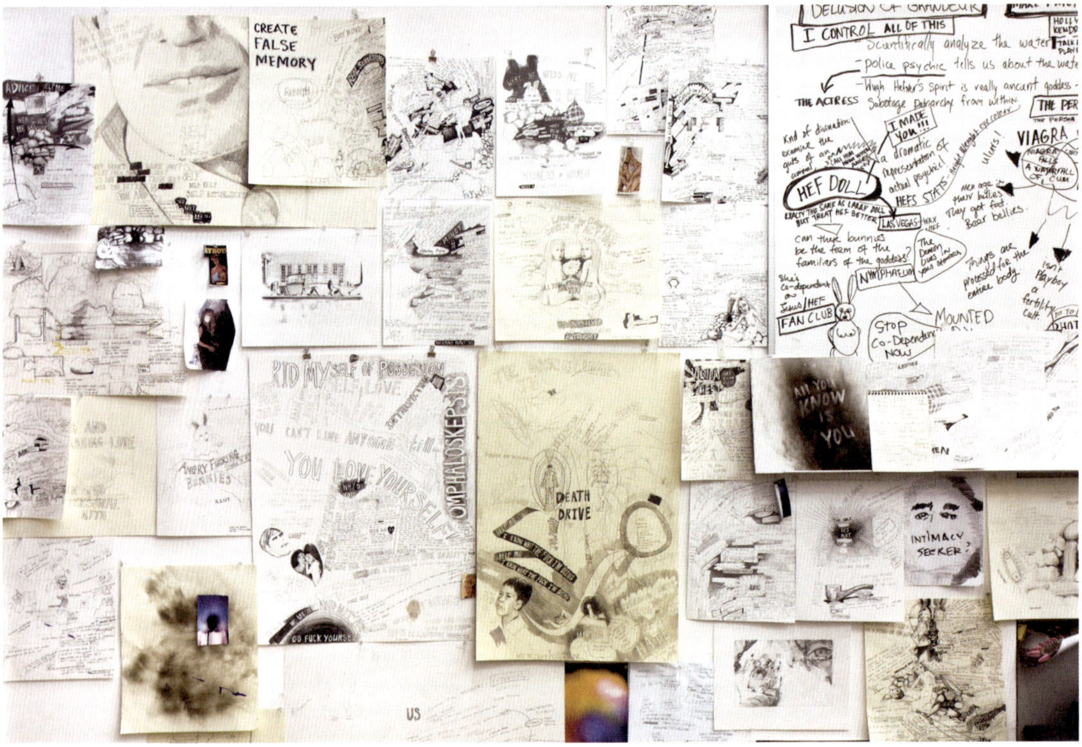

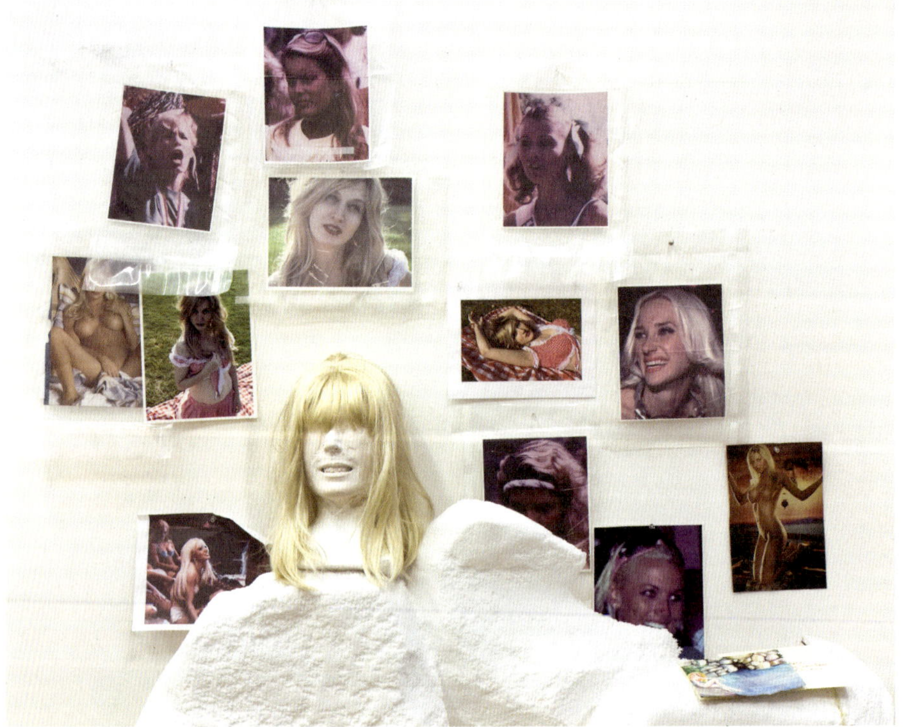

Top: Detail of drawings on the studio wall, 2008. Ink and graphite on paper. Dimensions variable. Courtesy the artist and Maccarone Gallery, New York.

Bottom: *Research for Angry Bunnies* (detail), 2008. Mixed media. Dimensions variable. Courtesy the artist and Maccarone Gallery, New York.

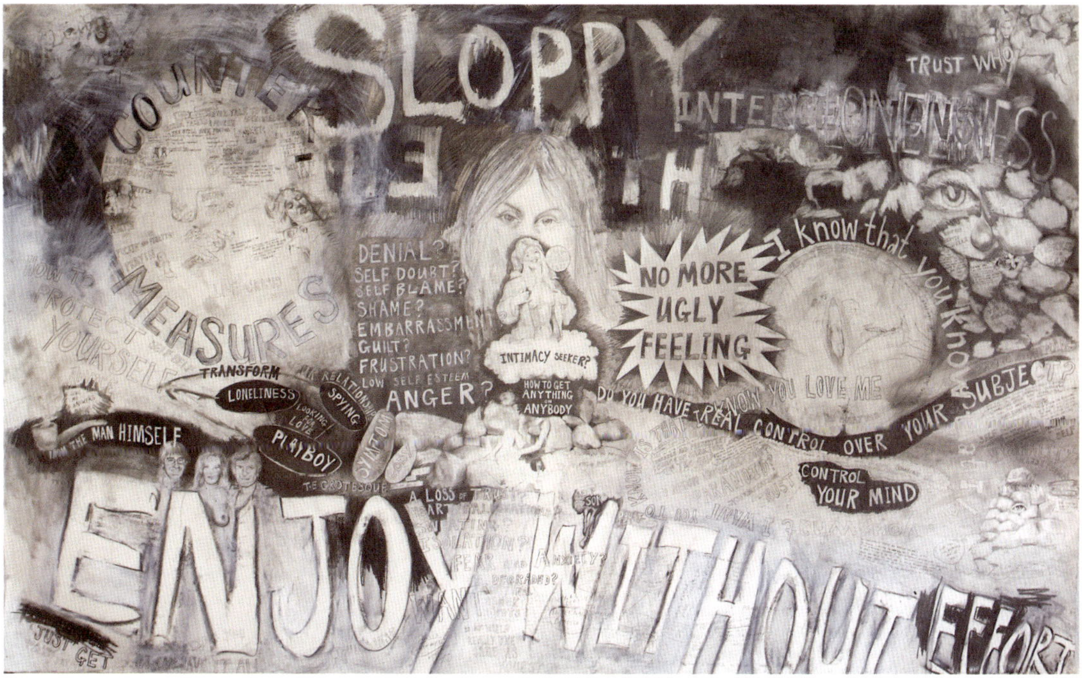

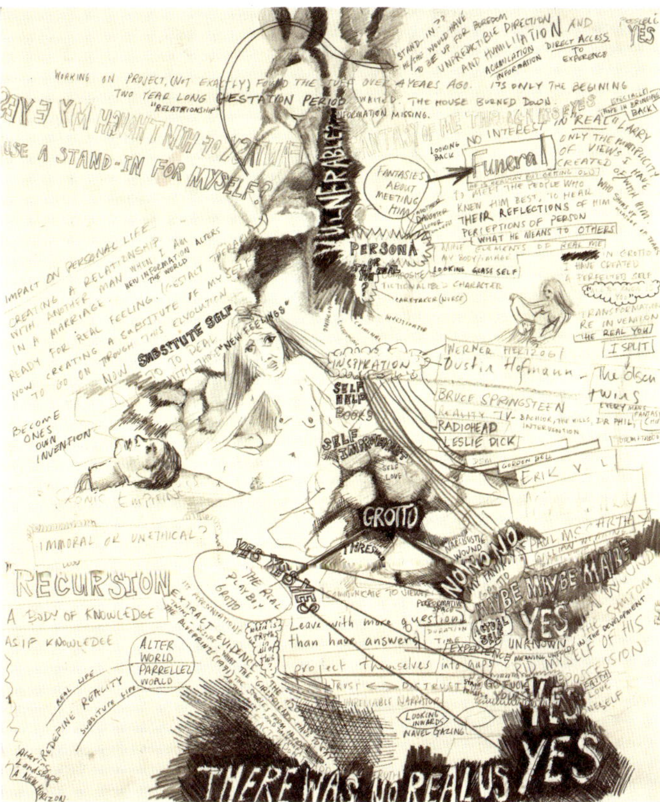

Top: *Sloppy Interceptions*, 2008. Pencil on paper. 48 x 72 in. (121.9 x 182.9 cm). Courtesy the artist and Maccarone Gallery, New York.

Bottom: Untitled, 2008. Graphite and ink on paper. 48 x 72 in. (121.9 x 182.9 cm). Courtesy the artist and Maccarone Gallery, New York.

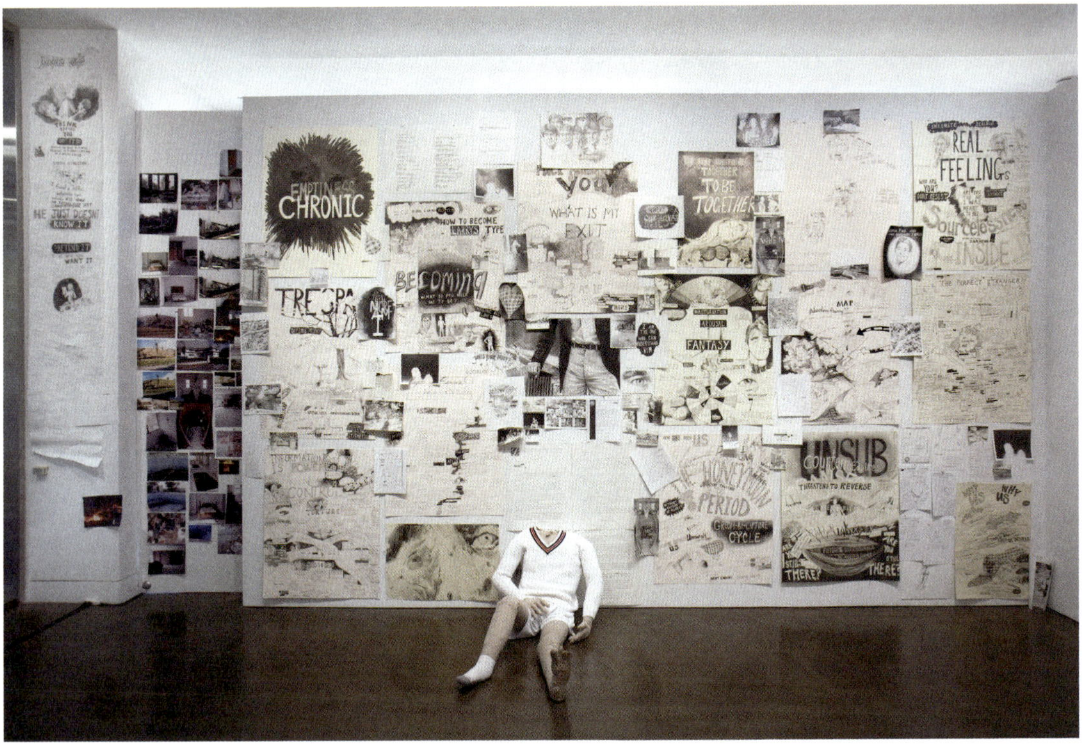

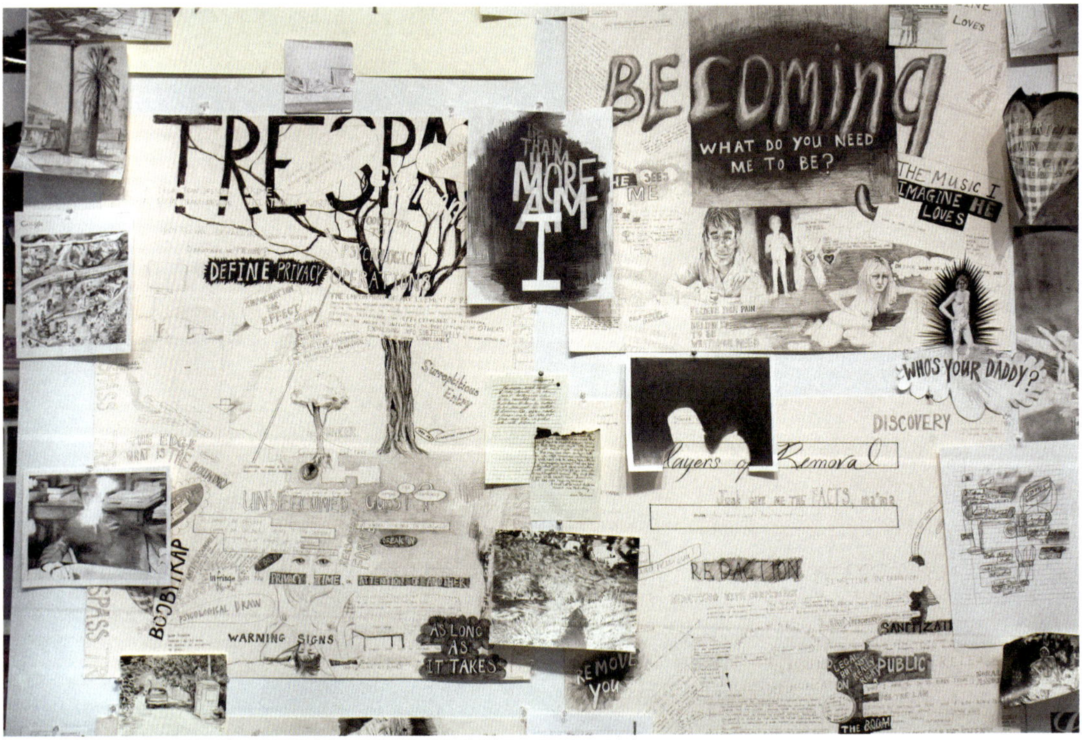

Top: *The Larry Project*, 2007. Installation view, *Hammer Projects: Kaari Upson*, Hammer Museum, Los Angeles, November 27, 2007–February 17, 2008.

Bottom: Untitled drawing installation (detail), 2007. Pencil and ink on paper. 120 x 192 in. (304.8 x 487.7 cm). Hammer Museum, Los Angeles, Purchased with funds provided in part by Dean Valentine and Amy Adelson and John Rubeli.

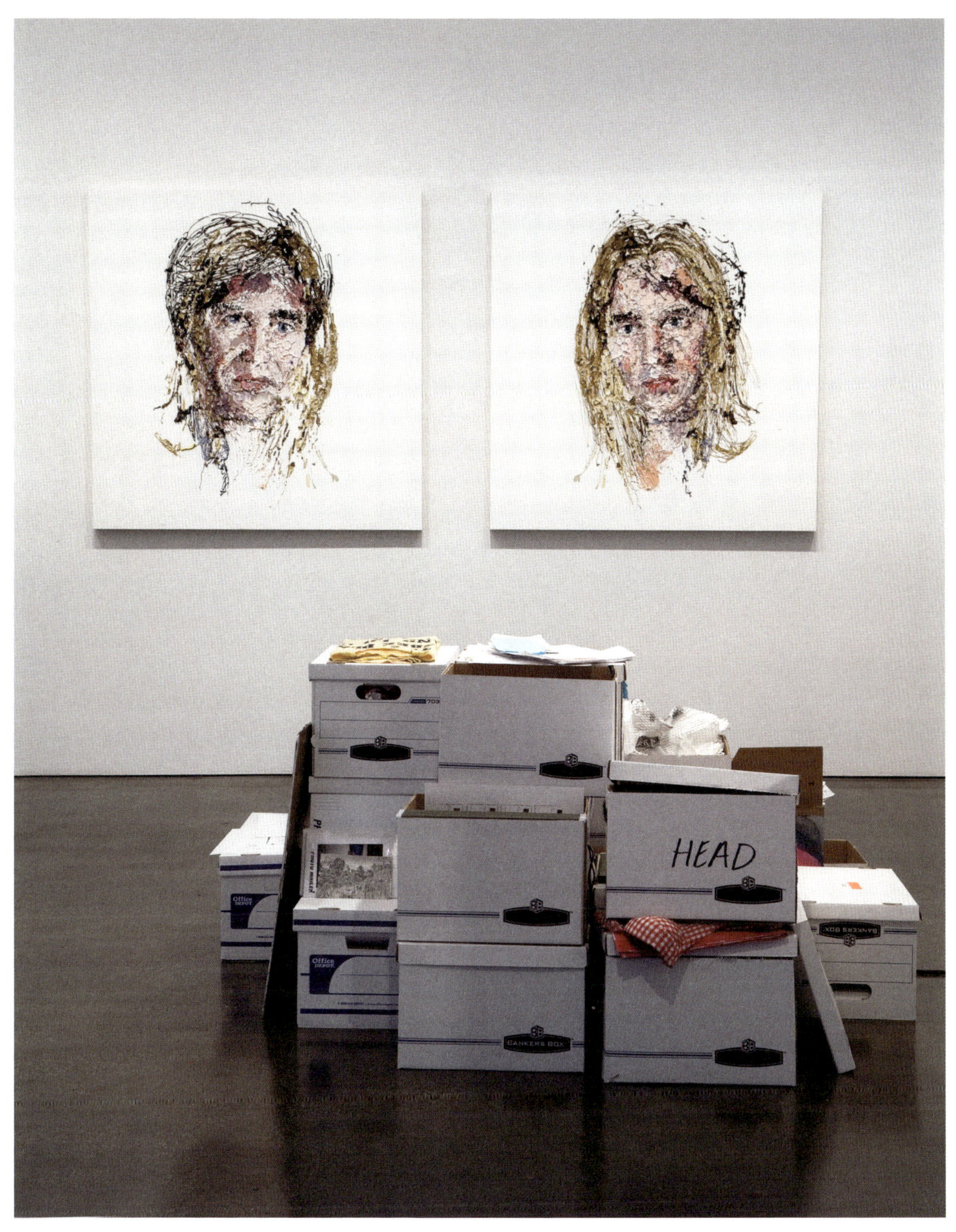

The Larry Project, 2007. Installation view, *Hammer Projects: Kaari Upson*, Hammer Museum, Los Angeles, November 27, 2007–February 17, 2008. The artist made the paintings shown here, called Kiss paintings, by smashing together still-wet portraits of Larry and herself, to further merge the two characters. Upson has produced nearly thirty of these Kiss diptychs to date.

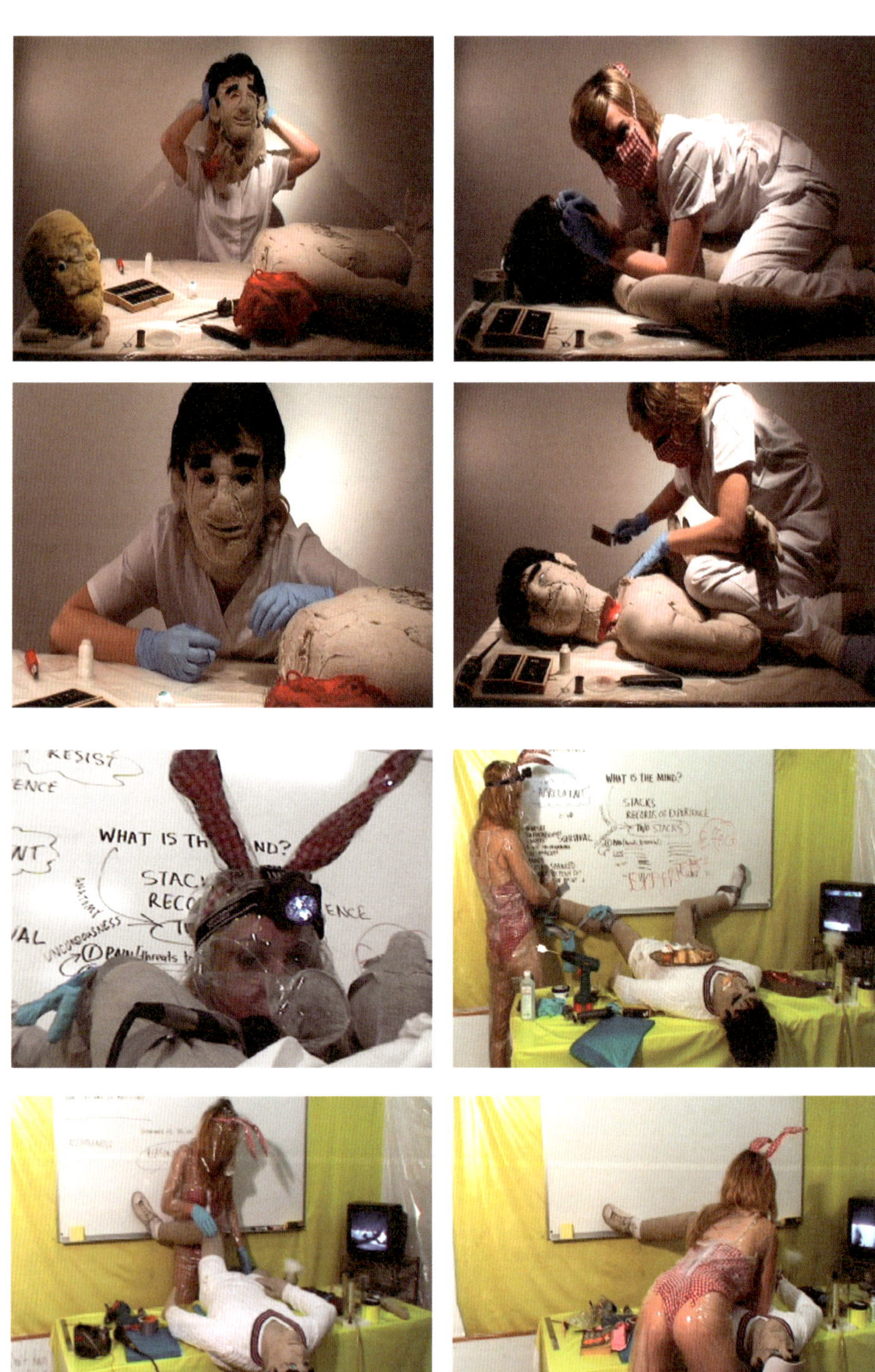

Two top rows: Stills from *As Long as It Takes—Part I: The Head*, 2007. DVD, color, sound. 56 min. Courtesy the artist and Maccarone Gallery, New York.

Two bottom rows: Stills from *As Long as It Takes—Part II: The Ass*, 2007. DVD, color, sound. 22 min. Courtesy the artist and Maccarone Gallery, New York.

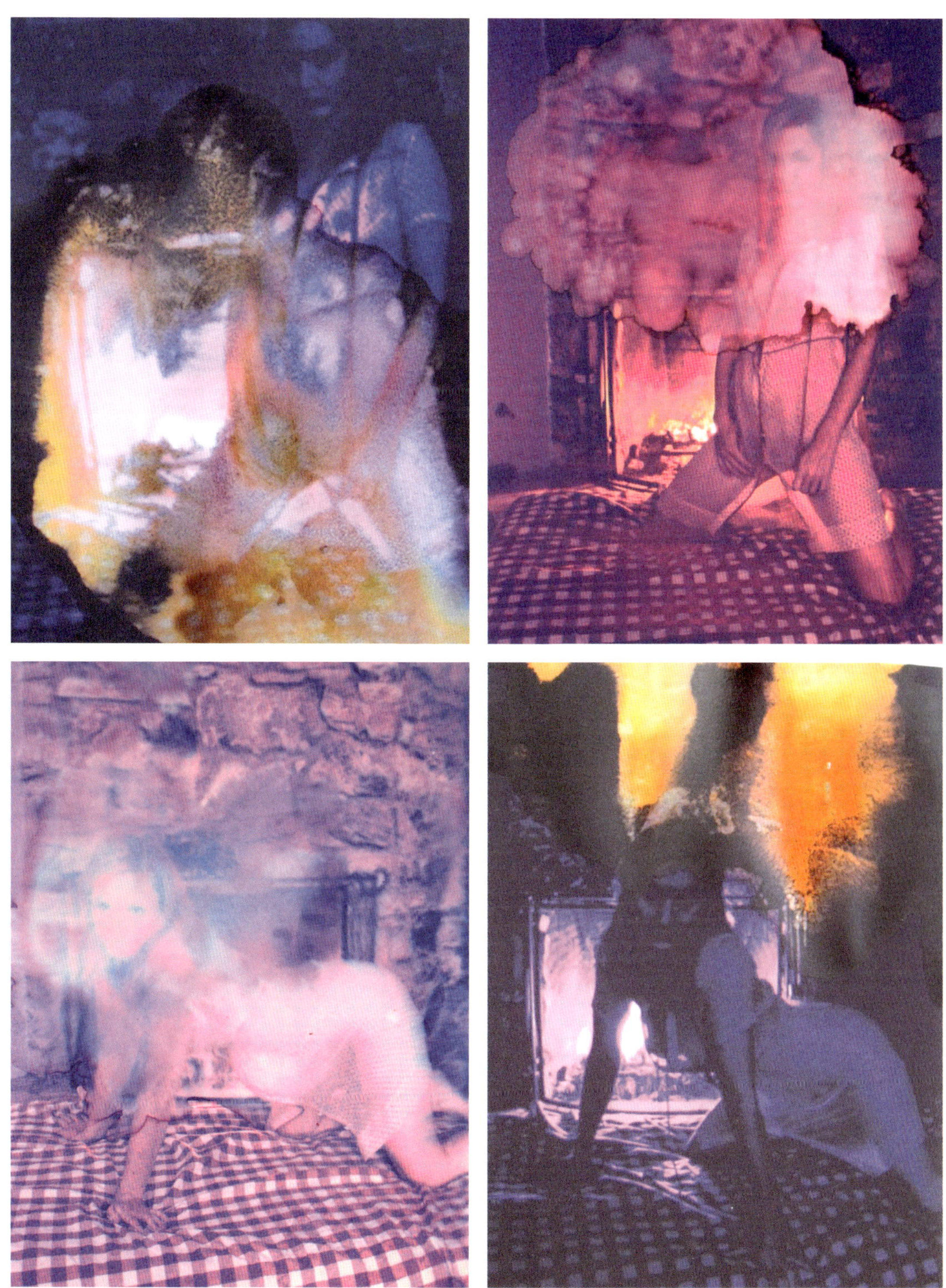

Stills from *Calm down I am not trying to destroy you*, 2008. DVD, color, sound. Approx. 30 min. Courtesy the artist and Maccarone Gallery, New York.

Charlie White

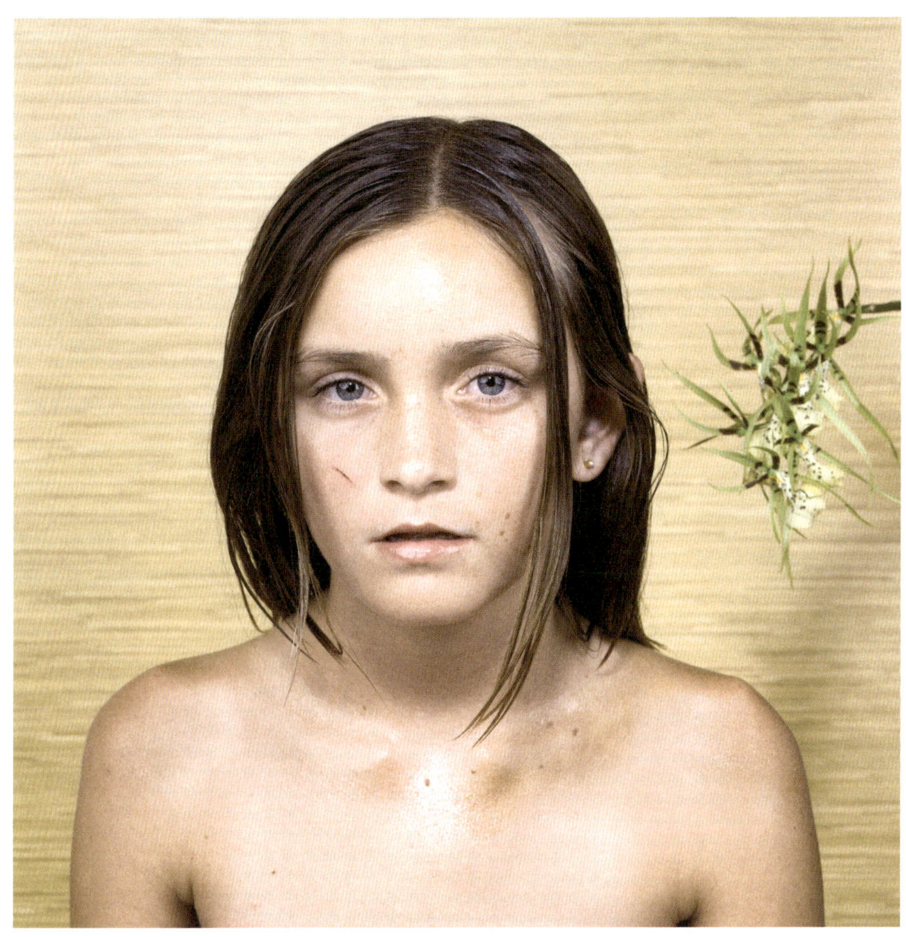

Jody, 2005, from Everything Is American. Chromogenic print. 30 x 30 in. (76.2 x 76.2 cm). Courtesy the artist.

Charlie White precociously burst on the scene with soft-core pornographic photos of a veiny, blue-skinned female alien in the late 1990s (Femalien, 1996). His next photo series, In a Matter of Days (1999), explored Hollywood clichés such as monster and disaster movies. The photos are so expertly produced that they look like commercial advertisements or movie stills, but there is always something slightly off or some missing information that distinguishes them from mere promotional materials. Reminiscent of a 1970s horror film still, *The Inland Empire* (1999) depicts a woman fighting off a skeletal monster with a stick. In *Highland Park* (1999) a man hoists a decapitated monster head while a boy pokes a stick into its nostrils and a girl looks on from behind a chain-link fence. The series Understanding Joshua (2001) features a pathetic alien puppet named Joshua, cast as the high school dork. We see Joshua being forced to watch an innocent blond girl get doused with milk (*Getting Lindsay Linton*, 2001) or slumping dejectedly, naked on a toilet as a girl's bare legs are visible in the shower and a wig and pile of clothes sit on the floor nearby (*Her Place*, 2000). The works are caught somewhere between Hollywood high production and sophomoric jokes—we are left to fill in the blanks between the images we see in order to complete the narratives.

White, who grew up in Philadelphia and later lived in New York, doesn't believe that he knew how much his thinking related to Los Angeles until he lived here. For White, Hollywood is a complicated model. He's experienced some of the ugliness of the industry, which is "defined by its lack of freedom, and its lack of experimentation."[1] Hollywood inspires him to dismantle ideas. "I see it as a sickness in many people in Los Angeles; it rots things, good things, good people, good ideas, it whores them, and helps them erode down to a memory of what they once were or planned to be. People who love Hollywood adore it, crave it; they are sick." He's obsessed with the *product* of the entertainment industry and feeds off it: "I do not see myself as free from it; I see myself as tormented by it, like most people."

In constructing his elaborate scenarios, White visually references the shallow sets of porn films, the three walls of the sitcom, and the flatness of children's television. His own personal history and insecurities provide fodder for his photographs. *Three Heartfelt Singers & Autobiographical Television Posters* (2003) depicts a children's television show, *Harry in the Hospital*, inspired by White's own childhood heart surgeries. In the last few years White has become interested in the *image* of the adolescent/teen girl, as well as the teen boy. In 2003 he began the work titled *Leda*, which was "a reinterpretation of Ovid's 'Leda and the Swan' through an American teen-princess lens." During the casting for *Leda*, White met another young girl named Cyrilla Strothers. Intrigued by this girl, who for him represented a mysterious other, White gave Cyrilla's friends and family members cameras so that they could document her daily routine and capture her activities, gestures, and expressions. Through these photos he was able to get inside the head of a "typical" adolescent girl. *The Cyrilla Strothers Project* (2004–6) eventually comprised an extensive database of about eleven thousand images examining the life of one exurban American girl.

This project led White to make his first film, *American Minor* (2008), which depicts a restless teenage girl as she sits around the house, eats cereal, and watches TV, bored but heavily burdened by something. The actress embodies the angst of anticipation and the trauma of impending change over which young teenagers have absolutely no control. If you don't feel anxious and uncomfortable watching this video, you were never an adolescent. It might lead you to label White the next Humbert Humbert searching for his very own Lolita, or to applaud him for so eerily capturing the indescribable feeling of being a thirteen-year-old girl.

White took things further with Teen and Transgender Comparative Study (2008), a series of five photographs.[2] The double portraits pair adolescent girls and pre-op transwomen (male-to-female transgender people) who share an uncanny resemblance to each other. The arresting images highlight the awkwardness of that moment when they are on the brink of transformation. The series began almost accidentally after White had made a series of refined portraits of teenagers that he felt had mostly failed. He did, however, find interesting a series of teenagers and one transwoman. He realized that he didn't know how to view the transgender subject in an unexploitative manner. He became obsessed with both teen and transgender imagery and began to sort out how to look at teens and transwomen from the perspective of an adult male. "I had a jpeg on my computer from 2004; it was a grid of pictures that I had made, placing one of my teen models next to my M-to-F model, Tina, because they seemed alike in some way. It took a few years to realize that this grid was the answer to how to look at both groups, and even once I could see the parallel, I was not clear on how to stage the portraits." Fascinated by that transitional moment in the life of a teenager, he juxtaposes adolescents on the verge of womanhood with transwomen, also on the verge of womanhood. The similarities are uncanny. The background of the grid also became important for this new series. Because of its blankness, it could be both something and nothing at once and situates the subjects in a neutral, almost specimen-like context. The remarkable resemblance and shared awkwardness of these portraits makes them unsettling and hard to look at, but at the same time they are hard to turn away from and impossible to forget. In this series White is looking at two puberties, two girls, two faces, and two ideas that for him become one, and in that singularity we find many of society's desires.

In the process of White's research he has ventured into a new culture, completely outside his day-to-day life. In getting to know his transgender and teen models and the worlds they inhabit, he's decreased the distance between himself and his subjects, which was a distinct aspect of his previous photographs. In a few cases he traveled deeply into "two separate but similar worlds at once: the space of the tween and that of transgender." He began to see himself in them or to see how much he shared with teen girls and transwomen and those in-between states that are malleable and unfixed. "I feel like a tourist in all parts of my life, so no one area feels more natural than the other." Nonetheless the work is clearly coming from the viewpoint of a male observer: "I can't deny that. I do not want to deny that, or my relation to the photographs would be misleading."

NOTES

1. All quotations from the artist are from conversations with the author.

2. The Teen and Transgender Comparative Study was funded in part through the USC Advancing Scholarship in the Humanities and Social Sciences Research Grant.

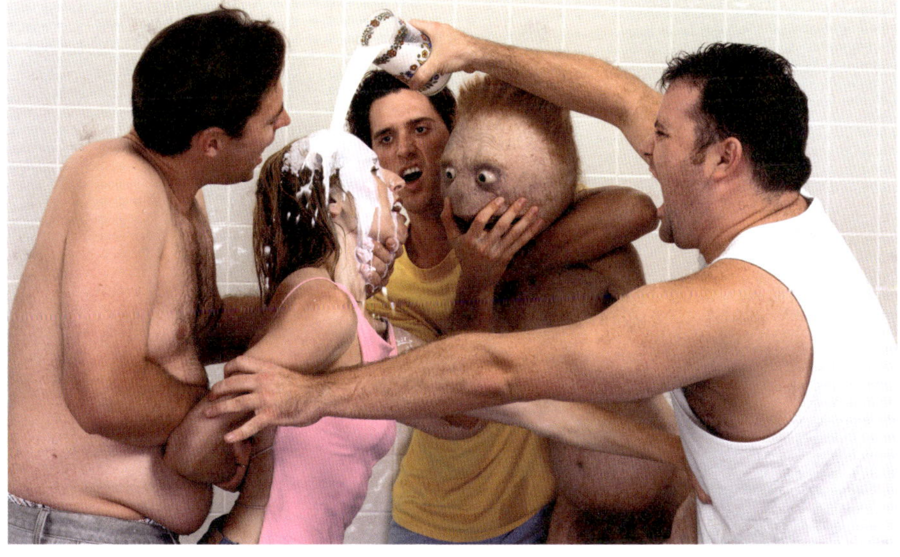

Getting Lindsay Linton, 2001, from Understanding Joshua. Chromogenic print. 36 x 60 in. (91.4 x 152.4 cm). Courtesy the artist.

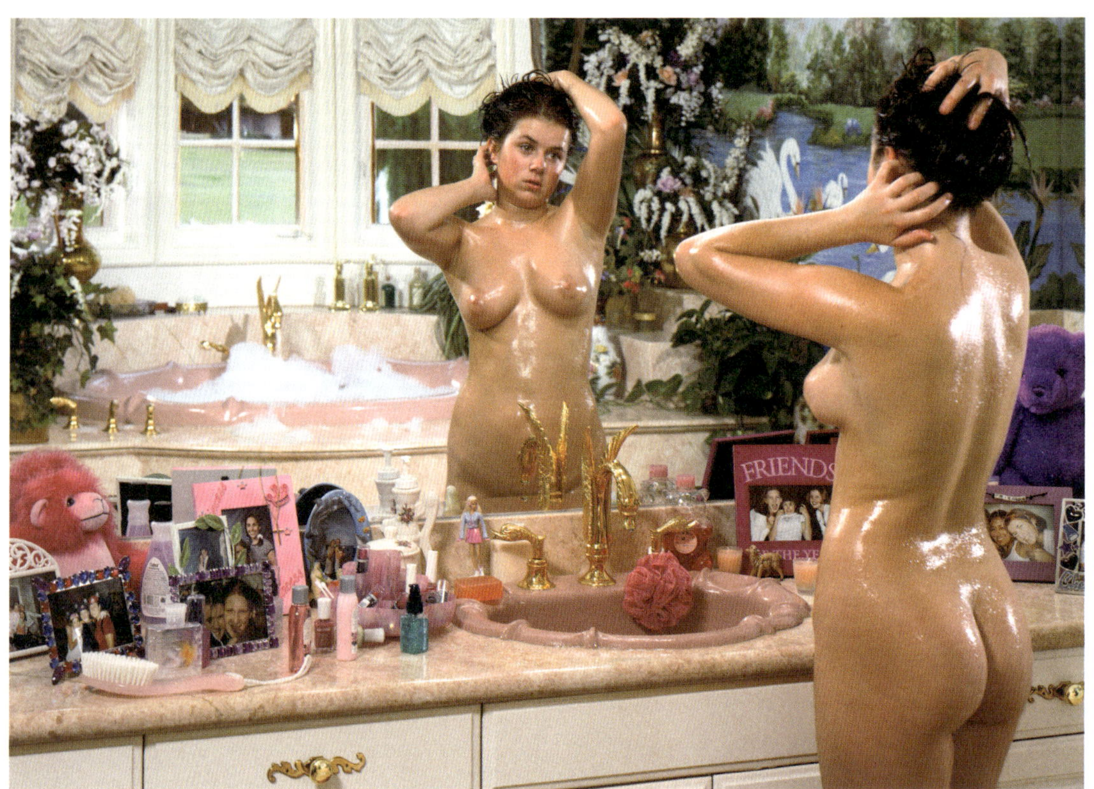

Leda, 2003, from And Jeopardize the Integrity of the Hull. Chromogenic print. 42 x 60 in. (106.7 x 152.4 cm). Courtesy the artist.

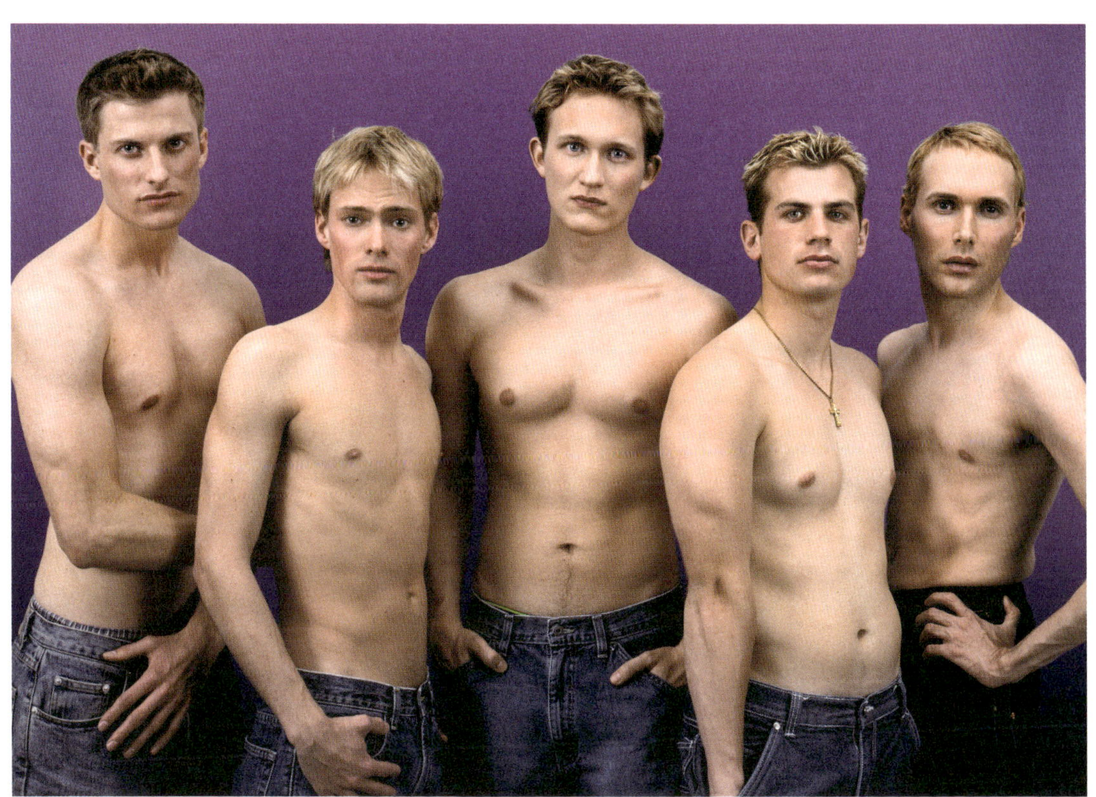

Plum, 2003, from And Jeopardize the Integrity of the Hull. Chromogenic print. 42 x 60 in. (106.7 x 152.4 cm). Courtesy the artist.

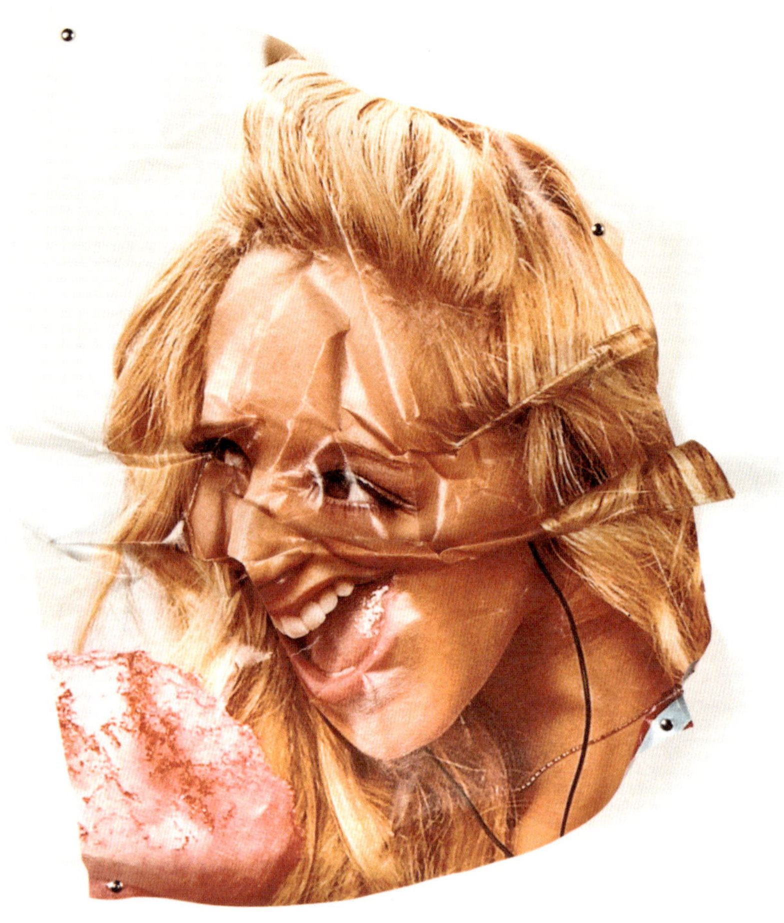

Teen Idols #2, 2008, from The Girl Studies. Cibachrome print. 20 x 16 in. (50.8 x 40.6 cm). Courtesy the artist.

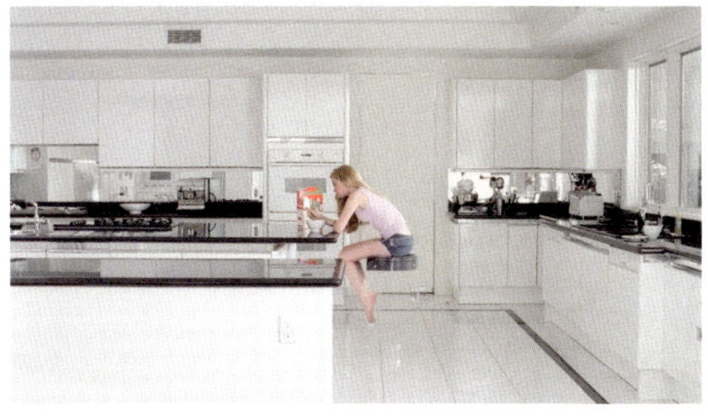
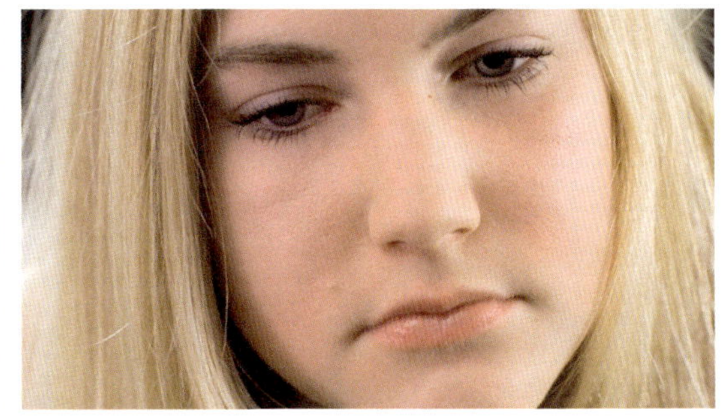
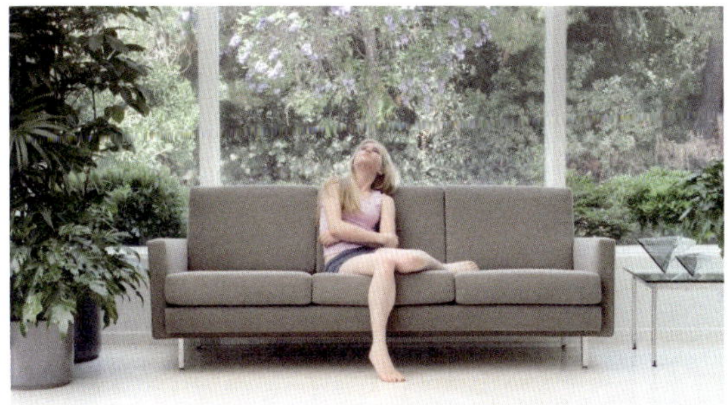
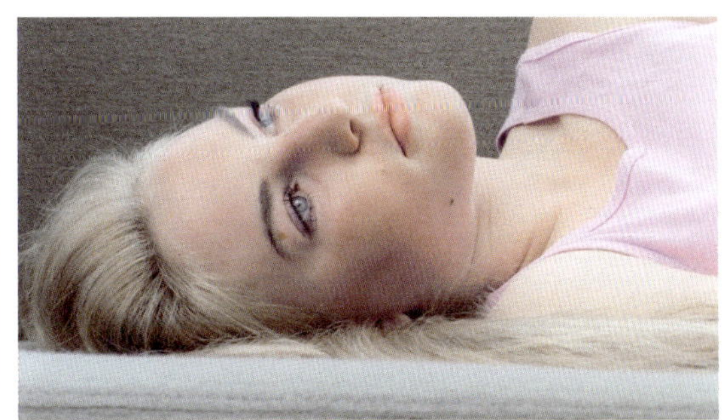
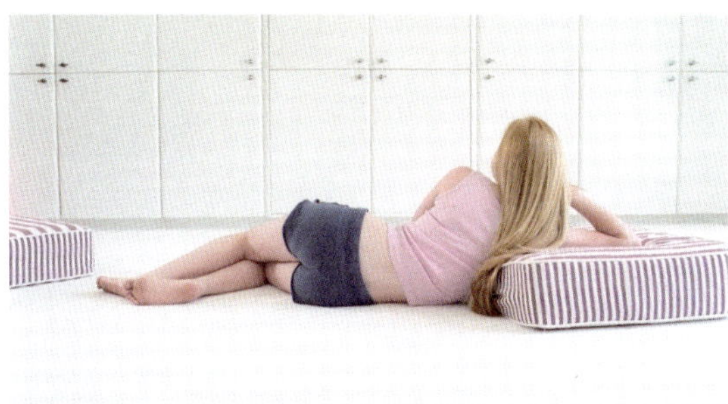
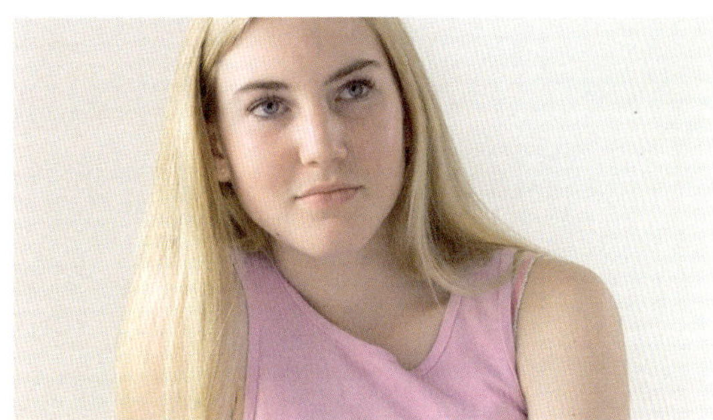
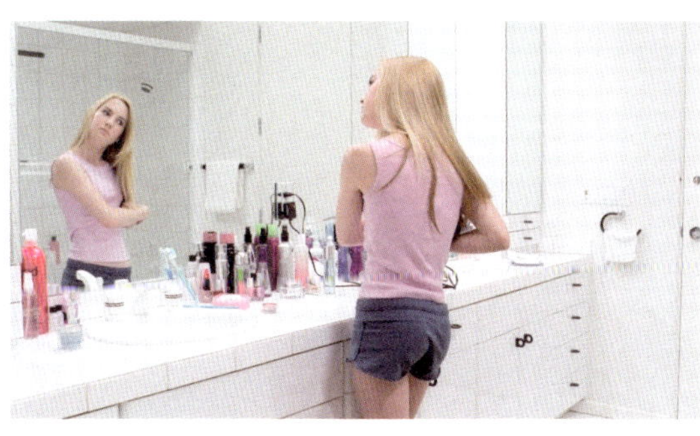
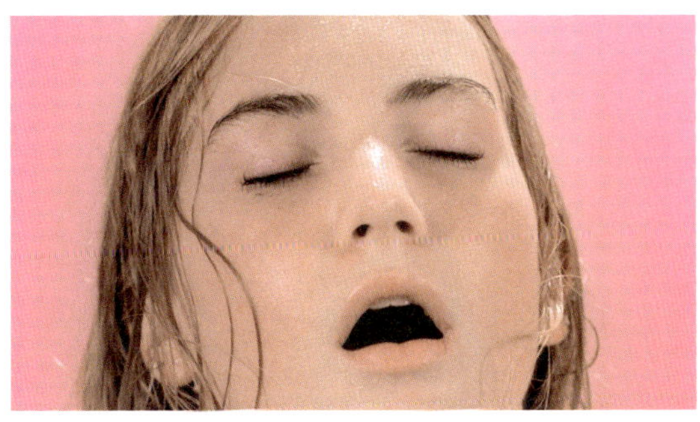

Stills from *American Minor*, 2008. 35mm film transferred to Blu-ray disc, color, sound. 7:44 min. Courtesy Loock Gallery, Berlin. Top row: scene 1; second row: scene 2; third row: scene 3; bottom row: scene 4.

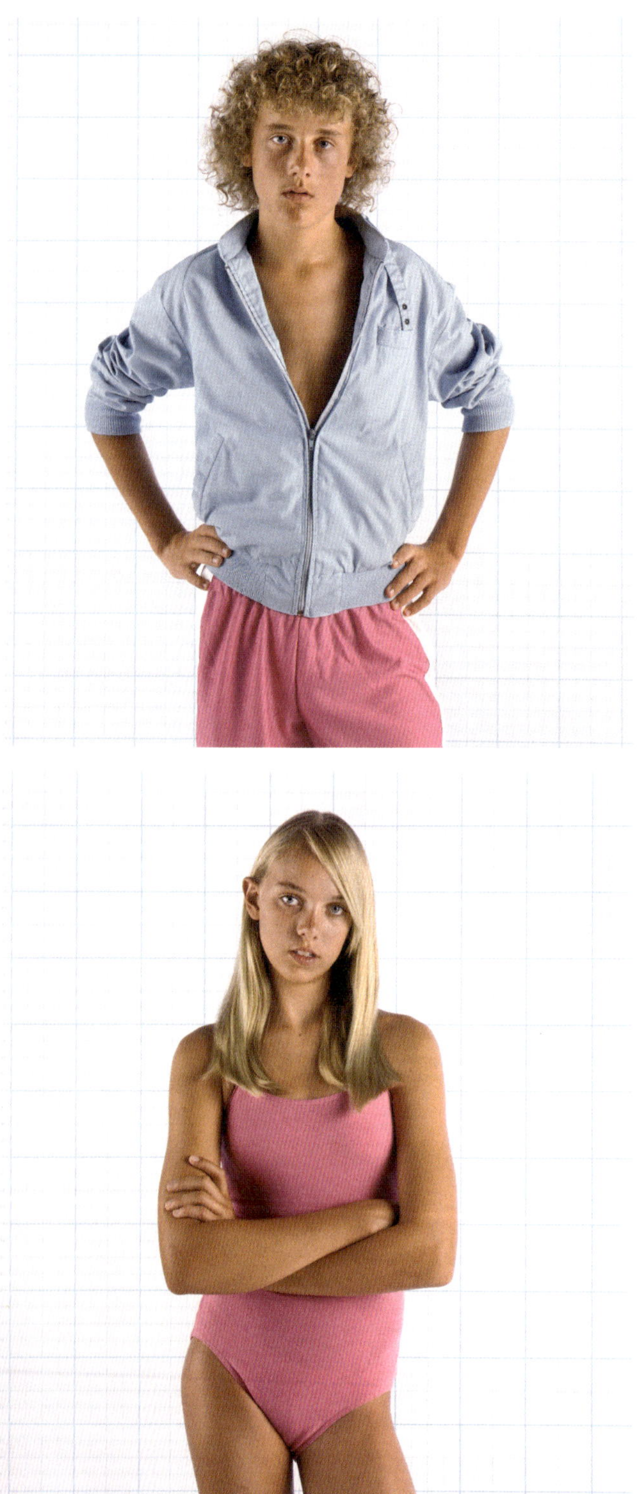

Top: *Boy Posed*, 2008, from The Girl Studies. Chromogenic print. 50 x 45 in. (127 x 114.3 cm). Courtesy Loock Gallery, Berlin.
Bottom: *Girl Posed*, 2008, from The Girl Studies. Chromogenic print. 50 x 45 in. (127 x 114.3 cm). Courtesy Loock Gallery, Berlin.

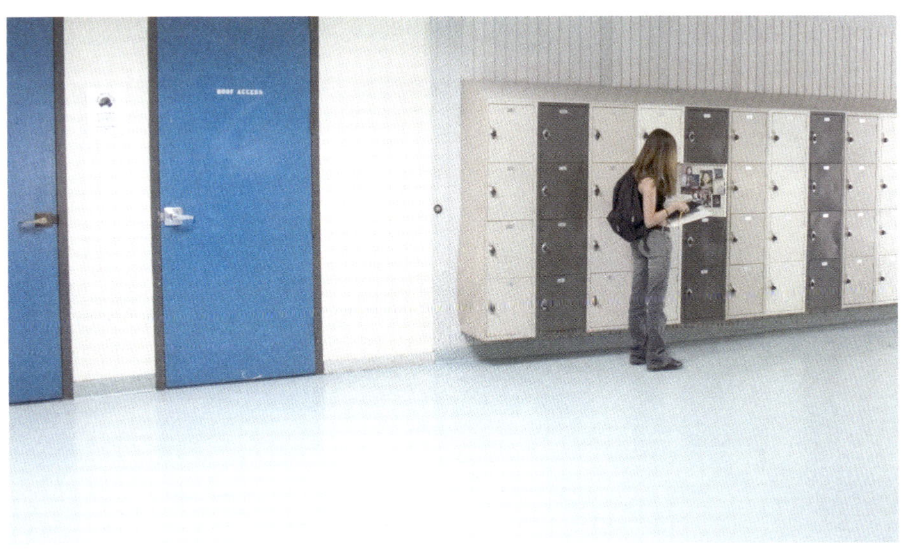

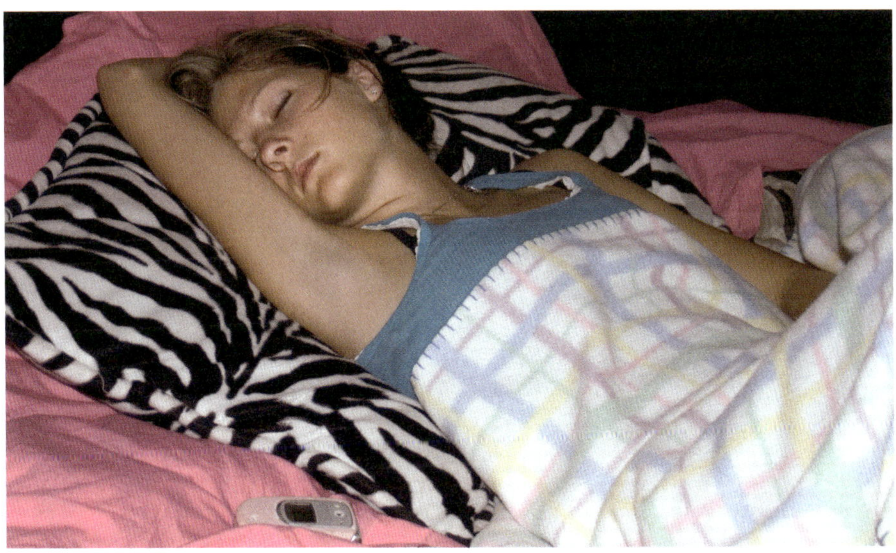

Selections from *The Cyrilla Strothers Project*, 2004–6. Archive of 11,000 images chronicling the life of Cyrilla Strothers from ages sixteen to eighteen. Courtesy the artist.

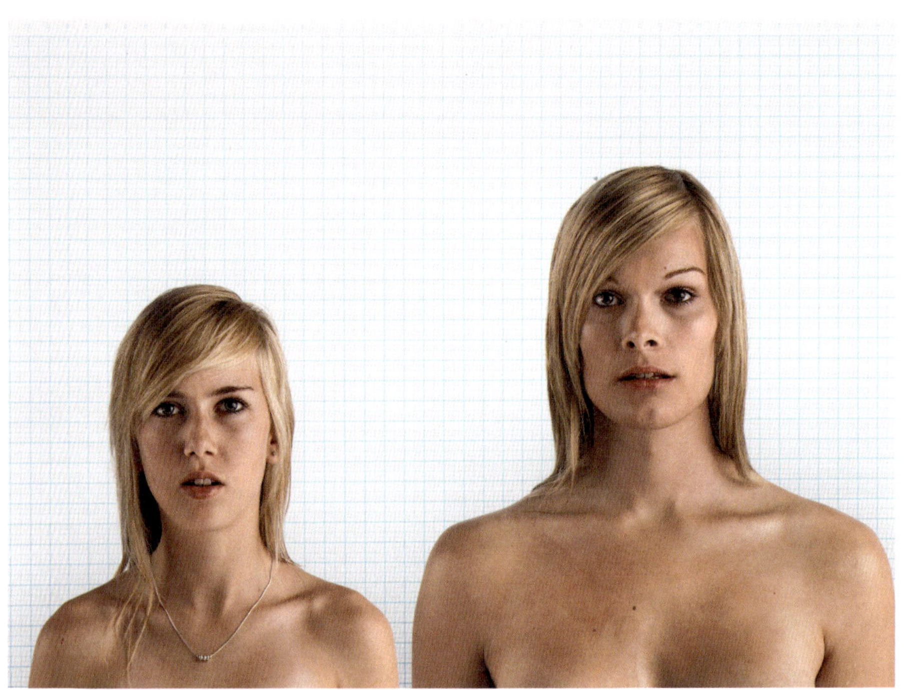

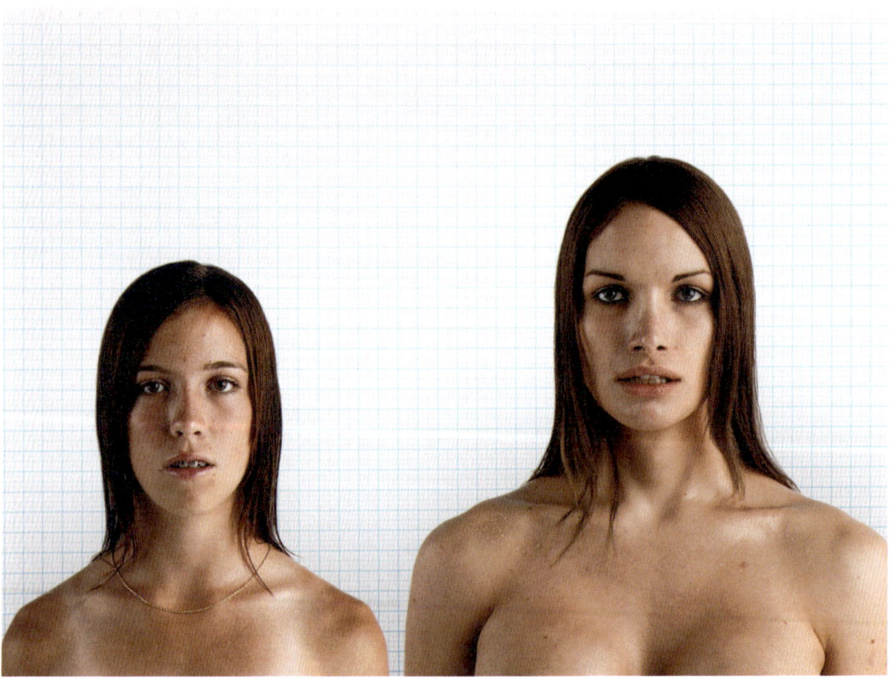

Top: *Teen and Transgender Comparative Study #1*, 2008. Chromogenic print. 26 1/2 x 36 in. (67.3 x 91.4 cm). Courtesy Loock Gallery, Berlin.
Bottom: *Teen and Transgender Comparative Study #2*, 2008. Chromogenic print. 26 1/2 x 36 in. (67.3 x 91.4 cm). Courtesy Loock Gallery, Berlin.

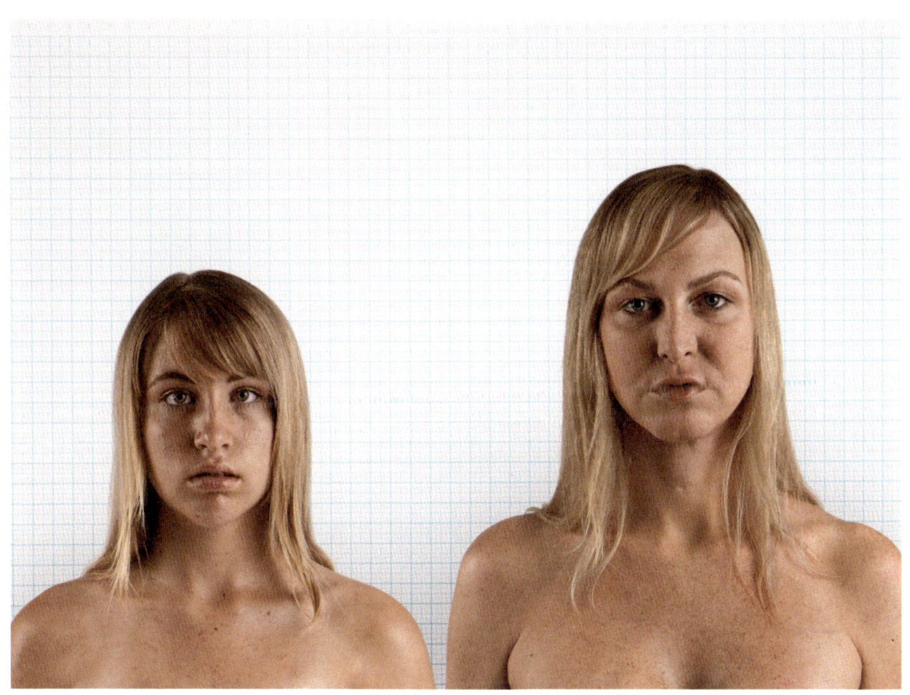

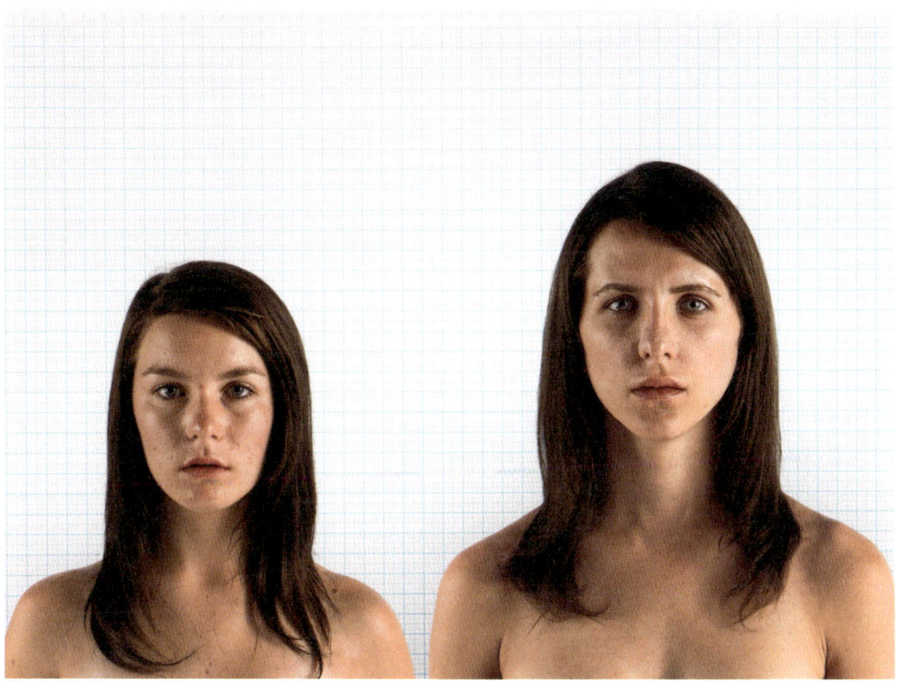

Top: *Teen and Transgender Comparative Study #3*, 2008. Chromogenic print. 26 1/2 x 36 in. (67.3 x 91.4 cm). Courtesy Loock Gallery, Berlin.
Bottom: *Teen and Transgender Comparative Study #4*, 2008. Chromogenic print. 26 1/2 x 36 in. (67.3 x 91.4 cm). Courtesy Loock Gallery, Berlin.

Jeffrey Vallance

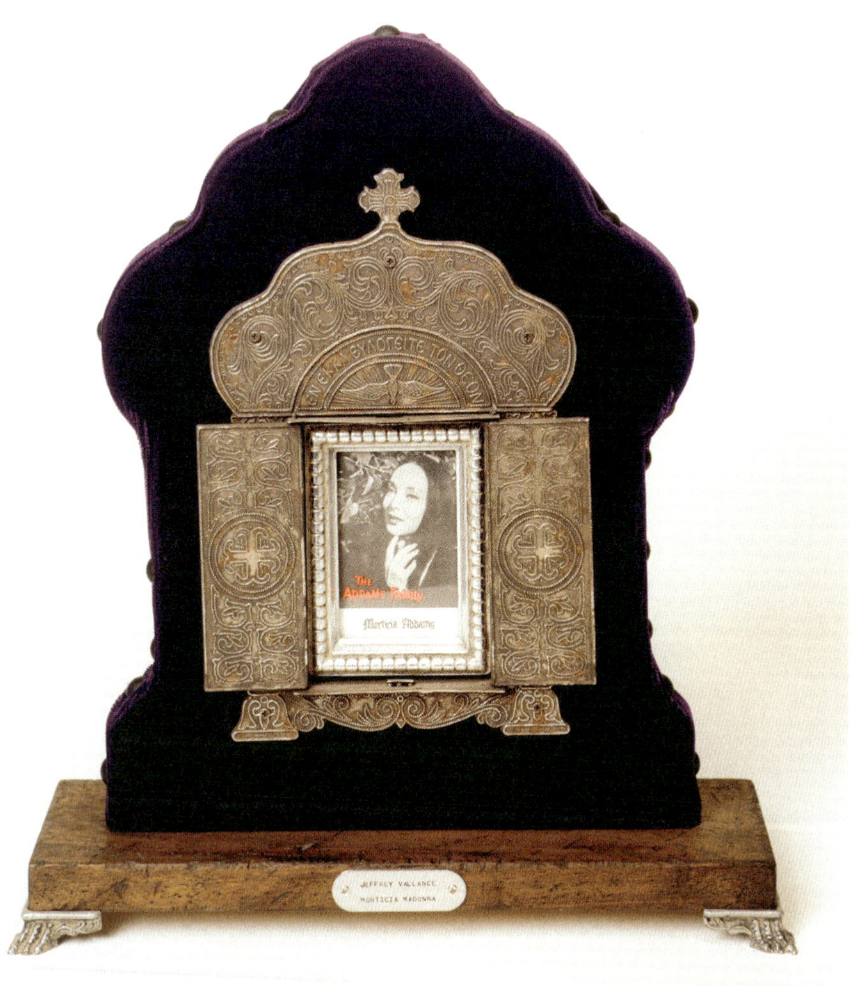

Morticia Madonna, 2007. Mixed-media sculpture. 13 1/2 x 12 x 3 5/8 in. (33.7 x 30.5 x 9.2 cm). Courtesy the artist and Margo Leavin Gallery, Los Angeles.

Jeffrey Vallance is a story collector, recounting enchanting tales and adventures. Thirty years ago, for his project *Blinky the Friendly Hen* (1978), he bought a frozen hen at Ralph's supermarket, named it Blinky, and gave it a complete burial at a pet cemetery, which he documented in a book.[1] And then there are his travels to meet the king of Tonga, his correspondence with politicians, and his recent relics and reliquaries that enshrine objects of personal value. His unique view of the world, nurtured by a fascinating wealth of knowledge regarding the most obscure rituals and traditions, is astounding.

Vallance is hard to define in simple art-world terms. He's often described as an amateur anthropologist. He did study anthropology briefly in college, but unlike many anthropologists, he is not searching for the pure, unadulterated culture. He "likes to see how different cultures interact with each other, and seeks out cultural impurities—mostly contamination by Western culture."[2] For example, when he traveled through Polynesia, he looked at junk food packaging and tin cans that washed up on the beach. While most tourists would collect the shells and ignore the trash, Vallance zeroed in on the overlooked treasures of everyday life. He's also interested in ancient clashes of cultures. At the Vatican gift shop, for example, he found a tiki carving among the rosaries, which reminded him that when missionaries in Polynesia came upon a new island, one of the first things they would do was pile up all the tiki carvings and burn them. "So first the missionaries burned all the native tikis, and now they have natives carving them again, as Vatican souvenirs. So that's how I've studied anthropology."

A large portion of his work is research based, and Vallance has a special aptitude for finding the most obscure peoples, objects, or traditions to explore. "When I begin research on a new subject, I have no idea what medium the final form will take. I let each project determine the appropriate medium. I might paint; draw; make prints, photography, video, sculpture, objects, artifacts, performance art; use collections; curate; or write a text—each exhibition might be any of these or a mix of several. Sometimes the final version of a project will be a published text, and there will be no formal exhibition." He mixes up the formats and tries to keep things fresh by not sticking with any formula or medium for too long. "Sometimes my work will be a hybrid or a cross-pollination of two or more different mediums, and it can be difficult for the art world to define, because the art world and art history are organized in terms of categories, and many times my work falls outside of their definitions."

Since he was a child, he has been especially fascinated by island cultures. His parents decorated the house in which he grew up with plastic tikis, tapa cloth, and other South Pacific island decorations. As an adult he became curious about the real origins of these designs and set out on a series of voyages to Polynesia in search of the origins of the myth of tiki. After spending time in the South Pacific, he wanted to experience an island culture that was its polar opposite, so he went to Iceland. "In a sense, I'd gone full circle: My ancestors came to Southern California from northern Norway and decorated their home with Polynesian pop, which aroused my curiosity and inspired me to travel to Polynesia, which in turn inspired me to return to my ancestral Nordic homeland."

When Vallance and his wife moved into their home in the San Fernando Valley, they encountered a strange brown wall. Puzzled by the peculiar wall, Vallance suggested "going with a brown theme and putting all brown artifacts on the wall, so it looks intentional." Vallance theorizes that "sometime during the 1970s the tenants decided to do some remodeling and covered one wall in the house with real wood paneling, creating a recessed shelf display area in the center. Then, later, someone else painted a lighter color over the real wood, to brighten up the room. Finally, a later resident tried to re-create the look of wood by covering it with a horrible brownish green faux-wood finish." For this exhibition Vallance decided to turn the wall into an artwork and made a life-size replica of it complete with the objects he's been collecting. So far he's assembled more than a hundred brown objects, mostly from his travels—tikis from Polynesia, wood carvings from Switzerland and Lapland, Lutheran emblems, artifacts from Tasmania, and relics from *Blinky the Friendly Hen*. There are also thrift-store portraits of dogs and cats; mounted antlers from all over the world; miscellaneous artifacts from Venice, Norway, Greenland, Iceland, and Las Vegas; a shrine to the Virgin of Guadalupe; and a coconut (coco de mer) from the Seychelles shaped like human buttocks.

The Brown Wall (2009) is a perfect illustration of his penchant for collecting. As a child he collected relics from what he calls "personal tragicomic events," an accident or disturbing psychological event, for example. He also collected objects that he "couldn't believe humans would ever make." Later in life he realized that these collections could be divided into specific categories: pop-culture symbols, anthropological artifacts, political campaign memorabilia, and hundreds of others. He had a large collection of Nixon memorabilia, which he'd started collecting in the 1960s at Nixon campaign headquarters and rallies, and eventually it became his *Richard Nixon Museum* (1991). He has a special admiration for political leaders, especially those who function as cultural symbols for their society, and those who fall from grace—Nixon and former Washington, D.C., mayor Marion Barry, for example. As an adult he has collected mainly objects that support his art theories, and amassed research archives on tikis; the king of Tonga; symbols from Switzerland, Iceland, Lapland, and Tasmania; and chickens, to name a few.

Vallance's philosophical approach to edification always brings a smile to your face. *I try to set up layers of perception that are similar to real-world situations and hope that the viewer can participate in traveling through and between the layers. Often the first layer is humor. I think humor is a good doorway into the work—it makes the work more accessible. The second layer is usually irony, where somehow the viewer can see that the humor is connected to a real idea or concept in the world. Irony transitions into seriousness, the third layer, where the viewer can see that there are cultural issues involved in the piece. And the fourth layer is, hopefully, one of transcendence—even a spiritual aspect of the work, which circles back on itself and becomes humorous again, and the viewer is caught in some kind of paradox.*

Vallance reminds us to explore our curiosities and regain our childlike wonder at and appreciation of the seemingly simple and meaningful treasures of everyday life.

NOTES

1. The *Blinky the Friendly Hen* (1978) project was inspired by Evelyn Waugh's book *The Loved One*, which grew out of Waugh's essay "Death in Hollywood." Blinky has since been exhumed and spawned a chapel full of relics.

2. All quotations from the artist are from conversations or e-mail correspondence with the author.

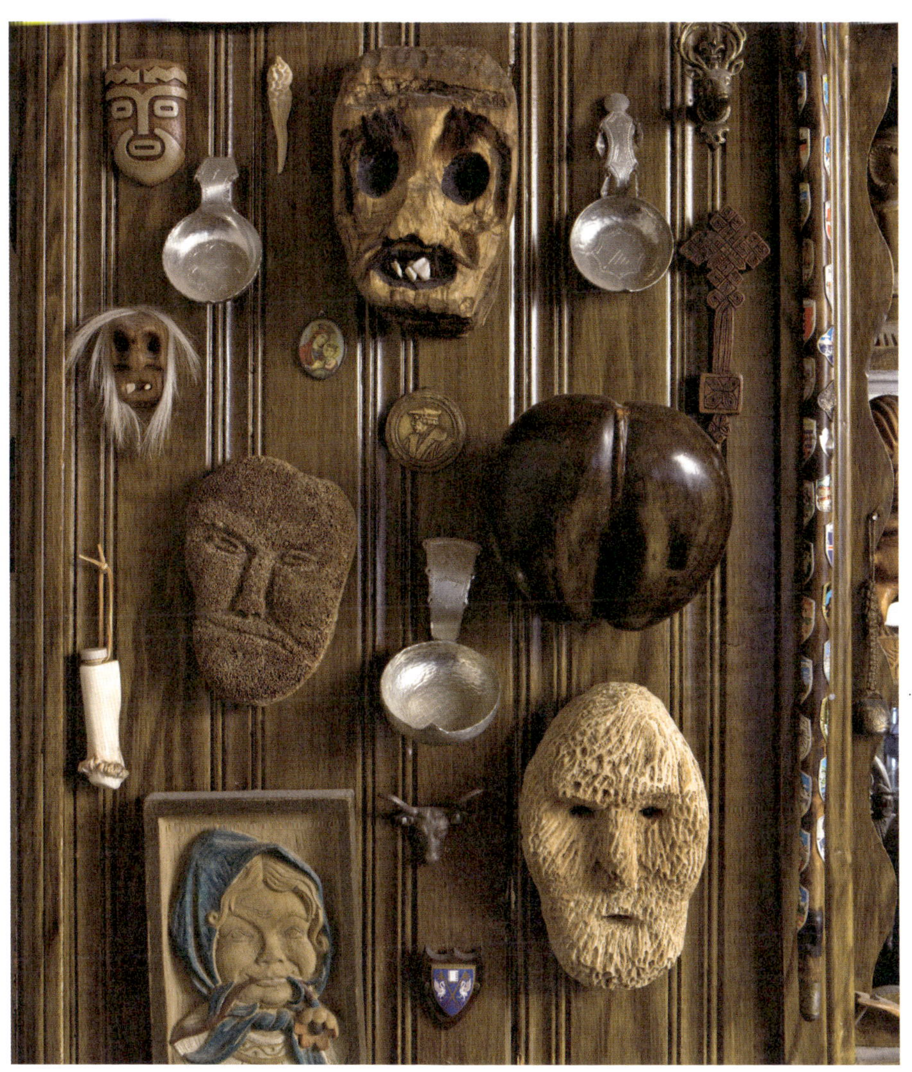

Detail of the Brown Wall, photographed in situ at the home of Jeffrey Vallance, 2008.

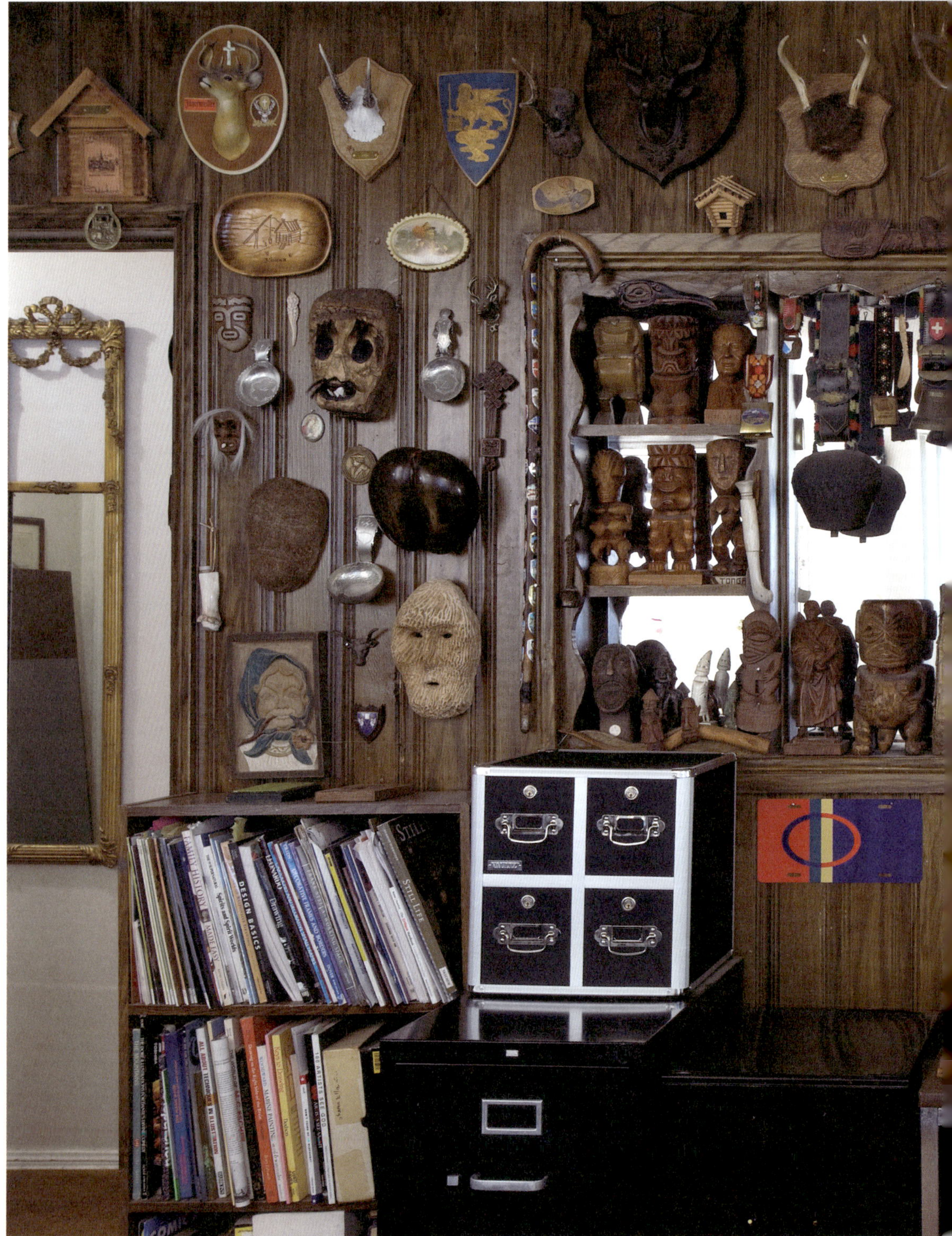

 The Brown Wall, photographed in situ at the home of Jeffrey Vallance, 2008.

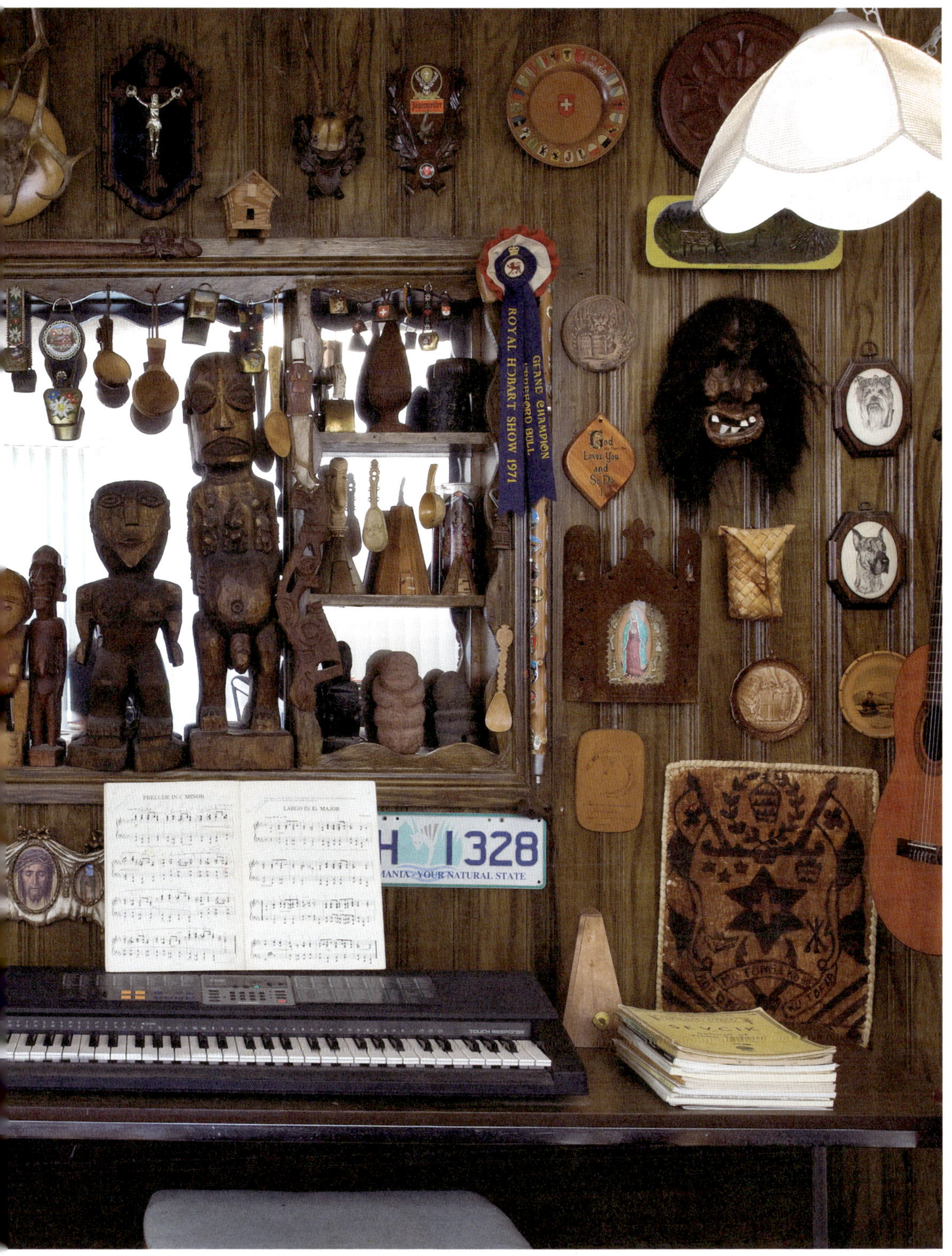

GRAND CHAMPION
ROYAL HOBART SHOW 1971
God Loves You and So Do
PRELUDE IN C MINOR
LARGO IN E♭ MAJOR
H 1328
MANIA - YOUR NATURAL STATE
TOUCH RESPONSE

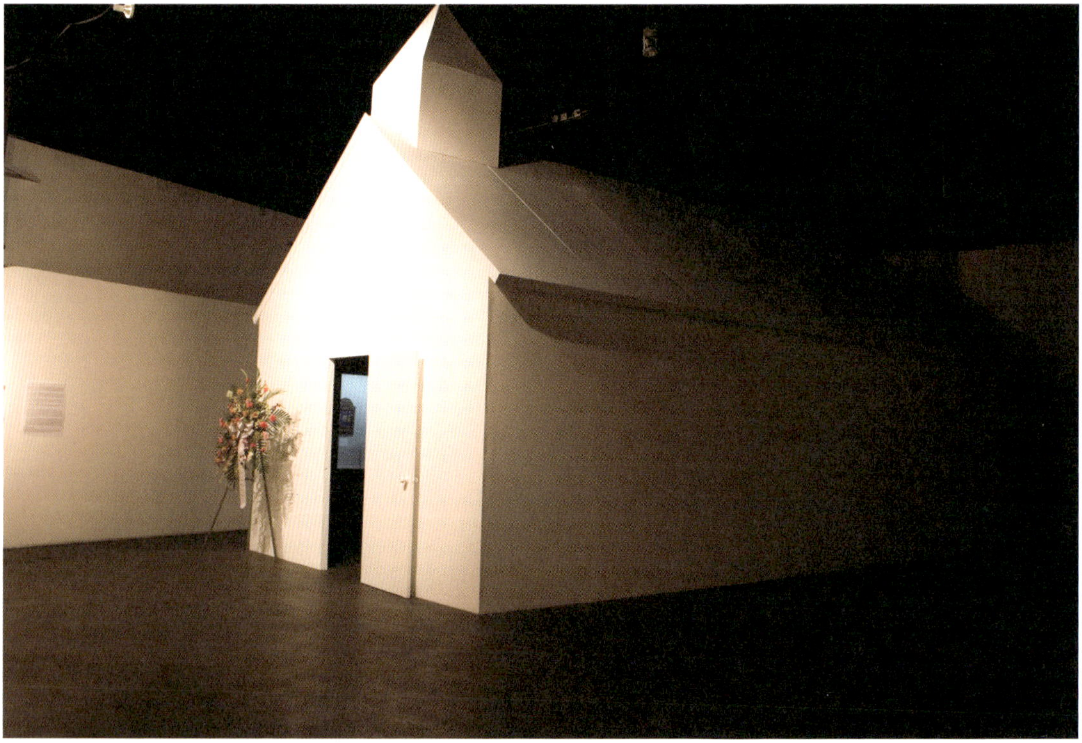

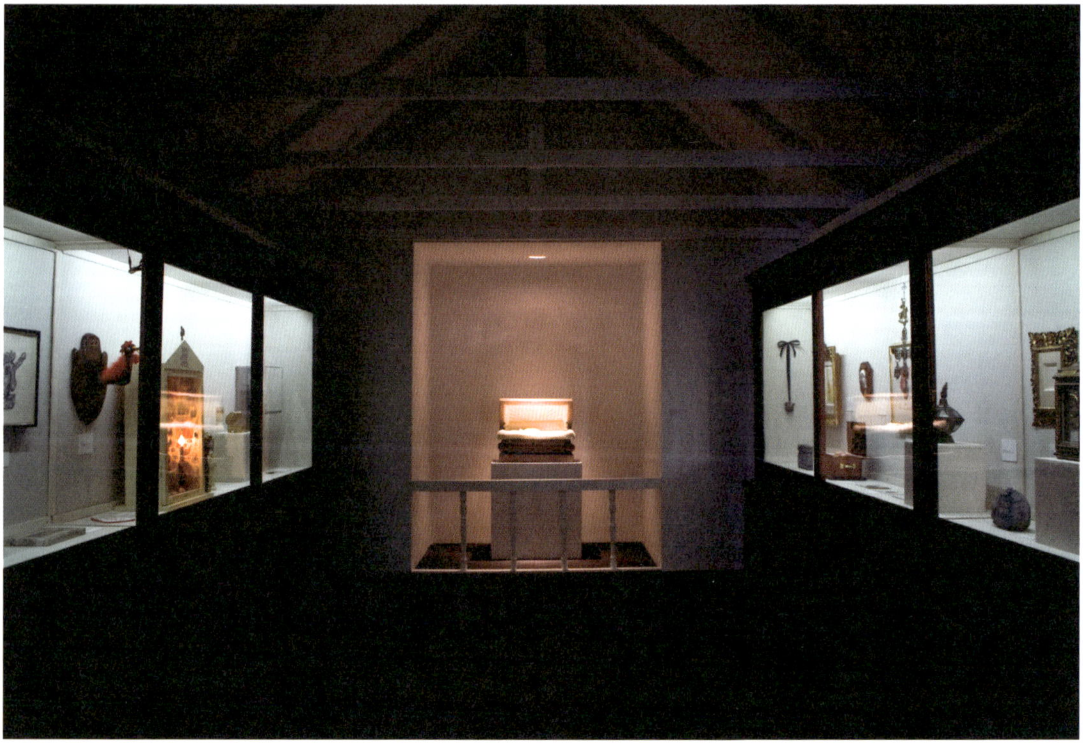

Blinky Chapel (exterior and interior), 2008. Installation views from *Blinky the Friendly Hen 30th Anniversary Exhibition*, Track 16 Gallery, Santa Monica, California, 2008. Courtesy the artist.

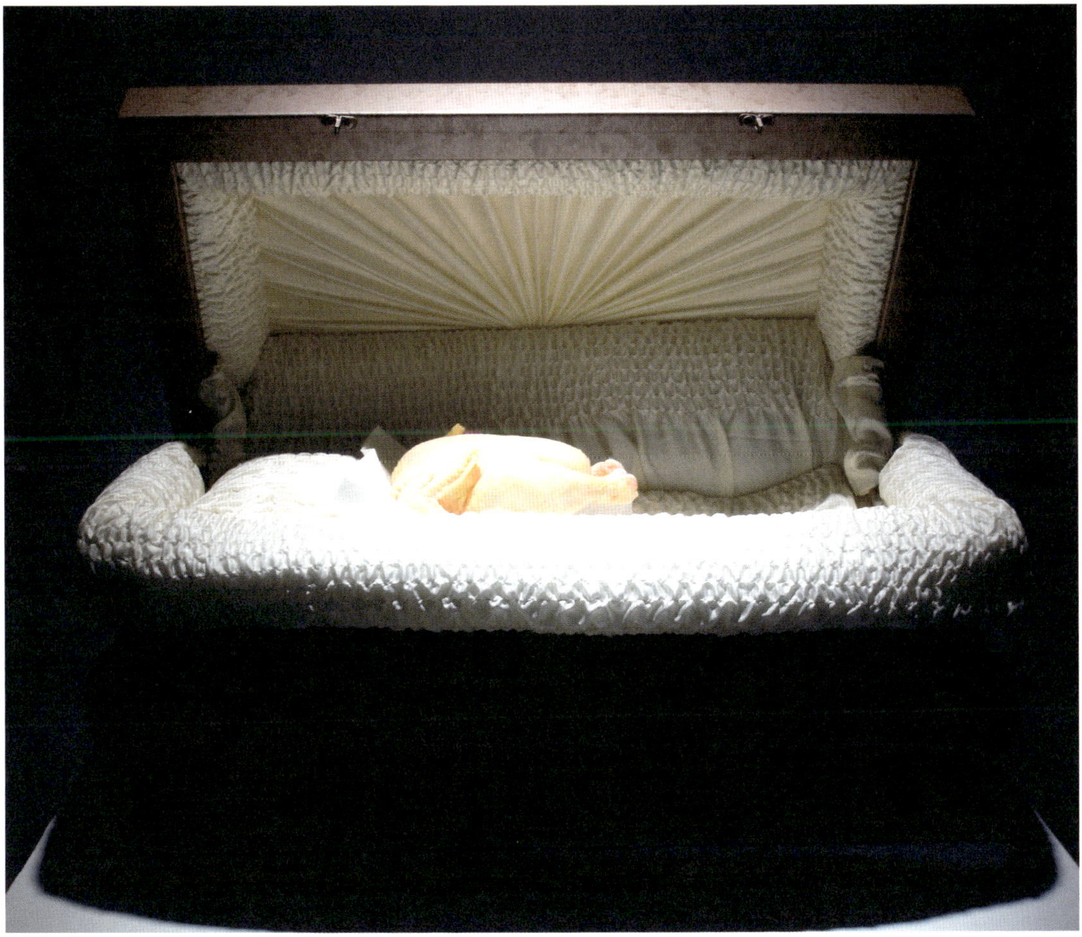

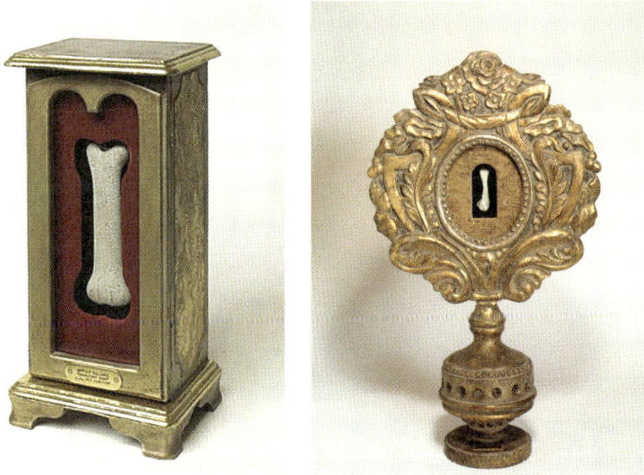

Top: *Blinky's Coffin*, 1989. Mixed-media sculpture. 17 x 22 3/4 x 27 in. (43.2 x 57.8 x 68.6 cm). Installation view inside the *Blinky Chapel*, 2008, in *Blinky the Friendly Hen 30th Anniversary Exhibition*, Track 16 Gallery, Santa Monica, California, 2008. Collection of Barry Sloane.

Bottom left: *Crematory Bone (L.A. Pet Cemetery)*, 2006. Mixed-media sculpture. 12 x 5 1/4 x 4 3/4 in. (30 x 12.7 x 10.1 cm). Courtesy the artist and Galerie Nathalie Obadia, Paris.

Bottom right: *Blinky Bone*, 2006. Mixed media. 23 x 13 3/4 x 5 1/2 in. (58.4 x 34.9 x 14 cm). Courtesy the artist and Margo Leavin Gallery, Los Angeles.

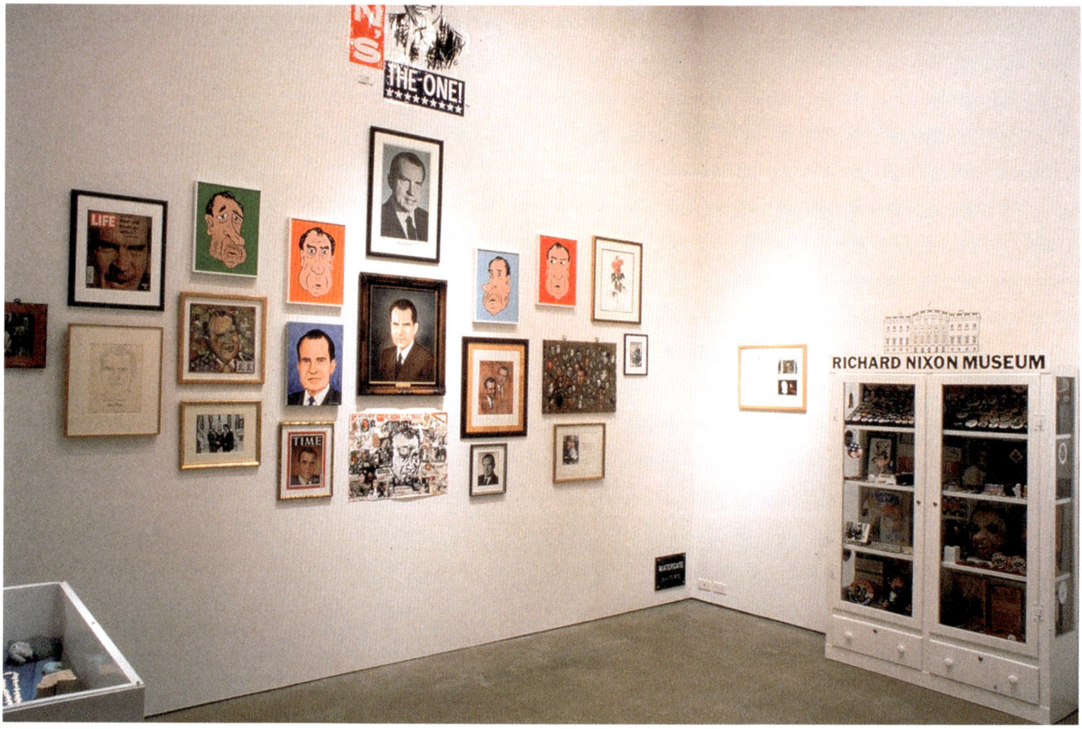

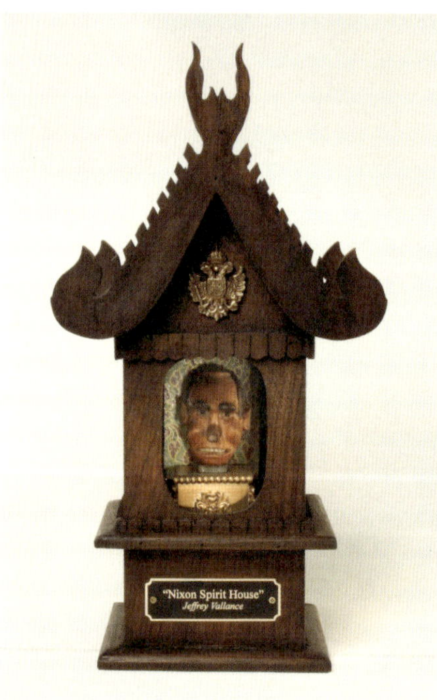

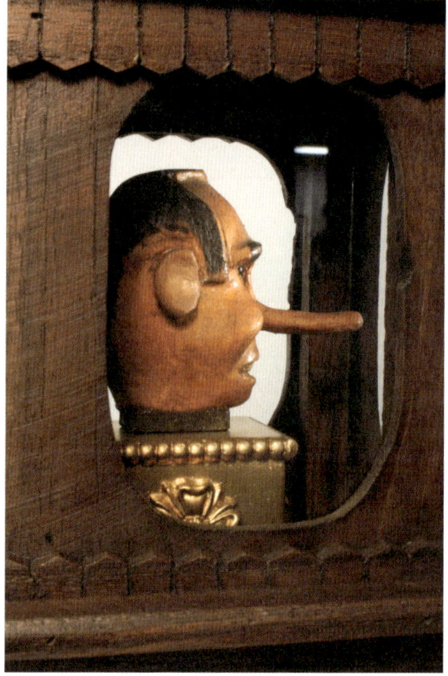

Top: *Jeffrey Vallance Presents the Richard Nixon Museum*, 1991. Installation view, Rosamund Felsen Gallery, Los Angeles, 1991. Courtesy the artist.

Bottom left: *Nixon Spirit House*, 2007. Mixed media. 14 1/4 x 7 3/4 x 6 1/4 in. (36.2 x 19.7 x 15.9 cm). Courtesy the artist and Galerie Nathalie Obadia, Paris.

Bottom right: *Nixon Spirit House* (detail), 2007. Mixed media. 14 1/4 x 7 3/4 x 6 1/4 in. (36.2 x 19.7 x 15.9 cm). Courtesy the artist and Galerie Nathalie Obadia, Paris.

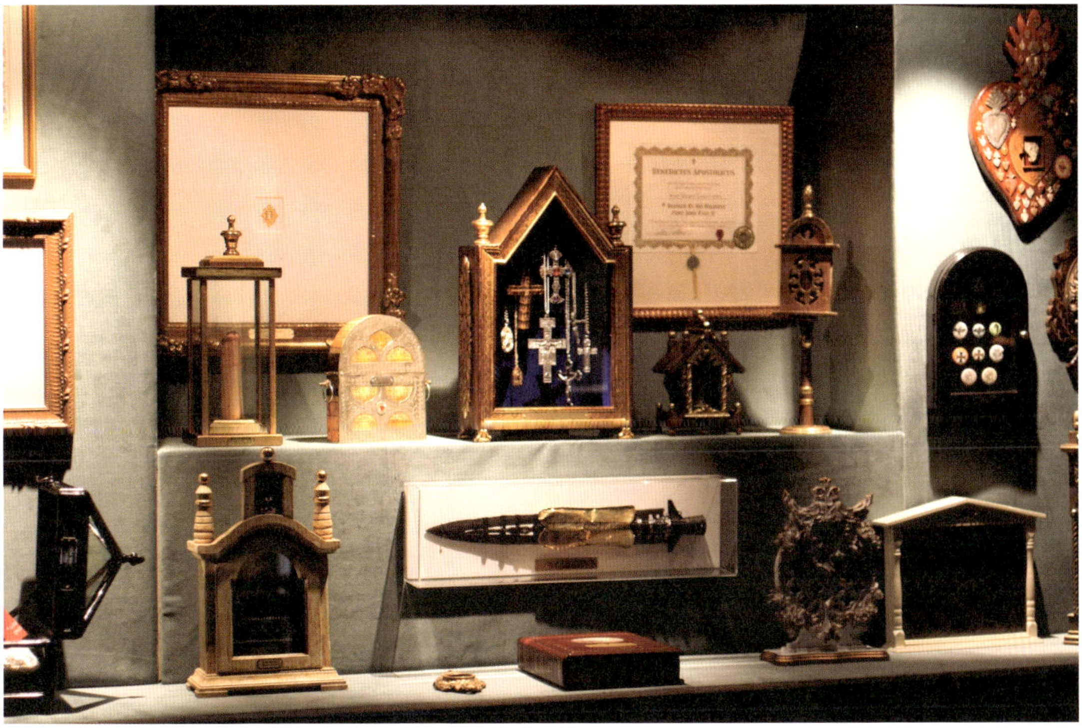

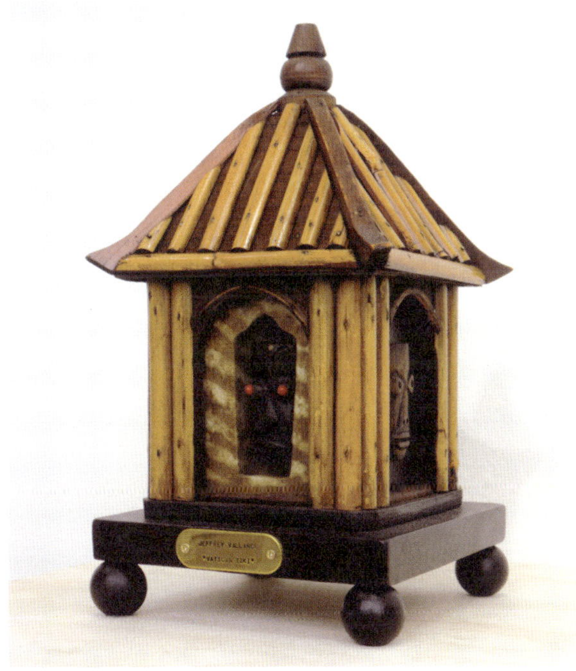

Top: *Relics & Reliquaries*, 2007. Installation view, California State University Fullerton Grand Central Art Center, Santa Ana. Courtesy the artist.
Bottom: *Vatican Tiki Relic*, 2006. Mixed media. 5 3/4 x 10 x 5 3/4 in. (14.6 x 25.4 x 14.6 cm). Courtesy the artist and Margo Leavin Gallery, Los Angeles.

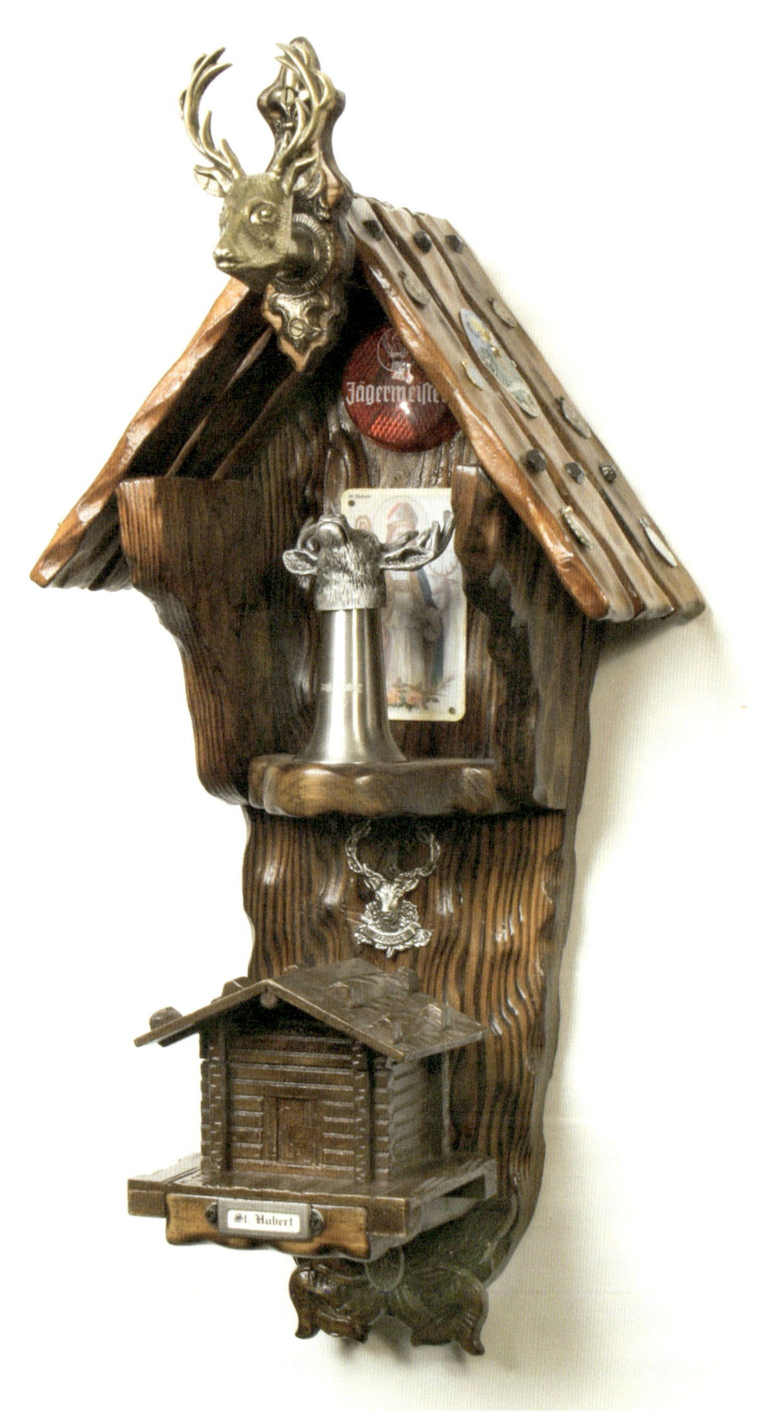

Above: *Jägermeister: St. Hubert Relics*, 2007. Mixed media. 16 3/4 x 8 7/8 x 7 in. (42.5 x 22.5 x 17.8 cm). Courtesy the artist and Galerie Nathalie Obadia, Paris.
Opposite: Jeffrey Vallance in his Bedroom Museum, ca. 1980.

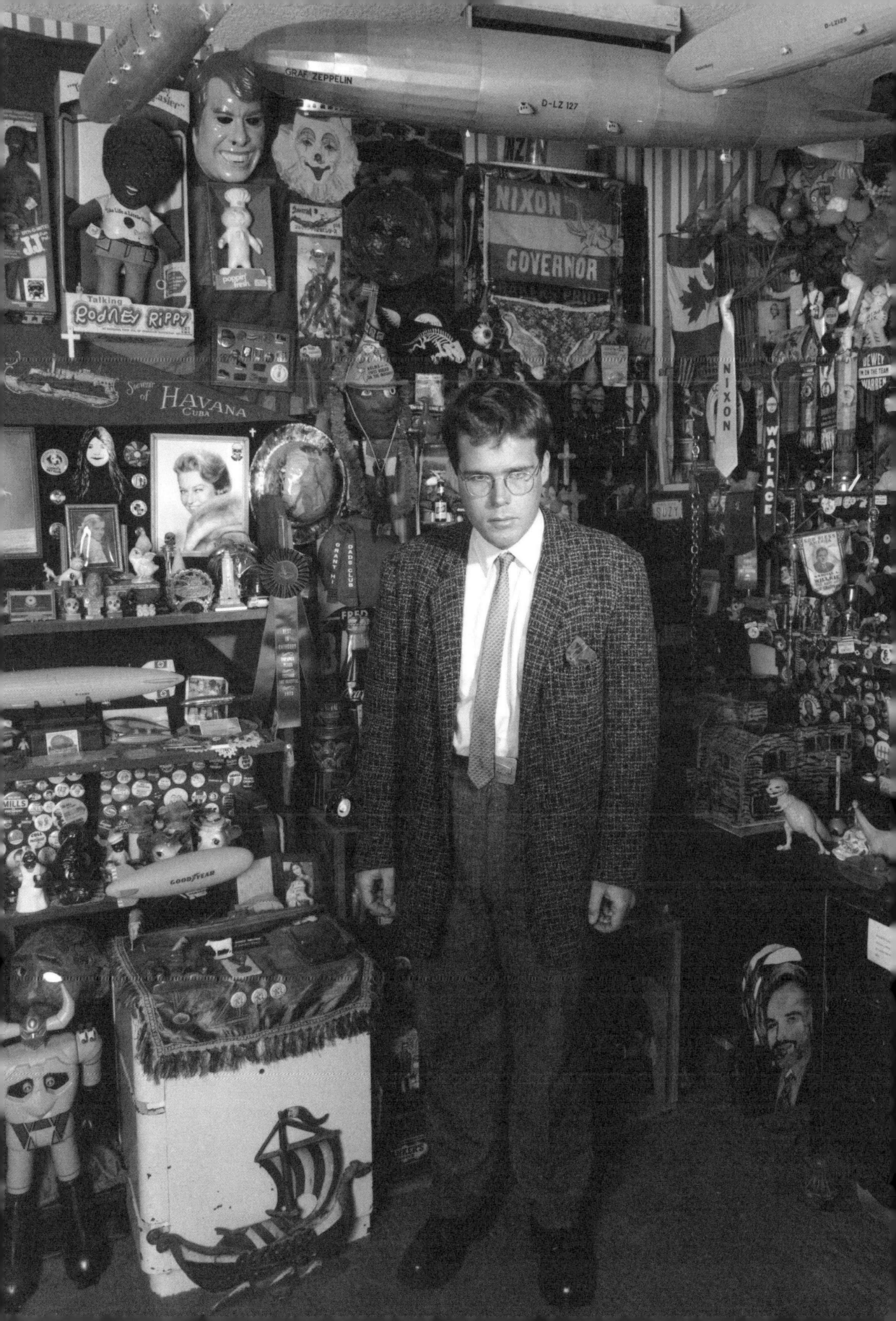
GRAF ZEPPELIN
D-LZ 127
D-LZ129
NIXON
GOVERNOR
Talking
RODNEY RIPPY
Souvenir of HAVANA
CUBA
NIXON
WALLACE
DEWEY
WARREN
SUZY
FRED
GOODYEAR

Lisa Anne Auerbach

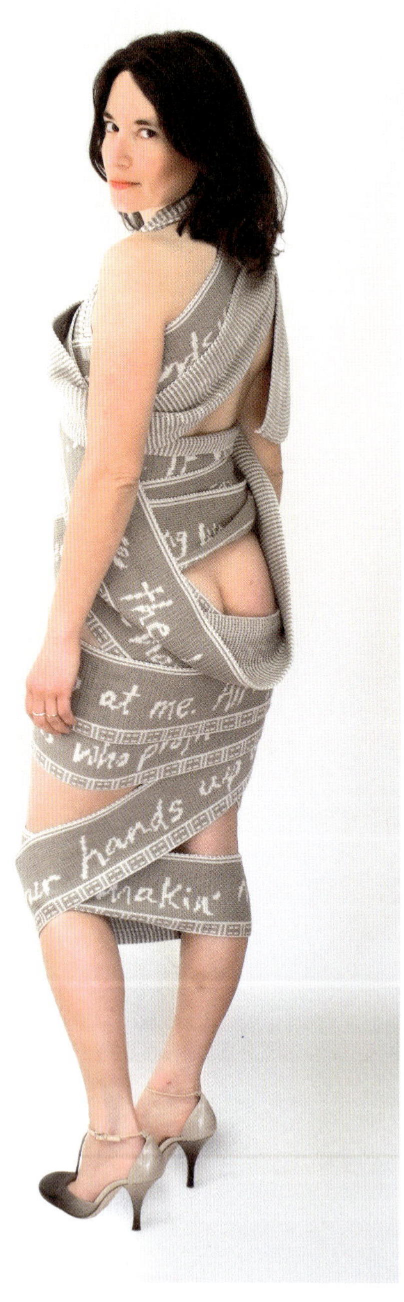

Independent Woman, 2006. Ultrachrome print. 7 1/4 x 18 in. (18.4 x 45.7 cm). Courtesy the artist and Gavlak, West Palm Beach, Florida.

I just suck the world in through a straw and shit it out in a million different ways. I am such a product of my environment, of what's around me. I am just a mollusk.

—Lisa Anne Auerbach[1]

Lisa Anne Auerbach's work makes you laugh and gets you to think about things you probably would never have even considered if it weren't for her provocations. She is incredibly prolific, producing countless works in a multitude of media, from knitting to photography to publishing and more—she even makes soap. She's a shining example of the do-it-yourself approach to life. She transitions naturally from one craft to another, motivated by frugality and a belief that it isn't necessary to have money to make things. Like an Energizer bunny, she is always active, making and doing something. "I am interested in people taking the reins, making their own reality, changing their own world, and thereby changing everyone's world."

Auerbach happened upon knitting almost accidentally. When she graduated from school, she lost access to a darkroom, so she couldn't make color photographs as easily anymore. She obsessed over custom-knit sweaters that Rick Nielsen, lead guitarist of Cheap Trick, wore. "Nielsen's sweaters were like T-shirts, but because they were sweaters, they were more serious, more urgent, more meaningful." Some simply displayed the band's name, and others had ridiculous sayings, such as "Don't Steal My Girlfriend." She explains: "Cheap Trick is the whole reason I started making sweaters in the first place. I wanted to knit so I could make myself a customized Cheap Trick sweater. Their music was catchy, but I cared more about their costumes and personas."[2] So Auerbach checked out some knitting books from the library and taught herself to knit. Her second sweater (*Sandy Koufax Sweater*, 1996) is a simple blue cardigan bearing a huge white Star of David on the back. She photographed herself modeling the sweater wearing a short white latex tennis skirt, standing on a forklift, her back toward the camera to show off the star. This started an ongoing series of photographs in which she models her knitwear, and she can't help but spice things up with saucy catalog poses. For her it's logical, motivated by necessity rather than vanity—she's there and free, so why not use herself as the model?

Auerbach has co-opted the traditional female craft of knitting and turned it into a tool for wry, pointed political messages. One knit skirt and sweater set looks innocuous, until you read the text. On the front: "Did you hear what Bush said when asked about Roe vs. Wade?" And on the reverse: "I don't care how they get out of New Orleans." Knitted into the body of another sweater is a design that resembles a belt of explosives that might be worn by a suicide bomber, but airport security doesn't even take a second look—to them it's another reindeer or lamb sweater that Grandma made. Auerbach knows how easy it is to take things for granted, and she puts these messages out into the world in a subtle, almost subliminal fashion that slowly penetrates our consciousness. She's gently prodding and poking at a complacent public: "I like to convince people gently, lure them into seeing things from my perspective, and change the world slowly, virally." With her knit works, Auerbach has entered into an entire subculture of knitting fanatics. She is incredibly prolific and has made nearly one hundred sweaters to date.

For a series of self-portrait photographs (without the knit products) Auerbach plays quirky and traditional female characters with a humorous twist: she's a housewife greeting the UPS man, a modern-day superhero hoisting a rifle, or a mannequin in a sex doll factory. She's like the Tina Fey of the art world—totally deadpan, cute, and spot-on with her impressions. She began posing for photos when she and fellow artist Daniel Marlos worked on slide mounting and copy work at the photo lab of the Griffith Observatory and published a zine called *The Casual Observer*. They took turns being on the cover, adopting a stiff but casual, cheeky but upstanding style for the publication. The cover-girl persona then morphed into a naughty version. For the cover of an unpublished zine called *Knit & Shit*, she's sitting on a toilet knitting; for her biking zine, *Saddlesore*, we see her sexily lying in the dirt next to her bike after a fall, with the cover line: "Oops, I did it again." Another issue features Auerbach in a hilarious postcoital embrace, under a sheet with her bicycle.

Writing is also a major component of Auerbach's practice. She edits several Web sites with blogs and regular project updates.[3] In the mid-1990s she began reviewing porn for an industry trade magazine. She went in thinking it would be the greatest opportunity ever to make the best art about porn. But it was actually less exciting than she thought it would be. She lost interest in the idea of making art about porn; it became more of a side job or an anthropological experiment. She did, however, love going to totally nondescript locations and "finding five bored nude women playing Twister, talking about body hair in some master bedroom of a rented house. It helped me to imagine that behind every boring facade there is something going on that you might never expect." Auerbach also wrote for ski and art magazines. "I felt like I was living in some holy triumvirate of culture." She'd bring parts of each industry together, sharing porn with the skiers and impressing the art world with her porn experience. "I loved seeing how all three worlds were nearly identical; people throwing themselves literally into their work, physically, in terms of skiers and porn stars, but artists too, to a certain extent, becoming a public persona, putting themselves out there in their work. And all three perceived of their world as the center of the universe. They had their own magazines, their own conventions, their own superstars." Auerbach soon realized that she preferred the independence of her self-published zines and journals, even though the readership is smaller. She hasn't turned her back entirely on mainstream media, though; she recently published an article about tract publishing in the *Los Angeles Times Book Review*.

Auerbach is consumed by the blend of the banality of everyday life and curious humor, "especially humor combined with anger or humor combined with the everyday or humor combined with anger and the everyday." She uses humor to disarm and seduce: "Humor is the spoonful of sugar that helps the medicine go down. If you prattle on about something complex, everyone falls asleep, but if you make a joke about it, maybe they'll actually pause to think." Auerbach has already lived more than nine lives, and she doesn't seem to be slowing down at all. If her work wasn't so funny and relevant and engaging, it might make you feel lazy.

NOTES

Lisa Anne Auerbach's projects for this exhibition were funded in part through the Artists' Resource for Completion grant from The Durfee Foundation.

1. Unless otherwise noted, all quotations from the artist are from conversations or e-mail correspondence with the author.
2. Lisa Anne Auerbach, "I Want You to Want Me on Wilshire," The Little Red Blog of Revolutionary Knitting, November 2, 2006, http://stealthissweater.blogspot.com/2006/11/i-want-you-to-want-me-on-wilshire.html.
3. Auerbach's Web projects include an artist's site (http://www.lisaanneauerbach.com/), The Little Red Blog of Revolutionary Knitting (http://stealthissweater.blogspot.com/), and The Tract House (http://www.thetracthouse.com/), as well as others that she has contributed to (http://www.knittersforkerry.com, http://www.highdeserttestsites.com, http://www.hamburgerla.com, http://www.whatsthatbug.com, and http://www.americanhomebody.com).

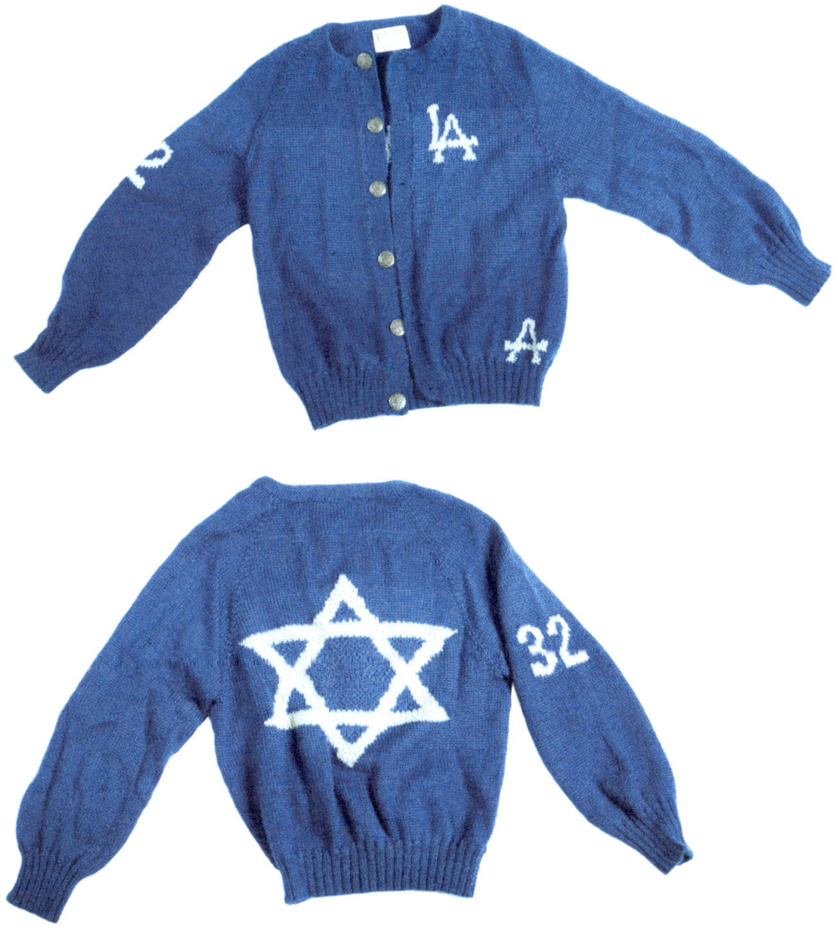

Sandy Koufax Sweater, 1996. Wool and mohair. Medium. Courtesy the artist and Gavlak, West Palm Beach, Florida.

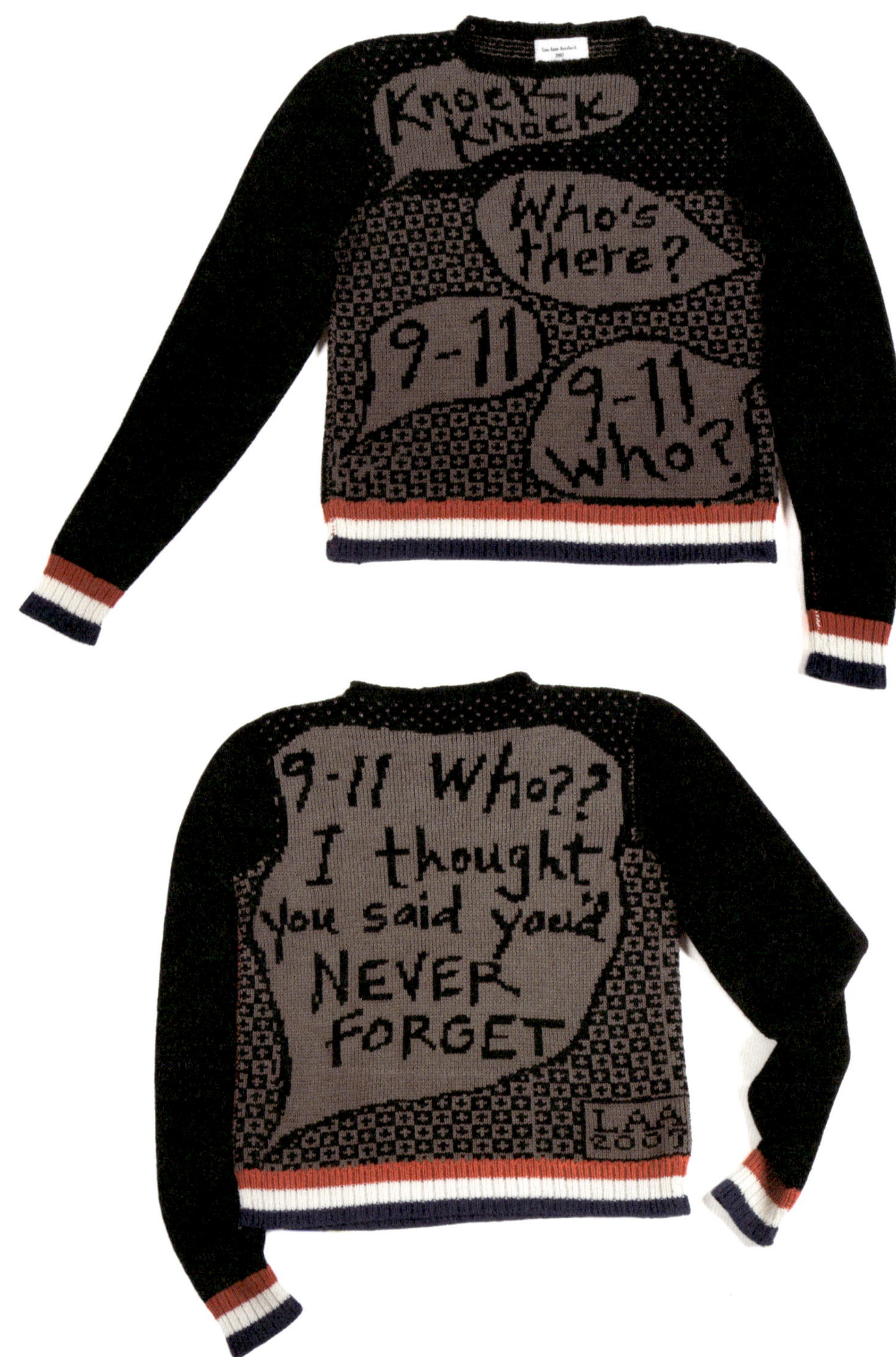

Never Forget, 2007. Merino wool. Medium. Courtesy the artist and Gavlak, West Palm Beach, Florida.

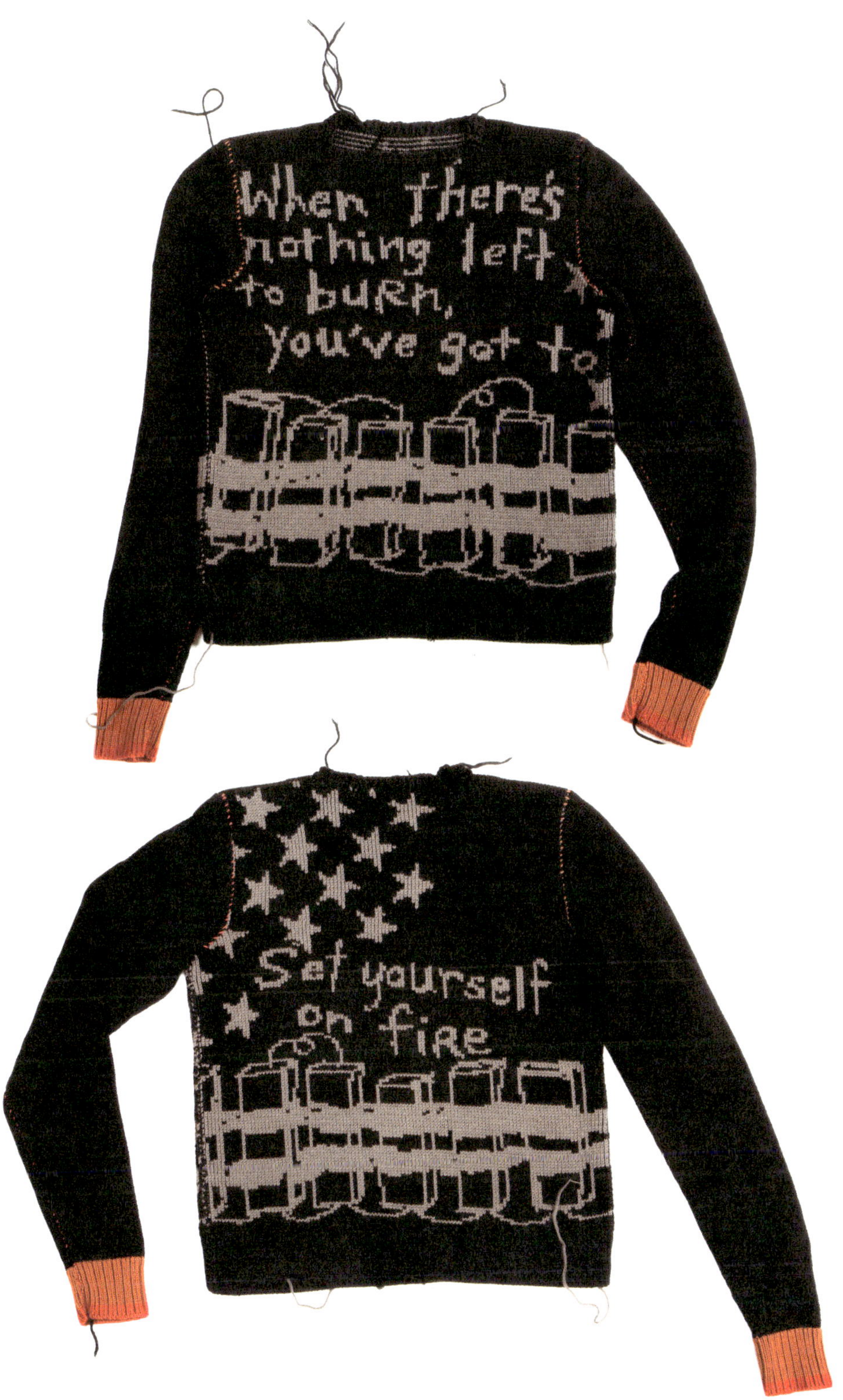

When there's nothing left to burn, you've got to set yourself on fire, 2007. Merino wool. Medium. Courtesy the artist and Gavlak, West Palm Beach, Florida.

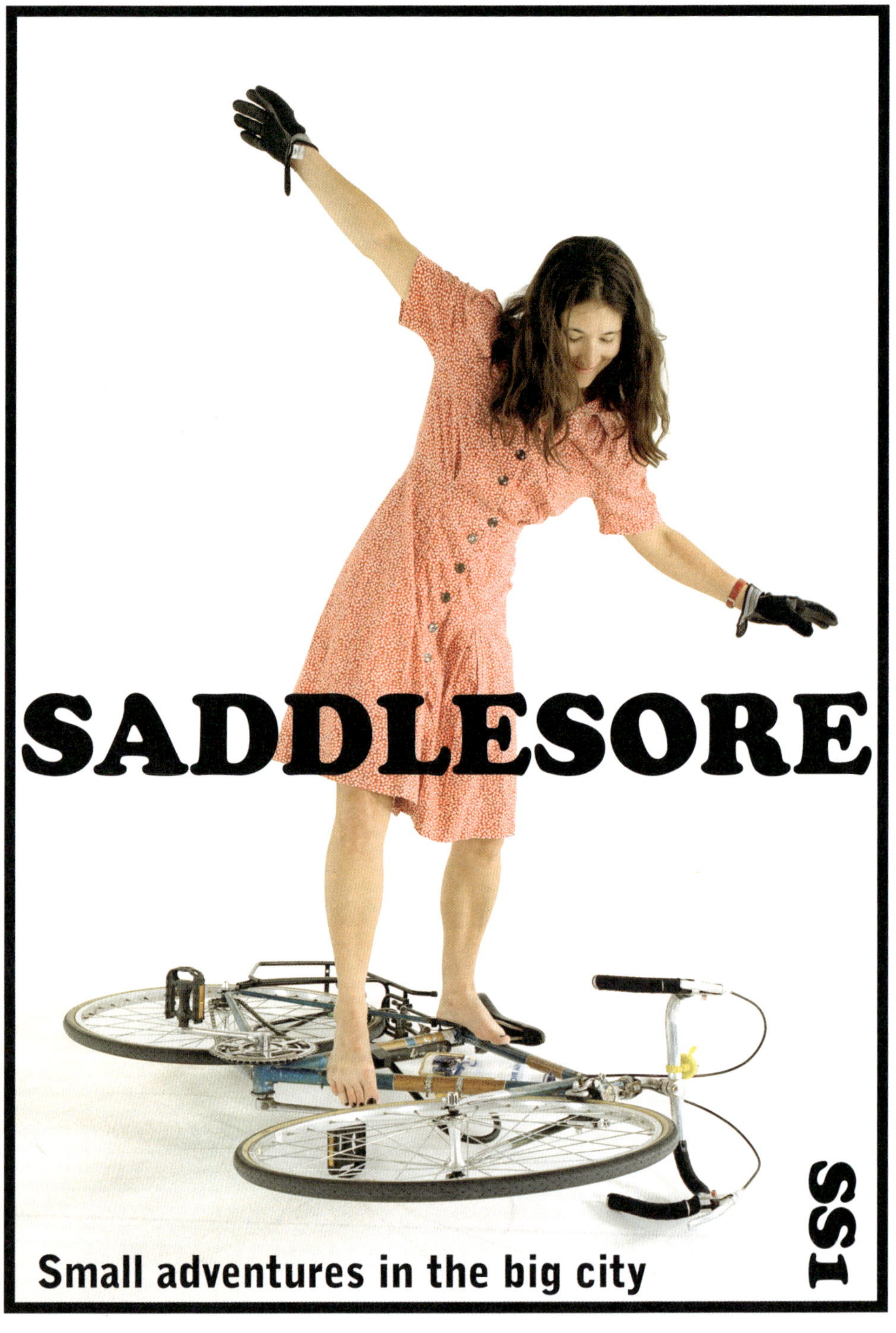
SADDLESORE
Small adventures in the big city
ISSI

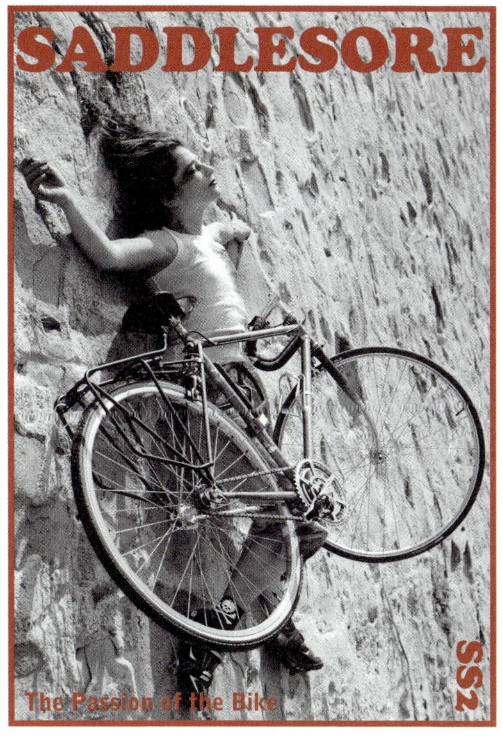

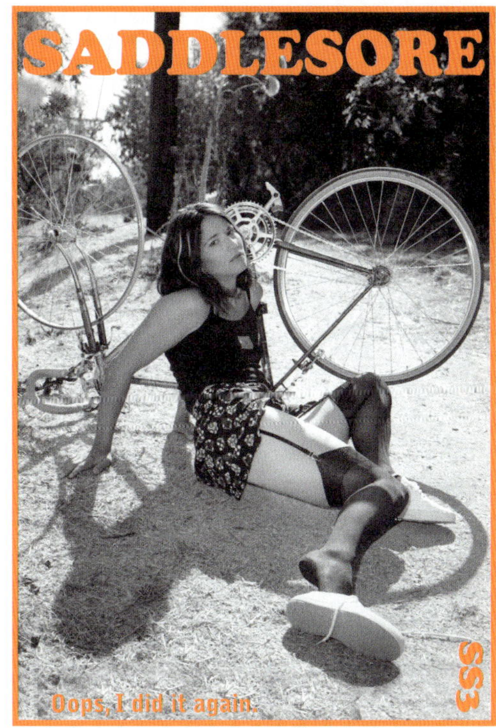

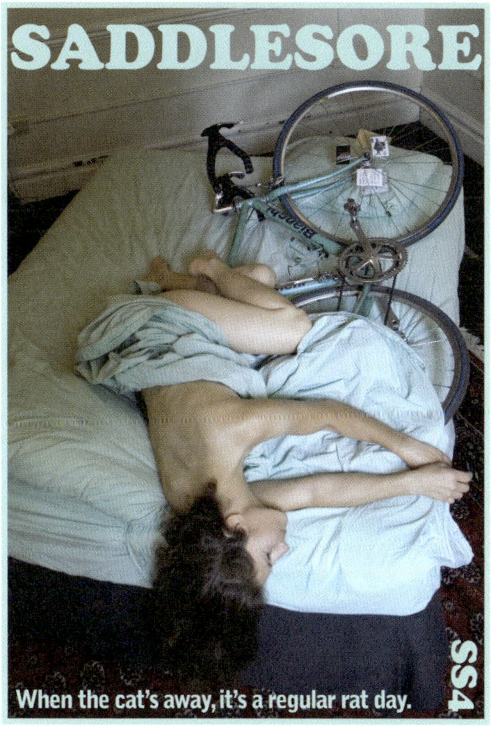

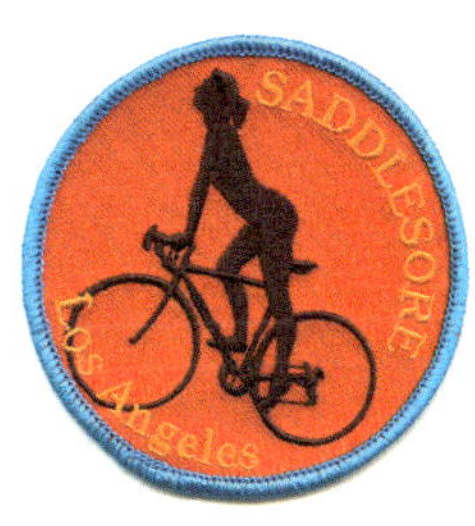

Opposite: Lisa Anne Auerbach and Chris Buck. Cover of *Saddlesore #1*, 2004. Courtesy the artist and Gavlak, West Palm Beach, Florida.
Top left: Lisa Anne Auerbach and Daniel Marlos. Cover of *Saddlesore #2*, 2005. Courtesy the artist and Gavlak, West Palm Beach, Florida.
Top right: Lisa Anne Auerbach and Daniel Marlos. Cover of *Saddlesore #3*, 2006. Courtesy the artist and Gavlak, West Palm Beach, Florida.
Bottom left: Cover of *Saddlesore #4*, 2007. Courtesy the artist and Gavlak, West Palm Beach, Florida.
Bottom right: *Saddlesore Patch*, 2005. Fabric. 3 x 3 in. (7.6 x 7.6 cm). Courtesy the artist and Gavlak, West Palm Beach, Florida.

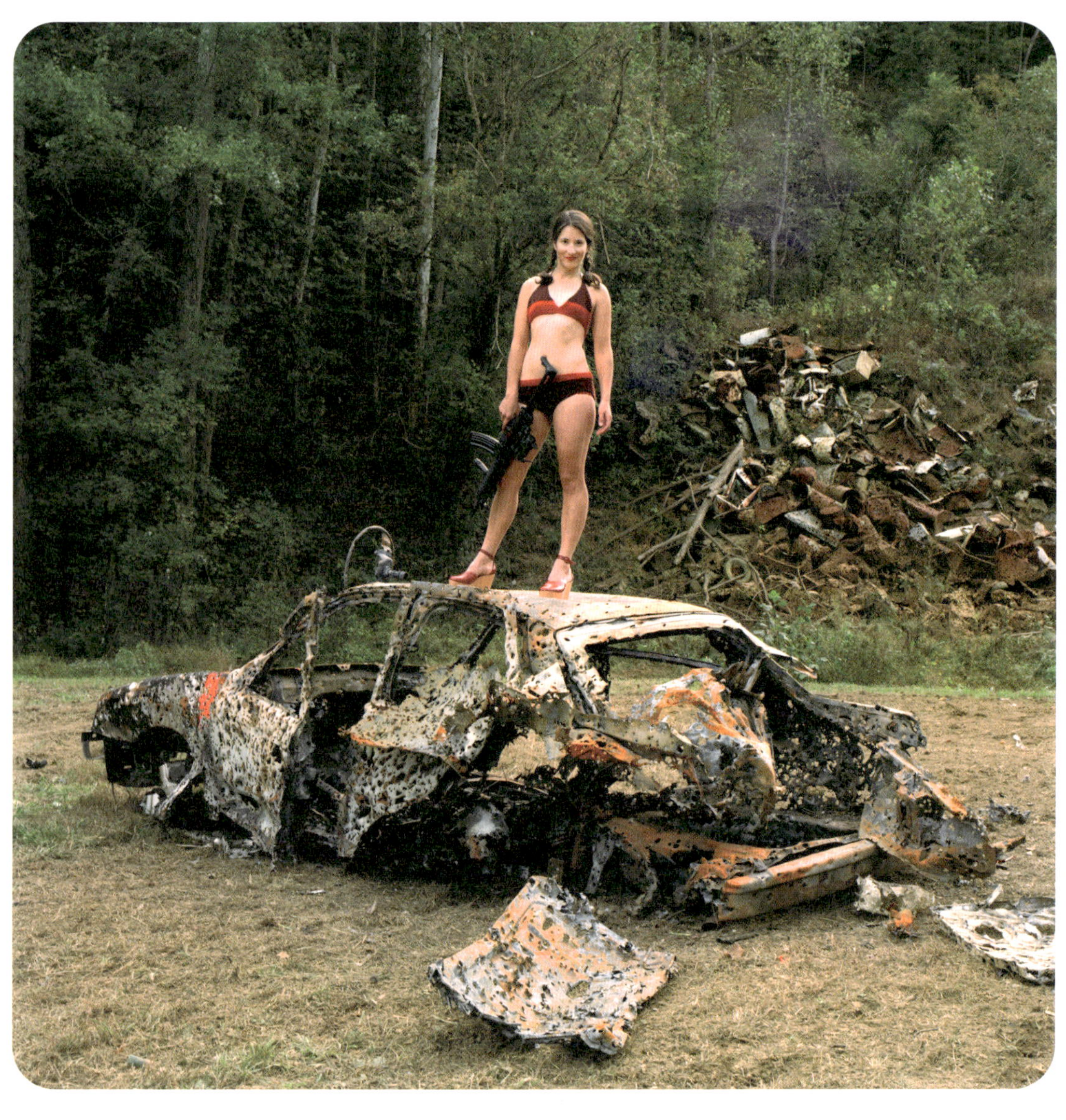

Hand-Knit Bikini, 2002/2008. Ultrachrome print. 16 1/2 x 16 1/2 in. (41.9 x 41.9 cm). Courtesy the artist and Gavlak, West Palm Beach, Florida.

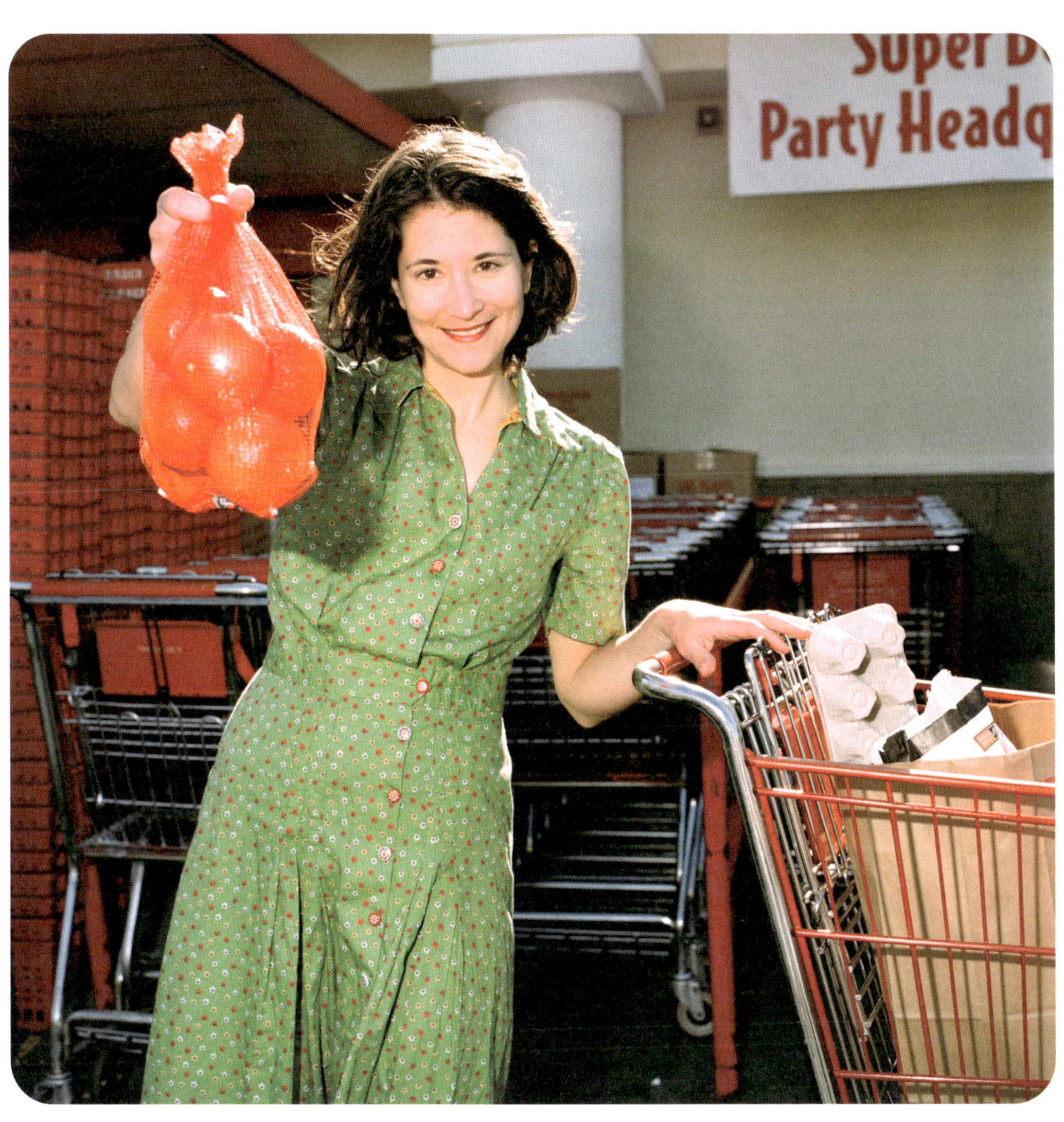

Lisa Anne Auerbach and Daniel Marlos. *December*, from *American Homebody "Sweetheart" Calendar 2001–2002*, 2001/2008. Ultrachrome print. 16 1/2 x 16 1/2 in. (41.9 x 41.9 cm). Courtesy the artist and Gavlak, West Palm Beach, Florida.

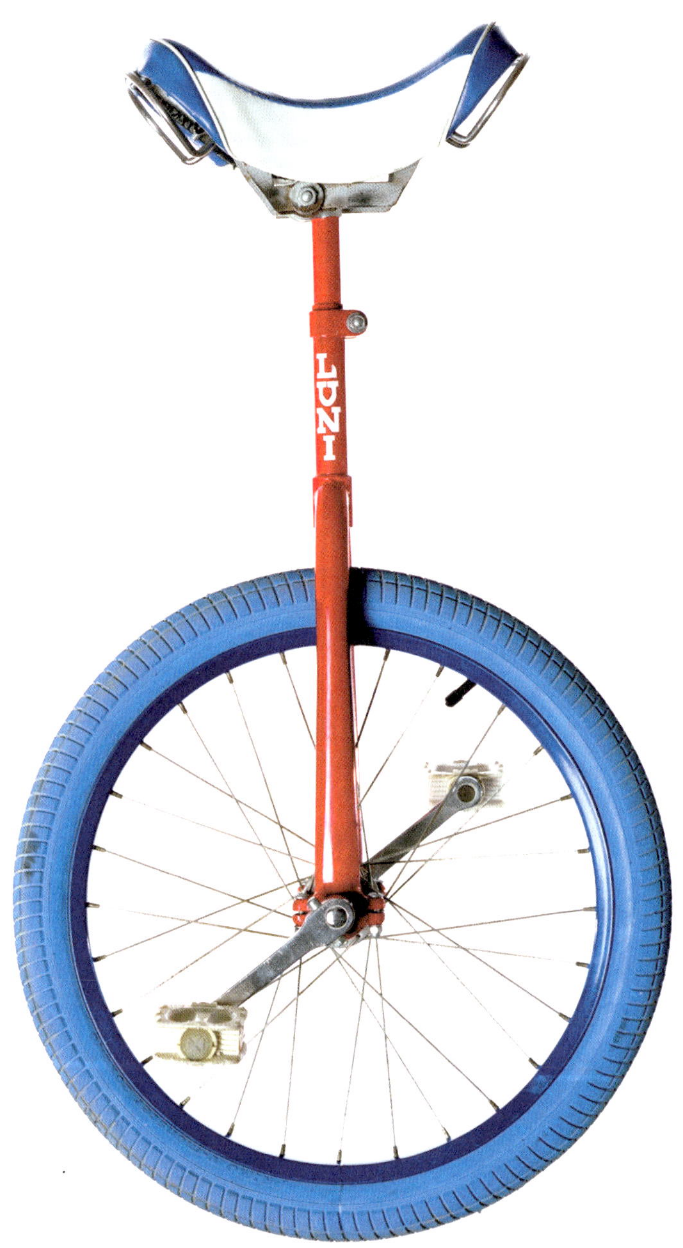

Cookie Monster, 2007. Chromogenic print. 20 x 16 in. (50.8 x 40.6 cm). Courtesy the artist and Gavlak, West Palm Beach, Florida.

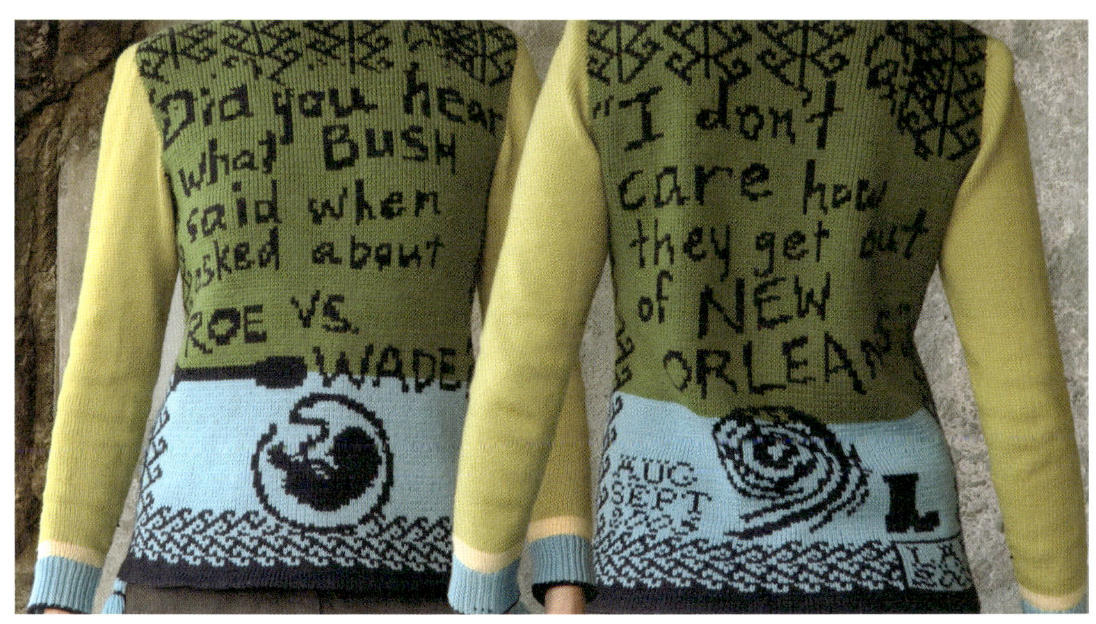

Did You Hear What Bush Said When Asked about Roe vs. Wade? 2005. Wool. Dimensions variable. Beth Rudin DeWoody; courtesy the artist and Gavlak, West Palm Beach, Florida.

Golden Land

WILLIAM FAULKNER

If he had been thirty, he would not have needed the two aspirin tablets and the half glass of raw gin before he could bear the shower's needling on his body and steady his hands to shave. But then when he had been thirty neither could he have afforded to drink as much each evening as he now drank; certainly he would not have done it in the company of the men and the women in which, at forty-eight, he did each evening, even though knowing during the very final hours filled with the breaking of glass and the shrill cries of drunken women above the drums and saxophones—the hours during which he carried a little better than his weight both in the amount of liquor consumed and in the number and sum of checks paid—that six or eight hours later he would rouse from what had not been sleep at all but instead that dreamless stupefaction of alcohol out of which last night's turgid and licensed uproar would die, as though without any interval for rest or recuperation, into the familiar shape of his bedroom—the bed's foot silhouetted by the morning light which entered the bougainvillaea-bound windows beyond which his painful and almost unbearable eyes could see the view which might be called the monument to almost twenty-five years of industry and desire, of shrewdness and luck and even fortitude—the opposite canyonflank dotted with the white villas halfhidden in imported olive groves or friezed by the sombre spaced columns of cypress like the façades of eastern temples, whose owners' names and faces and even voices were glib and familiar in back corners of the United States and of America and of the world where those of Einstein and Rousseau and Esculapius had never sounded.

He didn't waken sick. He never wakened ill nor became ill from drinking, not only because he had drunk too long and too steadily for that, but because he was too tough even after the thirty soft years; he came from too tough stock on that day thirty-four years ago when at fourteen he had fled, on the brakebeam of a westbound freight, the little lost Nebraska town named for, permeated with, his father's history and existence—a town to be sure, but only in the sense that any shadow is larger than the object which casts it. It was still frontier even as he remembered it at five and six—the projected and increased shadow of a small outpost of sodroofed dugouts on the immense desolation of the plains where his father, Ira Ewing too, had been first to essay to wring wheat during the six days between those when, outdoors in spring and summer and in the fetid halfdark of a snowbound dugout in the winter and fall, he preached. The second Ira Ewing had come a long way since then, from that barren and treeless village which he had fled by a night freight to where he now lay in a hundred-thousand-dollar house, waiting until he knew that he could rise and go to the bath and put the two aspirin tablets into his mouth. They—his mother and father—had tried to explain it to him—something about fortitude, the will to endure. At fourteen he could neither answer them with logic and reason nor explain what he wanted: he could only flee. Nor was he fleeing his father's harshness and wrath. He was fleeing the scene itself—the treeless immensity in the lost center of which he seemed to see the sum of his father's and mother's dead youth and bartered lives in a tiny forlorn spot which nature permitted to green into brief and niggard wheat for a season's moment before blotting it all with the primal and invincible snow as though (not even promise, not even threat) in grim and almost playful augury of the final doom of all life. And it was not even this that he was fleeing because he was not fleeing: it was only that absence, removal, was the only argument which fourteen knew how to employ against adults with any hope of success. He spent the next ten years half tramp half casual laborer as he drifted down the Pacific Coast to Los Angeles; at thirty he was married, to a Los Angeles girl, daughter of a carpenter, and father of a son and a daughter and with a foothold in real estate; at forty-eight he spent fifty thousand dollars a year, owning a business which he had built up unaided and preserved intact through nineteen-twenty-nine; he had given to his children luxuries and advantages which his own father not only could not have conceived in fact but would have condemned completely in theory—as it proved, as the paper which the Filipino chauffeur, who each morning carried him into the house and undressed him and put him to bed, had removed from the pocket of his topcoat and laid on the reading table proved, with reason. On the death of his father twenty years ago he had returned to Nebraska, for the first time, and fetched his mother back with him, and she was now established in a home of her own only the less sumptuous because she refused (with a kind of abashed and thoughtful unshakability which he did not remark) anything finer or more elaborate. It was the house in which they had all lived at first, though he and his wife and children had moved within the year. Three years ago they had moved again, into the house where he now waked in a select residential section of Beverly Hills, but not once in the nineteen years had he failed to stop (not even during the last five, when to move at all in the mornings required a terrific drain on that character or strength which the elder Ira had bequeathed him, which had enabled the other Ira to pause on the Nebraska plain and dig a hole for his wife to bear children in while he planted wheat) on his way to the office (twenty miles out of his way to the office) and spend ten minutes with her. She lived in as complete physical ease and peace as he could devise. He had arranged her affairs so that she did not even need to bother with money, cash, in order to live; he had arranged credit for her with a neighboring market and butcher so that the Japanese gardener who came each day to water and tend the flowers could do her shopping for her; she never even saw the bills. And the only reason she had no servant was that even at seventy she apparently clung stubbornly to the old habit of doing her own cooking and housework. So it would seem that he had been right. Perhaps there were times when, lying in bed like this and waiting for the will to rise and take the aspirin and the gin (mornings perhaps following evenings when he had drunk more than ordinarily and when even the six or seven hours of oblivion had not been sufficient to enable him to distinguish between reality and illusion) something of the old strong harsh Campbellite blood which the elder Ira must have bequeathed him might have caused him to see or feel or imagine his father looking down from somewhere upon him, the prodigal, and what he had accomplished. If this were so, then surely the elder Ira, looking down for the last two mornings upon the two tabloid papers which the Filipino removed from his master's topcoat and laid on the reading table, might have taken advantage of that old blood and taken his revenge, not just for that afternoon thirty-four years ago but for the entire thirty-four years.

When he gathered himself, his will, his body, at last and rose from the bed he struck the paper so that it fell to the floor and lay open at his feet, but he did not look at it. He just stood so, tall, in silk pajamas, thin where his father had been gaunt with the years of hard work and unceasing struggle with an unpredictable and implacable earth (even now, despite the life which he had led, he had very little paunch) looking at nothing while at his feet the black headline flared above the row of five or six tabloid photographs from which his daughter alternately stared back or flaunted long pale shins: APRIL LALEAR BARES ORGY SECRETS. When he moved at last he stepped on the paper, walking on his bare feet into the bath; now it was his trembling and jerking hands that he watched as he shook the two tablets onto the glass shelf and set the tumbler into the rack and unstoppered the gin bottle and braced his knuckles against the wall in order to pour into the tumbler. But he did not look at the paper, not even when, shaved, he re-entered the bedroom and went to the bed beside which his slippers sat and shoved the paper aside with his foot in order to step into them. Perhaps, doubtless, he did not need to. The trial was but entering its third tabloidal day now, and so for two days his daughter's face had sprung out at him, hard, blonde and inscrutable, from every paper he opened; doubtless he had never forgot her while he slept even, that he had waked into thinking about remembering her as he had waked into the dying drunken uproar of the evening eight hours behind him without any interval between for rest or forgetting.

Nevertheless as, dressed, in a burnt orange turtleneck sweater beneath his gray flannels, he descended the Spanish staircase, he was outwardly calm and possessed. The delicate iron balustrade and the marble steps coiled down to the tile-floored and barnlike living room beyond which he could hear his wife and son talking on the breakfast terrace. The son's name was Voyd. He and his wife had named the two children by what might have been called mutual contemptuous armistice—his wife called the boy Voyd, for what reason he never knew; he in his turn named the girl (the child whose woman's face had met him from every paper he touched for two days now beneath or above the name, April Lalear) Samantha, after his own mother. He could hear them talking—the wife between whom and himself there had been nothing save civility, and not always a great deal of that, for ten years now; and the son who one afternoon two years ago had been delivered at the door drunk and insensible by a car whose occupants he did not see and, it devolving upon him to undress the son and put him to bed, whom he discovered to be wearing, in place of underclothes, a woman's brassière and step-ins. A few minutes later, hearing the blows perhaps, Voyd's mother ran in and found her husband beating the still unconscious son with a series of towels which a servant was steeping in rotation in a basin of ice-water. He was beating the son hard, with grim and deliberate fury. Whether he was trying to sober the son up or was merely beating him, possibly he himself did not know. His wife though jumped to the latter conclusion. In his raging disillusionment he tried to tell her about the woman's garments but she refused to listen; she assailed him in turn with virago fury. Since that day the son had contrived to see his father only in his mother's presence (which neither the son nor the mother found very difficult, by the way) and at which times the son treated his father with a blend of cringing spite and vindictive insolence half a cat's and half a woman's.

He emerged onto the terrace; the voices ceased. The sun, strained by the vague high soft almost nebulous California haze, fell upon the terrace with a kind of treacherous unbrightness. The terrace, the sundrenched terra cotta tiles, butted into a rough and savage shear of canyonwall bare yet without dust, on or against which a solid mat of flowers bloomed in fierce lush myriad-colored paradox as though in place of being rooted into and drawing from the soil they lived upon air alone and had been merely leaned intact against the sustenanceless lavawall by someone who would later return and take them away. The son, Voyd, apparently naked save for a pair of straw-colored shorts, his body brown with sun and scented faintly by the depilatory which he used on arms, chest and legs, lay in a wicker chair, his feet in straw beach shoes, an open newspaper across his brown legs. The paper was the highest class one of the city, yet there was a black headline across half of it too, and even without pausing, without even being aware that he had looked, Ira saw there too the name which he recognized. He went on to his place; the Filipino who put him to bed each night, in a white service jacket now, drew his chair. Beside the glass of orange juice and the waiting cup lay a neat pile of mail topped by a telegram. He sat down and took up the telegram; he had not glanced at his wife until she spoke:

"Mrs. Ewing telephoned. She says for you to stop in there on your way to town."

He stopped; his hands opening the telegram stopped. Still blinking a little against the sun he looked at the face opposite him across the table—the smooth dead makeup, the thin lips and the thin nostrils and the pale blue unforgiving eyes, the meticulous platinum hair which looked as though it had been transferred to her skull with a brush from a book of silver leaf such as window painters use. "What?" he said. "Telephoned? Here?"

"Why not? Have I ever objected to any of your women telephoning you here?"

The unopened telegram crumpled suddenly in his hand. "You know what I mean," he said harshly. "She never telephoned me in her life. She don't have to. Not that message. When have I ever failed to go by there on my way to town?"

"How do I know?" she said. "Or are you the same model son you have been a husband and seem to be a father?" Her voice was not shrill yet, nor even very loud, and none could have told how fast her breathing was because she sat so still, rigid beneath the impeccable and unbelievable hair, looking at him with that pale and outraged unforgiveness. They both looked at each other across the luxurious table—the two people who at one time twenty years ago would have turned as immediately and naturally and unthinkingly to one another in trouble, who even ten years ago might have done so.

"You know what I mean," he said, harshly again, holding himself too against the trembling which he doubtless believed was from last night's drinking, from the spent alcohol. "She don't read papers. She never even sees one. Did you send it to her?"

"I?" she said. "Send what?"

"Damnation!" he cried. "A paper! Did you send it to her? Don't lie to me."

"What if I did?" she cried. "Who is she, that she must not know about it? Who is she, that you should shield her from knowing it? Did you make any effort to keep me from knowing it? Did you make any effort to keep it from happening? Why didn't you think about that all those years while you were too drunk, too besotted with drink, to know or notice or care what Samantha was—"

"Miss April Lalear of the cinema, if you please," Voyd said. They paid no attention to him; they glared at one another across the table.

"Ah," he said, quiet and rigid, his lips scarcely moving. "So I am to blame for this too, am I? I made my daughter a bitch, did I? Maybe you will tell me next that I made my son a f—"

"Stop!" she cried. She was panting now; they glared at one another across the suave table, across the five feet of irrevocable division.

"Now, now," Voyd said. "Don't interfere with the girl's career. After all these years, when at last she seems to have found a part that she can—" He ceased; his father had turned and was looking at him. Voyd lay in his chair, looking at his father with that veiled insolence that was almost feminine. Suddenly it became completely feminine; with a muffled halfscream he swung his legs out to spring up and flee but it was too late; Ira stood above him, gripping him not by the throat but by the face with one hand, so that Voyd's mouth puckered and slobbered in his father's hard, shaking hand. Then the mother sprang forward and tried to break Ira's grip but he flung her away and then caught and held her, struggling too, with the other hand when she sprang in again.

"Go on," he said. "Say it." But Voyd could say nothing because of his father's hand gripping his jaws open, or more than likely because of terror. His body was free of the chair now, writhing and thrashing while he made his slobbering, moaning sound of terror while his father held him with one hand and held his screaming mother with the other one. Then Ira flung Voyd free, onto the terrace; Voyd rolled once and came onto his feet, crouching, retreating toward the French windows with one arm flung up before his face while he cursed his father. Then he was gone. Ira faced his wife, holding her quiet too at last, panting too, the skillful map of makeup standing into relief now like a paper mask trimmed smoothly and pasted onto her skull. He released her.

"You sot," she said. "You drunken sot. And yet you wonder why your children—"

"Yes," he said quietly. "All right. That's not the question. That's all done. The question is, what to do about it. My father would have known. He did it once." He spoke in a dry light pleasant voice: so much so that she stood, panting still but quiet, watching him. "I remember. I was about ten. We had rats in the barn. We tried everything. Terriers. Poison. Then one day father said, 'Come.' We went to the barn and stopped all the cracks, the holes. Then we set fire to it. What do you think of that?" Then she was gone too. He stood for a moment, blinking a little, his eyeballs beating faintly and steadily in his skull with the impact of the soft unchanging sunlight, the fierce innocent mass of the flowers. "Philip!" he called. The Filipino appeared, brownfaced, impassive, with a pot of hot coffee, and set it beside the empty cup and the icebedded glass of orange juice. "Get me a drink," Ira said. The Filipino glanced at him, then he became busy at the table, shifting the cup and setting the pot down and shifting the cup again while Ira watched him. "Did you hear me?" Ira said. The Filipino stood erect and looked at him.

"You told me not to give it to you until you had your orange juice and coffee."

"Will you or won't you get me a drink?" Ira shouted.

"Very good, sir," the Filipino said. He went out. Ira looked after him; this had happened before: he knew well that the brandy would not appear until he had finished the orange juice and the coffee, though just where the Filipino lurked to watch him he never knew. He sat again and opened the crumpled telegram and read it, the glass of orange juice in the other hand. It was from his secretary: MADE SETUP BEFORE I BROKE STORY LAST NIGHT STOP THIRTY PERCENT FRONT PAGE STOP MADE APPOINTMENT FOR YOU COURTHOUSE THIS P.M. STOP WILL YOU COME TO OFFICE OR CALL ME. He read the telegram again, the glass of orange juice still poised. Then he put both down and rose and went and lifted the paper from the terrace where Voyd had flung it, and read the half headline: LALEAR WOMAN DAUGHTER OF PROMINENT LOCAL FAMILY. Admits Real Name Is Samantha Ewing, Daughter of Ira Ewing, Local Realtor. He read it quietly; he said quietly, aloud:

"It was that Jap that showed her the paper. It was that damned gardener." He returned to the table. After a while the Filipino came, with the brandy-and-soda, and wearing now a jacket of bright imitation tweed, telling him that the car was ready.

II

His mother lived in Glendale; it was the house which he had taken when he married and later bought, in which his son and daughter had been born—a bungalow in a cul-de-sac of pepper trees and flowering shrubs and vines which the Japanese tended, backed into a barren foothill combed and curried into a cypress-and-marble cemetery dramatic as a stage set and topped by an electric sign in red bulbs which, in the San Fernando valley fog, glared in broad sourceless ruby as though just beyond the crest lay not heaven but hell. The length of his sports model car in which the Filipino sat reading a paper dwarfed it. But she would have no other, just as she would have neither servant, car, nor telephone—a gaunt spare slightly stooped woman upon whom even California and ease had put no flesh, sitting in one of the chairs which she had insisted on bringing all the way from Nebraska. At first she had been content to allow the Nebraska furniture to remain in storage, since it had not been needed (when Ira moved his wife and family out of the house and into the second one, the intermediate one, they had bought new furniture too, leaving the first house furnished complete for his mother) but one day, he could not recall just when, he discovered that she had taken the one chair out of storage and was using it in the house. Later, after he began to sense that quality of unrest in her, he had suggested that she let him clear the house of its present furniture and take all of hers out of storage but she declined, apparently preferring or desiring to leave the Nebraska furniture where it was. Sitting so, a knitted shawl about her shoulders, she looked less like she lived in or belonged to the house, the room, than the son with his beach burn and his faintly theatrical gray temples and his bright expensive suavely antiphonal garments did. She had changed hardly at all in the thirty-four years; she and the older Ira Ewing too, as the son remembered him, who, dead, had suffered as little of alteration as while he had been alive. As the sod Nebraska outpost had grown into a village and then into a town, his father's aura alone had increased, growing into the proportions of a giant who at some irrevocable yet recent time had engaged barehanded in some titanic struggle with the pitiless earth and endured and in a sense conquered—it too, like the town, a shadow out of all proportion to the gaunt gnarled figure of the actual man. And the actual woman too as the son remembered them back in that time. Two people who drank air and who required to eat and sleep as he did and who had brought him into the world, yet were strangers as though of another race, who stood side by side in an irrevocable loneliness as though strayed from another planet, not as husband and wife but as blood brother and sister, even twins, of the same travail because they had gained a strange peace through fortitude and the will and strength to endure.

"Tell me again what it is," she said. "I'll try to understand."

"So it was Kazimura that showed you the damned paper," he said. She didn't answer this; she was not looking at him.

"You tell me she has been in the pictures before, for two years. That that was why she had to change her name, that they all have to change their names."

"Yes. They call them extra parts. For about two years, God knows why."

"And then you tell me that this—that all this was so she could get into the pictures—"

He started to speak, then he caught himself back out of some quick impatience, some impatience perhaps of grief or despair or at least rage, holding his voice, his tone, quiet: "I said that that was one possible reason. All I know is that the man has something to do with pictures, giving out the parts. And that the police caught him and Samantha and the other girl in an apartment with the doors all locked and that Samantha and the other woman were naked. They say that he was naked too and he says he was not. He says in the trial that he was framed—tricked; that they were trying to blackmail him into giving them parts in a picture; that they fooled him into coming there and arranged for the police to break in just after they had taken off their clothes; that one of them made a signal from the window. Maybe so. Or maybe they were all just having a good time and were innocently caught." Unmoving, rigid, his face broke, wrung with faint bitter smiling as though with indomitable and impassive suffering, or maybe just smiling, just rage. Still his mother did not look at him.

"But you told me she was already in the pictures. That that was why she had to change her—"

"I said, extra parts," he said. He had to catch himself again, out of his jangled and outraged nerves, back from the fierce fury of the impatience. "Can't you understand that you don't get into the pictures just by changing your name? and that you don't even stay there when you get in? that you can't even stay there by being female? that they come here in droves on every train—girls younger and prettier than Samantha and who will do anything to get into the pictures? So will she, apparently; but who know or are willing to learn to do more things than even she seems to have thought of? But let's don't talk about it. She has made her bed; all I can do is to help her up: I can't wash the sheets. Nobody can. I must go, anyway; I'm late." He rose, looking down at her. "They said you telephoned me this morning. Is this what it was?"

"No," she said. Now she looked up at him; now her gnarled hands began to pick faintly at one another. "You offered me a servant once."

"Yes. I thought fifteen years ago that you ought to have one. Have you changed your mind? Do you want me to—"

Now she stopped looking at him again, though her hands did not cease. "That was fifteen years ago. It would have cost at least five hundred dollars a year. That would be—"

He laughed, short and harsh. "I'd like to see the Los Angeles servant you could get for five hundred dollars a year. But what—" He stopped laughing, looking down at her.

"That would be at least five thousand dollars," she said.

He looked down at her. After a while he said, "Are you asking me again for money?" She didn't answer nor move, her hands picking slowly and quietly at one another. "Ah," he said, "You want to go away. You want to run from it. So do I!" he cried, before he could catch himself this time; "so do I! But you did not choose me when you elected a child; neither did I choose my two. But I shall have to bear them and you will have to bear all of us. There is no help for it." He caught himself now, panting, quieting himself by will as when he would rise from bed, though his voice was still harsh: "Where would you go? Where would you hide from it?"

"Home," she said.

"Home?" he repeated; he repeated in a kind of amazement: "home?" before he understood. "You would go back there? with those winters, that snow and all? Why, you wouldn't live to see the first Christmas: don't you know that?" She didn't move nor look up at him. "Nonsense," he said. "This will blow over. In a month there will be two others and nobody except us will even remember it. And you don't need money. You have been asking me for money for years, but you don't need it. I had to worry about money so much at one time myself that I swore that the least I could do was to arrange your affairs so you would never even have to look at the stuff. I must go; there is something at the office today. I'll see you tomorrow."

It was already one o'clock. "Courthouse," he told the Filipino, settling back into the car. "My God, I want a drink." He rode with his eyes closed against the sun; the secretary had already sprung onto the running board before he realized that they had reached the courthouse. The secretary, bareheaded too, wore a jacket of authentic tweed; his turtleneck sweater was dead black, his hair was black too, varnished smooth to his skull; he spread before Ira a dummy newspaper page laid out to embrace the blank space for the photograph beneath the caption: APRIL LALEAR'S FATHER. Beneath the space was the legend: IRA EWING, PRESIDENT OF THE EWING REALTY CO.,—WILSHIRE BOULEVARD, BEVERLY HILLS.

"Is thirty percent all you could get?" Ira said. The secretary was young; he glared at Ira for an instant in vague impatient fury.

"Jesus, thirty percent is thirty percent. They are going to print a thousand extra copies and use our mailing list. It will be spread all up and down the Coast and as far East as Reno. What do you want? We can't expect them to put under your picture, 'Turn to page fourteen for halfpage ad,' can we?" Ira sat again with his eyes closed, waiting for his head to stop.

"All right," he said. "Are they ready now?"

"All set. You will have to go inside. They insisted it be inside, so everybody that sees it will know it is the courthouse."

"All right," Ira said. He got out; with his eyes half closed and the secretary at his elbow he mounted the steps and entered the courthouse. The reporter and the photographer were waiting but he did not see them yet; he was aware only of being enclosed in a gaping crowd which he knew would be mostly women, hearing the secretary and a policeman clearing the way in the corridor outside the courtroom door.

"This is O.K.," the secretary said. Ira stopped; the darkness was easier on his eyes though he did not open them yet; he just stood, hearing the secretary and the policeman herding the women, the faces, back; someone took him by the arm and turned him; he stood obediently; the magnesium flashed and glared, striking against his painful eyeballs like blows; he had a vision of wan faces craned to look at him from either side of a narrow human lane; with his eyes shut tight now he turned, blundering until the reporter in charge spoke to him:

"Just a minute, chief. We better get another one just in case." This time his eyes were tightly closed; the magnesium flashed, washed over them; in the thin acrid smell of it he turned and with the secretary again at his elbow he moved blindly back and into the sunlight and into his car. He gave no order this time, he just said, "Get me a drink." He rode with his eyes closed again while the car cleared the downtown traffic and then began to move quiet, powerful and fast under him; he rode so for a long while before he felt the car swing into the palmbordered drive, slowing. It stopped; the doorman opened the door for him, speaking to him by name. The elevator boy called him by name too, stopping at the right floor without direction; he followed the corridor and knocked at a door and was fumbling for the key when the door opened upon a woman in a bathing suit beneath a loose beach cloak—a woman with treated hair also and brown eyes, who swung the door back for him to enter and then to behind him, looking at him with the quick bright faint serene smiling which only a woman nearing forty can give to a man to whom she is not married and from whom she has had no secrets physical and few mental over a long time of pleasant and absolute intimacy. She had been married though and divorced; she had a child, a daughter of fourteen, whom he was now keeping in boarding school. He looked at her, blinking, as she closed the door.

"You saw the papers," he said. She kissed him, not suddenly, without heat, in a continuation of the movement which closed the door, with a sort of warm envelopment; suddenly he cried, "I can't understand it! After all the advantages that... after all I tried to do for them—"

"Hush," she said. "Hush, now. Get into your trunks; I'll have a drink ready for you when you have changed. Will you eat some lunch if I have it sent up?"

"No. I don't want any lunch. —after all I have tried to give—"

"Hush, now. Get into your trunks while I fix you a drink. It's going to be swell at the beach." In the bedroom his bathing trunks and robe were laid out on the bed. He changed, hanging his suit in the closet where her clothes hung, where there hung already another suit of his and clothes for the evening. When he returned to the sitting room she had fixed the drink for him, she held the match to his cigarette and watched him sit down and take up the glass, watching him still with that serene impersonal smiling. Now he watched her slip off the cape and kneel at the cellarette, filling a silver flask, in the bathing costume of the moment, such as ten thousand wax female dummies wore in ten thousand shop windows that summer, such as a hundred thousand young girls wore on California beaches; he looked at her, kneeling—back, buttocks and flanks trim enough, even firm enough (so firm in fact as to be a little on the muscular side, what with unremitting and perhaps even rigorous care) but still those of forty. But I don't want a young girl, he thought. Would to God that all young girls, all young female flesh, were removed, blasted even, from the earth. He finished the drink before she had filled the flask.

"I want another one," he said.

"All right," she said. "As soon as we get to the beach."

"No. Now."

"Let's go on to the beach first. It's almost three o'clock. Won't that be better?"

"Just so you are not trying to tell me I can't have another drink now."

"Of course not," she said, slipping the flask into the cape's pocket and looking at him again with that warm, faint, inscrutable smiling. "I just want to have a dip before the water gets too cold." They went down to the car; the Filipino knew this too: he held the door for her to slip under the wheel, then he got himself into the back. The car moved on; she drove well. "Why not lean back and shut your eyes," she told Ira, "and rest until we get to the beach? Then we will have a dip and a drink."

"I don't want to rest," he said. "I'm all right." But he did close his eyes again and again the car ran powerful, smooth, and fast beneath him, performing its afternoon's jaunt over the incredible distances of which the city was composed; from time to time, had he looked, he could have seen the city in the bright soft vague hazy sunlight, random, scattered about the arid earth like so many gay scraps of paper blown without order, with its curious air of being rootless—of houses bright beautiful and gay, without basements or foundations, lightly attached to a few inches of light penetrable earth, lighter even than dust and laid lightly in turn upon the profound and primeval lava, which one good hard rain would wash forever from the sight and memory of man as a firehose flushes down a gutter—that city of almost incalculable wealth whose queerly appropriate fate it is to be erected upon a few spools of a substance whose value is computed in billions and which may be completely destroyed in that second's instant of a careless match between the moment of striking and the moment when the striker might have sprung and stamped it out.

"You saw your mother today," she said. "Has she—"

"Yes." He didn't open his eyes. "That damned Jap gave it to her. She asked me for money again. I found out what she wants with it. She wants to run, to go back to Nebraska. I told her, so did I.... If she went back there, she would not live until Christmas. The first month of winter would kill her. Maybe it wouldn't even take winter to do it."

She still drove, she still watched the road, yet somehow she had contrived to become completely immobile. "So that's what it is," she said.

He did not open his eyes. "What what is?"

"The reason she has been after you all this time to give her money, cash. Why, even when you won't do it, every now and then she asks you again."

"What what..." He opened his eyes, looking at her profile; he sat up suddenly. "You mean, she's been wanting to go back there all the time? That all these years she has been asking me for money, that that was what she wanted with it?"

She glanced at him swiftly, then back to the road. "What else can it be? What else could she use money for?"

"Back there?" he said. "To those winters, that town, that way of living, where she's bound to know that the first winter would...You'd almost think she wanted to die, wouldn't you?"

"Hush," she said quickly. "Shhhhh. Don't say that. Don't say that about anybody." Already they could smell the sea; now they swung down toward it; the bright salt wind blew upon them, with the long-spaced sound of the rollers; now they could see it—the dark blue of water creaming into the blanched curve of beach dotted with bathers. "We won't go through the club," she said. "I'll park in here and we can go straight to the water." They left the Filipino in the car and descended to the beach. It was already crowded, bright and gay with movement. She chose a vacant space and spread her cape.

"Now that drink," he said.

"Have your dip first," she said. He looked at her. Then he slipped his robe off slowly; she took it and spread it beside her own; he looked down at her.

"Which is it? Will you always be too clever for me, or is it that every time I will always believe you again?"

She looked at him, bright, warm, fond and inscrutable. "Maybe both. Maybe neither. Have your dip; I will have the flask and a cigarette ready when you come out." When he came back from the water, wet, panting, his heart a little too hard and fast, she had the towel ready, and she lit the cigarette and uncapped the flask as he lay on the spread robes. She lay too, lifted to one elbow, smiling down at him, smoothing the water from his hair with the towel while he panted, waiting for his heart to slow and quiet. Steadily between them and the water, and as far up and down the beach as they could see, the bathers passed—young people, young men in trunks, and young girls in little more, with bronzed, unselfconscious bodies. Lying so, they seemed to him to walk along the rim of the world as though they and their kind alone inhabited it, and he with his forty-eight years were the forgotten last survivor of another race and kind, and they in turn precursors of a new race not yet seen on the earth: of men and women without age, beautiful as gods and goddesses, and with the minds of infants. He turned quickly and looked at the woman beside him—at the quiet face, the wise, smiling eyes, the grained skin and temples, the hairroots showing where the dye had grown out, the legs veined faint and blue and myriad beneath the skin. "You look better than any of them!" he cried. "You look better to me than any of them!"

III

The Japanese gardener, with his hat on, stood tapping on the glass and beckoning and grimacing until old Mrs. Ewing went out to him. He had the afternoon's paper with its black headline: LALEAR WOMAN CREATES SCENE IN COURTROOM. "You take," the Japanese said. "Read while I catch water." But she declined; she just stood in the soft halcyon sunlight, surrounded by the myriad and almost fierce blooming of flowers, and looked quietly at the headline without even taking the paper, and that was all.

"I guess I won't look at the paper today," she said. "Thank you just the same." She returned to the living room. Save for the chair, it was exactly as it had been when she first saw it that day when her son brought her into it and told her that it was now her home and that her daughter in law and her grandchildren were now her family. It had changed very little, and that which had altered was the part which her son knew nothing about, and that too had changed not at all in so long that she could not even remember now when she had added the last coin to the hoard. This was in a china vase on the mantel. She knew what was in it to the penny; nevertheless, she took it down and sat in the chair which she had brought all the way from Nebraska and emptied the coins and the worn timetable into her lap. The timetable was folded back at the page on which she had folded it the day she walked downtown to the ticket office and got it fifteen years ago, though that was so long ago now that the pencil circle about the name of the nearest junction point to Ewing, Nebraska, had faded away. But she did not need that either; she knew the distance to the exact halfmile, just as she knew the fare to the penny, and back in the early twenties when the railroads began to become worried and passenger fares began to drop, no broker ever watched the grain and utilities market any closer than she watched the railroad advertisements and quotations. Then at last the fares became stabilized with the fare back to Ewing thirteen dollars more than she had been able to save, and at a time when her source of income had ceased. This was the two grandchildren. When she entered the house that day twenty years ago and looked at the two babies for the first time, it was with diffidence and eagerness both. She would be dependent for the rest of her life, but she would give something in return for it. It was not that she would attempt to make another Ira and Samantha Ewing of them; she had made that mistake with her own son and had driven him from home. She was wiser now; she saw now that it was not the repetition of hardship: she would merely take what had been of value in hers and her husband's hard lives—that which they had learned through hardship and endurance of honor and courage and pride—and transmit it to the children without their having to suffer the hardship at all, the travail and the despairs. She had expected that there would be some friction between her and the young daughter-in-law, but she had believed that her son, the actual Ewing, would be her ally; she had even reconciled herself after a year to waiting, since the children were still but babies; she was not alarmed, since they were Ewings too: after she had looked that first searching time at the two puttysoft little faces feature by feature, she had said it was because they were babies yet and so looked like no one. So she was content to bide and wait; she did not even know that her son was planning to move until he told her that the other house was bought and that the present one was to be hers until she died. She watched them go; she said nothing; it was to begin then. It did not begin for five years, during which she watched her son making money faster and faster and easier and easier, gaining with apparent contemptible and contemptuous ease that substance for which in niggard amounts her husband had striven while still clinging with undeviating incorruptibility to honor and dignity and pride, and spending it, squandering it, in the same way. By that time she had given up the son and she had long since learned that she and her daughter-in-law were irrevocable and implacable moral enemies. It was in the fifth year. One day in her son's home she saw the two children take money from their mother's purse lying on a table. The mother did not even know how much she had in the purse; when the grandmother told her about it she became angry and dared the older woman to put it to the test. The grandmother accused the children, who denied the whole affair with perfectly straight faces. That was the actual break between herself and her son's family; after that she saw the two children only when the son would bring them with him occasionally on his unfailing daily visits. She had a few broken dollars which she had brought from Nebraska and had kept intact for five years, since she had no need for money here; one day she planted one of the coins while the children were there, and when she went back to look, it was gone too. The next morning she tried to talk to her son about the children, remembering her experience with the daughter-in-law and approaching the matter indirectly, speaking generally of money. "Yes," the son said. "I'm making money. I'm making it fast while I can. I'm going to make a lot of it. I'm going to give my children luxuries and advantages that my father never dreamed a child might have."

"That's it," she said. "You make money too easy. This whole country is too easy for us Ewings. It may be all right for them that have been born here for generations; I don't know about that. But not for us."

"But these children were born here."

"Just one generation. The generation before that they were born in a sodroofed dugout on the Nebraska wheat frontier. And the one before that in a log house in Missouri. And the one before that in a Kentucky blockhouse with Indians around it. This world has never been easy for Ewings. Maybe the Lord never intended it to be."

"But it is from now on," he said; he spoke with a kind of triumph. "For you and me too. But mostly for them."

And that was all. When he was gone she sat quietly in the single Nebraska chair which she had taken out of storage—the first chair which the older Ira Ewing had bought for her after he built a house and in which she had rocked the younger Ira to sleep before he could walk, while the older Ira himself sat in the chair which he had made out of a flour barrel, grim, quiet and incorruptible, taking his earned twilight ease between a day and a day—telling herself quietly that that was all. Her next move was curiously direct; there was something in it of the actual pioneer's opportunism, of taking immediate and cold advantage of Spartan circumstance; it was as though for the first time in her life she was able to use something, anything, which she had gained by bartering her youth and strong maturity against the Nebraska immensity, and this not in order to live further but in order to die; apparently she saw neither paradox in it nor dishonesty. She began to make candy and cake of the materials which her son bought for her on credit, and to sell them to the two grandchildren for the coins which their father gave them or which they perhaps purloined also from their mother's purse, hiding the coins in the vase with the timetable, watching the niggard hoard grow. But after a few years the children outgrew candy and cake, and then she had watched railroad fares go down and down and then stop thirteen dollars away. But she did not give up, even then. Her son had tried to give her a servant years ago and she had refused; she believed that when the time came, the right moment, he would not refuse to give her at least thirteen dollars of the money which she had saved him. Then this had failed. "Maybe it wasn't the right time," she thought. "Maybe I tried it too quick. I was surprised into it," she told herself, looking down at the heap of small coins in her lap. "Or maybe he was surprised into saying No. Maybe when he has had time..." She roused; she put the coins back into the vase and set it on the mantel again, looking at the clock as she did so. It was just four, two hours yet until time to start supper. The sun was high; she could see the water from the sprinkler flashing and glinting in it as she went to the window. It was still high, still afternoon; the mountains stood serene and drab against it; the city, the land, lay sprawled and myriad beneath it—the land, the earth which spawned a thousand new faiths, nostrums and cures each year but no disease to even disprove them on—beneath the golden days unmarred by rain or weather, the changeless monotonous beautiful days without end countless out of the halcyon past and endless into the halcyon future.

"I will stay here and live forever," she said to herself.

Llyn Foulkes

In Memory of St. Vincent School, 1960
Assemblage: oil, charred wood, and plasticized ashes on blackboard, with chair
Blackboard: 66 x 72 1/4 in. (167.6 x 183.5 cm); chair: 26 1/4 x 13 x 12 1/2 in. (66.7 x 33 x 31.8 cm)
Norton Simon Museum; Gift of Dr. and Mrs. Harry Zlotnick

Flanders, 1961–62
Mixed media
Top part: 54 x 36 x 14 in. (137.2 x 91.4 x 35.6 cm); bottom part: 16 x 15 3/4 in. (40.6 x 40 cm)
Collection of Ernest and Eunice White

Geometry Teacher #1, 1973
Mixed media
15 1/2 x 13 1/2 in. (39.4 x 34.3 cm)
The Buck Collection, Laguna Beach, California

Made in Hollywood, 1983
Mixed media
66 5/8 x 66 7/8 x 7 1/4 in. (169.2 x 169.9 x 18.4 cm)
Museum of Contemporary Art San Diego; Promised gift of the Ruth Gribin Non-Exempt QTip Marital Trust
Courtesy Gribin Family Trust

The Crucifixion, 1985
Mixed media
29 x 21 in. (73.7 x 53.3 cm)
Hammer Museum, Los Angeles; Purchase with funds provided in part by Jean Stein

That Old Black Magic, 1985
Mixed media on board
67 x 57 in. (170.2 x 144.8 cm)
Laguna Art Museum Collection; Gift of Ruth and Murray Gribin

The Lost Frontier, 1997–2005
Mixed media
87 x 96 x 8 in. (221 x 243. 8 x 20.3 cm)
Courtesy the artist and Kent Gallery, New York

Dali and Me, 2006
Mixed media
33 x 26 in. (83.8 x 66 cm)
The Collection of Patrick and Soo Jin Jeong-Painter

Deliverance, 2007
Mixed media
72 x 84 in. (182.9 x 213.4 cm)
Courtesy the artist and Kent Gallery, New York

The Awakening (working title), 2009
(work in progress)
Mixed media
Dimensions unknown
Courtesy the artist and Kent Gallery, New York

Julie Becker

Leda and the Swan, 1993/2000
Video, color, sound
4:36 min.
Courtesy Greene Naftali Gallery, New York.

Octopus, 1997
Mixed media on paper
16 3/4 x 14 in. (42.5 x 35.6 cm)
Hammer Museum, Los Angeles; Gift of Dean Valentine and Amy Adelson

A Place Called Lovely, 1999
Mixed media
15 x 11 in. (38.1 x 27.9 cm)
Courtesy the artist and Greene Naftali Gallery, New York

Untitled, 1999
Ink, pencil, and mixed media on paper
8 1/2 x 11 in. (21.6 x 27.9 cm)
Tanya Bonakdar, New York

Untitled (Surrealism), 1999–2000
Artforum magazine, plastic, wood
14 x 13 1/2 x 3 1/4 in. (35.6 x 34.3 x 8.3 cm)
Courtesy the artist and Greene Naftali Gallery, New York

1910 West Sunset Blvd, 2000
Mixed-media sculpture
16 x 99 x 52 in. (40.6 x 251.5 x 132.1 cm)
Courtesy Greene Naftali Gallery, New York

Untitled (Whole Series) (Apocalypse), 2001
Mixed media on paper
17 3/4 x 23 1/4 in. (45.1 x 59.1 cm)
Courtesy Foundation 2021/Nyehaus, New York

Money Changer, 2002
Mixed media on paper
17 x 16 3/4 in. (43.1 x 42.6 cm)
Private collection, New York

Untitled (Roots), 2002
Mixed media on paper
17 3/4 x 23 1/2 in. (45.1 x 59.7 cm)
Private collection, New York

Pyramid Scheme, 2003
Mixed media on paper
17 x 14 in. (43.2 x 35.6 cm)
Ann and Mel Schaffer Family Collection

Untitled (Moon), 2003
Mixed media on paper
17 x 23 in. (43.2 x 58.4 cm)
Private collection, New York

Homemade Microphone, 2004
Mixed media
60 x 45 x 28 in. (152.4 x 114.3 x 71.1 cm)
Courtesy Tim Nye, New York

Untitled (mirror drawing), 2004
Mixed media on paper
14 x 17 in. (35.6 x 43.2 cm)
Courtesy Greene Naftali Gallery, New York

Hirsch Perlman

Animus Cat, 2008
Chromogenic print
72 x 97 in. (182.9 x 246.4 cm)
Courtesy the artist and Blum & Poe, Los Angeles

An Animus Cat Amok & Asunder, 2008
Chromogenic print
72 x 97 in. (182.9 x 246.4 cm)
Courtesy the artist and Blum & Poe, Los Angeles

An Animus Cat Antagonist, 2008
Chromogenic print
72 x 97 in. (182.9 x 246.4 cm)
Courtesy the artist and Blum & Poe, Los Angeles

An Animus Cat Apostate, 2008
Chromogenic print
97 x 72 in. (246.4 x 182.9 cm)
Courtesy the artist and Blum & Poe, Los Angeles

An Animus Cat Askant, 2008
Chromogenic print
72 x 97 in. (182.9 x 246.4 cm)
Courtesy the artist and Blum & Poe, Los Angeles

Charles Irvin

Chronology, 2006
Acrylic on canvas panel
18 x 14 in. (45.7 x 35.6 cm)
Courtesy the artist

Mandrake Party, 2006
Ink and acrylic on paper
30 x 22 1/2 in. (76.2 x 55.9 cm)
Courtesy the artist

Self-Portrait, 2006
Acrylic on canvas
24 x 30 in. (61 x 76.2 cm)
Courtesy the artist

Untitled, 2006
Acrylic on canvas panel
14 x 18 in. (35.6 x 45.7 cm)
Courtesy the artist

Dr. Smooth, 2007
Ink on paper
12 x 9 in. (30.5 x 22.9 cm)
Courtesy the artist

Egyptian Triptych, 2007
Mixed media on paper
17 x 14 in. (43.2 x 35.6 cm) each
Courtesy the artist

Shareholders Meeting, 2007
Ink and acrylic on paper
30 x 22 1/2 in. (76.2 x 55.9 cm)
Courtesy the artist

Symbolic Podium, 2007
Mixed media on paper
24 x 18 in. (61 x 45.7 cm)
Courtesy the artist

Untitled, 2007
Mixed media
19 x 13 in. (48.3 x 33 cm)
Courtesy the artist

Untitled (Masonic Apron), 2007
Mixed media on paper
14 x 11 in. (35.6 x 27.9 cm)
Courtesy the artist

Farty Man Sez, 2008
Prismacolor pencil on paper
18 x 24 in. (45.7 x 61 cm)
Courtesy the artist

Puzzle, 2008
Prismacolor pencil on paper
24 x 18 in. (61 x 45.7 cm)
Courtesy the artist

Smoky Rider, 2008
Ink on paper
24 x 18 in. (61 x 45.7 cm)
Courtesy the artist

Untitled, 2008
Mixed media on paper
14 x 17 in. (35.6 x 43.2 cm)
Courtesy the artist

Untitled, 2008
Ink and acrylic on paper
24 x 18 in. (61 x 45.7 cm)
Courtesy the artist

Untitled, 2008
Ink and acrylic on paper
18 x 24 in. (45.7 X 61 cm)
Courtesy the artist

Membrane Lane, 2009
Video, color, sound
Approx. 30 min.
Courtesy the artist

Victoria Reynolds

Beautiful Uteral Garlands, 1999
Oil on panel, frame
35 x 24 1/4 in. (88.9 x 61.6 cm)
Collection of Karol Howard and George Morton

For the Carnal in Dante's Hell, 1999
Oil on panel, frame
28 x 32 1/4 in. (71.1 x 81.9 cm)
Private collection, Hollywood, California

Fat of the Lamb, 2003
Oil on panel, frame
30 x 18 1/2 in. (76.2 x 47 cm)
Alan Power Collection

Flight of the Reindeer, 2003
Oil on panel, frame
32 x 43 1/4 in. (81.3 x 109.9 cm)
Collection of Barry Sloane

Tripe on the S-Curve, 2003
Oil on panel, frame
29 1/8 x 17 5/8 in. (74 x 44.8 cm)
Collection of Libby Lumpkin and Dave Hickey

Kiss the Fat, 2004
Oil on panel, frame
17 x 14 1/4 in. (43.2 x 36.2 cm)
Richard Heller Gallery; private collection

Fat Mouth, 2008
Oil on panel, frame
16 x 18 in. (40.6 x 45.7 cm)
Blaine Halvorson

Reindeer Burka Shroud, 2008
Graphite on BFK Rives
41 3/4 x 29 3/4 in. (106 x 75.6 cm)
Hammer Museum, Los Angeles; Purchase

Reindeer Priapus, 2008
Graphite on BFK Rives
41 3/4 x 29 3/4 in. (106 x 75.6 cm)
Courtesy the artist and Richard Heller Gallery, Santa Monica

Reindeer Shotput, 2008
Graphite on BFK Rives
41 3/4 x 29 3/4 in. (106 x 75.6 cm)
Hammer Museum, Los Angeles; Purchase

Reindeer Vision (Gievvot), 2008
Oil on panel, frame
44 x 32 in. (111.8 x 81.3 cm)
Collection of Ed Moses

Reindeer Vivification, 2008
Oil on panel, frame
44 x 32 in. (111.8 x 81.3 cm)
Courtesy the artist and Richard Heller Gallery, Santa Monica

Reindeer Voluptuary, 2008
Oil on panel, frame
44 x 32 in. (111.8 x 81.3 cm)
Collection of Richard S. and Alita Rogers

Resplendent Bung, 2008
Graphite on paper
17 x 14 in. (43.2 x 35.6 cm)
Collection of Karol Howard and George Morton

Uteral Bonnet, 2008
Oil on canvas, frame
26 x 26 in. (66 x 66 cm)
Courtesy the artist and Richard Heller Gallery, Santa Monica

Kaari Upson

Calm down I am not trying to destroy you, 2008
DVD, color, sound
Approximately 30 min.
Courtesy the artist and Maccarone Gallery, New York

The Grotto, 2008–9
Mixed-media sculptural installation with video projections
Dimensions variable
Courtesy the artist and Maccarone Gallery, New York

Charlie White

American Minor, 2008
35mm film transferred to Blu-ray disc, color, sound
7:44 min.
Courtesy Loock Gallery, Berlin

Teen and Transgender Comparative Study #1, 2008
Chromogenic print
26 1/2 x 36 in. (67.3 x 91.4 cm)
Courtesy Loock Gallery, Berlin

Teen and Transgender Comparative Study #2, 2008
Chromogenic print
26 1/2 x 36 in. (67.3 x 91.4 cm)
Courtesy Loock Gallery, Berlin

Teen and Transgender Comparative Study #3, 2008
Chromogenic print
26 1/2 x 36 in. (67.3 x 91.4 cm)
Courtesy Loock Gallery, Berlin

Teen and Transgender Comparative Study #4, 2008
Chromogenic print
26 1/2 x 36 in. (67.3 x 91.4 cm)
Courtesy Loock Gallery, Berlin

Teen and Transgender Comparative Study #5, 2008
Chromogenic print
26 1/2 x 36 in. (67.3 x 91.4 cm)
Courtesy Loock Gallery, Berlin

Jeffrey Vallance

Jeffrey Vallance in Audience with His Majesty King Taufa'ahau Tupou IV of Tonga, 1985
Hand-tinted photograph, framed with carved wooden coat of arms, enamel
36 x 26 1/4 in. (91.4 x 66.7 cm)
Courtesy the artist and Margo Leavin Gallery

Jeffrey Vallance Meeting with Vigdís Finnbogadóttir, President of Iceland, 1986
Hand-tinted photograph, framed
17 1/4 x 21 1/4 in. (43.8 x 54 cm)
Courtesy the artist and Margo Leavin Gallery

Jeffrey Vallance in Audience with His Majesty King Taufa'ahau Tupou IV of Tonga, 2000
Digital print
Approx. 16 x 20 1/4 in. (40.6 x 51.4 cm)
Courtesy the artist and Margo Leavin Gallery

Audience with His Holiness Pope John Paul II: Apostolic Blessing, 2001
Papal certificate with embossment and signature
Dimensions variable
Courtesy the artist and Margo Leavin Gallery

Jeffrey Vallance Meeting with Ólafur Ragnar Grímsson, President of Iceland, 2003
Digital print
Approx. 10 1/4 x 8 in. (26 x 20.3 cm)
Courtesy the artist and Margo Leavin Gallery

The Brown Wall, 2009
Mixed media with found objects
Approx. 96 x 168 in. (243.8 x 426.7 cm)
Courtesy the artist and Margo Leavin Gallery, Los Angeles

Lisa Anne Auerbach

Sandy Koufax Sweater, 1996
Wool and mohair
Size medium
Courtesy the artist and Gavlak, West Palm Beach, Florida

Lisa Anne Auerbach and Daniel Marlos
Cover photo for *American Homebody* (July 1998), 1998/2008
Ultrachrome print
16 1/2 x 16 1/2 in. (41.9 x 41.9 cm)
Courtesy the artist and Gavlak, West Palm Beach, Florida

Lisa Anne Auerbach and Daniel Marlos
Cover photo for *American Homebody* (September 1998), 1998/2008
Ultrachrome print
16 1/2 x 16 1/2 in. (41.9 x 41.9 cm)
Courtesy the artist and Gavlak, West Palm Beach, Florida

Lisa Anne Auerbach and Daniel Marlos
Cover photo for *American Homebody* (July 4, 1999), 1999/2008
Ultrachrome print
16 1/2 x 16 1/2 in. (41.9 x 41.9 cm)
Courtesy the artist and Gavlak, West Palm Beach, Florida

Lisa Anne Auerbach and Daniel Marlos
Cover photo for *American Homebody* (Autumn 1999, "Farmer's Daughter Issue"), 1999/2008
Ultrachrome print
16 1/2 x 16 1/2 in. (41.9 x 41.9 cm)
Courtesy the artist and Gavlak, West Palm Beach, Florida

Lisa Anne Auerbach and Daniel Marlos
Napping in Confederate Pajamas, 1999/2008
Ultrachrome print
16 1/2 x 16 1/2 in. (41.9 x 41.9 cm)
Courtesy the artist and Gavlak, West Palm Beach, Florida

Lisa Anne Auerbach and Daniel Marlos
Napping in Union Pajamas, 1999/2008
Ultrachrome print
16 1/2 x 16 1/2 in. (41.9 x 41.9 cm)
Courtesy the artist and Gavlak, West Palm Beach, Florida

Lisa Anne Auerbach and Daniel Marlos
Cover photo for *American Homebody* (January 2000, "We're Online"), 2000/2008
Ultrachrome print
16 1/2 x 16 1/2 in. (41.9 x 41.9 cm)
Courtesy the artist and Gavlak, West Palm Beach, Florida

Lisa Anne Auerbach and Daniel Marlos
December, from *American Homebody "Sweetheart" Calendar 2001–2002*, 2001/2008
Ultrachrome print
16 1/2 x 16 1/2 in. (41.9 x 41.9 cm)
Courtesy the artist and Gavlak, West Palm Beach, Florida

Lisa Anne Auerbach and Sharon Lockhart
February, from *American Homebody "Sweetheart" Calendar 2001–2002*, 2001/2008
Ultrachrome print
16 1/2 x 16 1/2 in. (41.9 x 41.9 cm)
Courtesy the artist and Gavlak, West Palm Beach, Florida

Lisa Anne Auerbach and Daniel Marlos
March, from *American Homebody "Sweetheart" Calendar 2001–2002*, 2001/2008
Ultrachrome print
16 1/2 x 16 1/2 in. (41.9 x 41.9 cm)
Courtesy the artist and Gavlak, West Palm Beach, Florida

Lisa Anne Auerbach and Sharon Lockhart
May, from *American Homebody "Sweetheart" Calendar 2001–2002*, 2001/2008
Ultrachrome print
16 1/2 x 16 1/2 in. (41.9 x 41.9 cm)
Courtesy the artist and Gavlak, West Palm Beach, Florida

Lisa Anne Auerbach and Charlie White
October, from *American Homebody "Sweetheart" Calendar 2001–2002*, 2001/2008
Ultrachrome print
16 1/2 x 16 1/2 in. (41.9 x 41.9 cm)
Courtesy the artist and Gavlak, West Palm Beach, Florida

Lisa Anne Auerbach and Sharon Lockhart
September, from *American Homebody "Sweetheart" Calendar 2001–2002*, 2001/2008
Ultrachrome print
16 1/2 x 16 1/2 in. (41.9 x 41.9 cm)
Courtesy the artist and Gavlak, West Palm Beach, Florida

Lisa Anne Auerbach, Fredrik Nilsen, and Charlie White
American Homebody Wallpaper, 2002/2008
Ultrachrome print
12 x 18 in. (30.5 x 45.7 cm)
Courtesy the artist and Gavlak, West Palm Beach, Florida

Hand-Knit Bikini, 2002/2008
Ultrachrome print
16 1/2 x 16 1/2 in. (41.9 x 41.9 cm)
Courtesy the artist and Gavlak, West Palm Beach, Florida

Lisa Anne Auerbach and Chris Buck
Cover of *Saddlesore #1*, 2004/2008
Ultrachrome print
21 x 14 1/2 in. (53.3 x 36.8 cm)
Courtesy the artist and Gavlak, West Palm Beach, Florida

Lisa Anne Auerbach and Daniel Marlos
Cover of *Saddlesore #2*, 2005/2008
Ultrachrome print
21 x 14 1/2 in. (53.3 x 36.8 cm)
Courtesy the artist and Gavlak, West Palm Beach, Florida

Did You Hear What Bush Said When Asked about Roe vs. Wade? 2005
Wool
Variable dimensions
Beth Rudin DeWoody

Lisa/Zoso, 2005
Wool
Variable dimensions
Ann Faison and Dave Muller

Smash Monogamy, 2005
Merino wool
Size medium
Courtesy the artist and Gavlak, West Palm Beach, Florida

Code Red, 2006
Merino wool
Size medium
Courtesy the artist and Gavlak, West Palm Beach, Florida

Lisa Anne Auerbach and Daniel Marlos
Cover of *Saddlesore #3*, 2006/2008
Ultrachrome print
21 x 14 1/2 in. (53.3 x 36.8 cm)
Courtesy the artist and Gavlak, West Palm Beach, Florida

Independent Woman, 2006/2008
Ultrachrome print
7 1/4 x 18 in. (18.4 x 45.7 cm)
Courtesy the artist and Gavlak, West Palm Beach, Florida

Bloodstorm, 2007
Chromogenic print
20 x 16 in. (50.8 x 40.6 cm)
Courtesy the artist and Gavlak, West Palm Beach, Florida

Cookie Monster, 2007
Chromogenic print
20 x 16 in. (50.8 x 40.6 cm)
Courtesy the artist and Gavlak, West Palm Beach, Florida

Cover of *Saddlesore #4*, 2007/2008
Ultrachrome print
21 x 14 1/2 in. (53.3 x 36.8 cm)
Courtesy the artist and Gavlak, West Palm Beach, Florida

Ensor, 2007
Chromogenic print
20 x 16 in. (50.8 x 40.6 cm)
Courtesy the artist and Gavlak, West Palm Beach, Florida

If nothing changes, it changes nothing, 2007
Merino wool
Size medium
Courtesy the artist and Gavlak, West Palm Beach, Florida

Jelly Roll, 2007
Chromogenic print
20 x 16 in. (50.8 x 40.6 cm)
Courtesy the artist and Gavlak, West Palm Beach, Florida

Never Forget, 2007
Merino wool
Size medium
Courtesy the artist and Gavlak, West Palm Beach, Florida

Larry Craig, Full of Love and a Wide Stance on the Shitter, 2007
Merino wool
Size medium
Courtesy the artist and Gavlak, West Palm Beach, Florida

Marvin, 2007
Chromogenic print
20 x 16 in. (50.8 x 40.6 cm)
Courtesy the artist and Gavlak, West Palm Beach, Florida

Pants Shitter, 2007
Chromogenic print
20 x 16 in. (50.8 x 40.6 cm)
Courtesy the artist and Gavlak, West Palm Beach, Florida

Sell Art Buy Shoes, 2007
Merino wool
Size medium
Courtesy the artist and Gavlak, West Palm Beach, Florida

Tricky Dick, 2007
Chromogenic print
20 x 16 in. (50.8 x 40.6 cm)
Courtesy the artist and Gavlak, West Palm Beach, Florida

Unibomber, 2007
Chromogenic print
20 x 16 in. (50.8 x 40.6 cm)
Courtesy the artist and Gavlak, West Palm Beach, Florida

When there's nothing left to burn, you've got to set yourself on fire, 2007
Merino wool
Size medium
Courtesy the artist and Gavlak, West Palm Beach, Florida

Widow Maker, 2007
Chromogenic print
20 x 16 in. (50.8 x 40.6 cm)
Courtesy the artist and Gavlak, West Palm Beach, Florida

Cunty First, 2008
Merino wool
Size medium
Courtesy the artist and Gavlak, West Palm Beach, Florida

My Jewish Grandma is voting for Obama / Chosen people choose Obama, 2008
Merino wool
Size medium
Courtesy the artist and Gavlak, West Palm Beach, Florida

Yes we can, No he Mccaint, 2008
Merino wool
Size medium
Courtesy the artist and Gavlak, West Palm Beach, Florida

Two vitrines with original publications (*American Homebody*, the *Casual Observer*, *Saddlesore*, etc.)

The artist is also producing several new sweaters for the exhibition.

Lenders to the Exhibition

Blum & Poe, Los Angeles
Tanya Bonakdar, New York
The Buck Collection, Laguna Beach, California
Beth Rudin DeWoody
Ann Faison and Dave Muller
Foundation 2021/Nyehaus, New York
Gavlak, West Palm Beach, Florida
Greene Naftali Gallery, New York
Blaine Halvorson
Richard Heller Gallery, Santa Monica
Karol Howard and George Morton
Kent Gallery, New York
Laguna Art Museum
Margo Leavin Gallery, Los Angeles
Loock Gallery, Berlin
Libby Lumpkin and Dave Hickey
Maccarone Gallery, New York
Ed Moses
Museum of Contemporary Art San Diego/
Gribin Family Trust
Tim Nye, New York
The Collection of Patrick and Soo Jin Jeong-Painter
Alan Power
Richard S. and Alita Rogers
Ann and Mel Schaffer
Norton Simon Museum of Art
Barry Sloane
Ernest and Eunice White
Several private collections

Lisa Anne Auerbach

Born in 1967 in Ann Arbor, Michigan

Education

MFA Art Center College of Design, Pasadena, California, 1994

BFA Rochester Institute of Technology, Rochester, New York, 1990

Boston University, School of Communications, 1988

Solo Exhibitions

2008 *Lisa Anne Auerbach*, Aspen Art Museum, Aspen, Colorado

2007 *Auerbachtoberfest*, David Patton Los Angeles

2006 *Right On, Weatherman*, CPK Kunsthal, Copenhagen

1995 *Self-Titled Debut*, Thomas Solomon's Garage, Los Angeles

1994 *Heaven Tonight*, Art Center College of Design, Pasadena

Group Exhibitions

2008 *Cottage Industry*, Contemporary Museum, Baltimore

The Way That We Rhyme, Yerba Buena Center for the Arts, San Francisco

2007 *Words Fail Me*, Museum of Contemporary Art, Detroit

2006 *Open Walls 2*, White Columns, New York

2004 *Publish and Be Damned*, Cubitt, London

Selected Articles and Essays

Bollen, Christopher. "Modern Art's Three Hot Trends." *Domino*, March 2006, 64.

Dambrot, Shana. "Lisa Anne Auerbach: Fear No Sweater." *FiberArts Magazine*, January–February 2006.

Gersten, Lana. "Political Stitch: Knitting for Obama." *Forward*, October 16, 2008, 2.

Gschwandtner, Sabrina. "Lisa Auerbach." In *KnitKnit: Profiles and Projects from Knitting's New Wave*, 8–13. New York: Stewart, Tabori and Chang STC Craft, 2007.

Holte, Michael Ned. "Preview: From California to the New York Island." *Artforum* 44 (May 2006): 123.

Morris, Barbara. "'Make You Notice' at SFAC Gallery" (review). *Artweek* 39 (June 2008): 12–13.

Oksenhorn, Stewart. "Poli-Knits: Lisa Auerbach Fashions a Message in Sweaters." *Aspen Times*, October 4, 2008.

Searle, Karen. *Knitting Art*. Osceola, Wis.: Voyageur Press, 2008, 104–11.

Summers, Marya. "Art Review." *New Times Broward Palm Beach*, April 20, 2006, http://www.browardpalmbeach.com/2006-04-20/culture/capsule-reviews-of-current-area-art-exhibitions/.

Williamson, Damien. "AAM Hosts a Different Kind of Voting Drive." *Aspen Daily News*, October 9, 2008.

Julie Becker

Born in 1972 in Los Angeles

Education

MFA California Institute of the Arts, Valencia, 1995

BFA California Institute of the Arts, Valencia, 1993

Solo Exhibitions

2000 *In Sync: Cinema and Sound in the Work of Julie Becker and Christian Marclay*, Whitney Museum of American Art, New York

1997 *Julie Becker: Researchers, Residents, a Place to Rest*, Kunsthalle Zürich, Zurich*

Group Exhibitions

2006 *Dark Places*, Santa Monica Museum of Art, Santa Monica, California

Seville Biennial, Seville, Spain

2003 *Sightings: Installation Art, 1969–2002*, Museum of Contemporary Art, Los Angeles

Sodium Dreams, Center for Curatorial Studies, Bard College, Annandale-on-Hudson, New York

2001 *Casino 2001: First Quadrennial of Contemporary Art*, S.M.A.K., Ghent, Belgium*

1999 *Peace*, Museum für Gegenwartskunst, Zurich, Switzerland

1997 *Gothic: Transmutations of Horror in Late Twentieth-Century Art*, Institute of Contemporary Art, Boston

New Works: Drawings Today, San Francisco Museum of Modern Art

1996 *Universalis: 23. Bienal Internacional São Paulo*, North American Section, São Paulo, Brazil*

Selected Articles and Essays

Bürgi, Bernhard. "Bernhard Bürgi in Conversation with Julie Becker." In *Julie Becker: Researchers, Residents, a Place to Rest*, 11–35. Zurich: Kunsthalle Zurich, 1997.

Hauptman, Jodi. "Imagining Cities." In *Fernand Léger*, by Carolyn Lanchner, 91–97. New York: Museum of Modern Art, 1998.

Kraus, Chris. "Julie Becker." In *Universalis: 23. Bienal Internacional São Paulo*. São Paulo: Bienal Internacional, 1996.

Von Schlegell, Mark. "Sparkle Girl." *artext*, no. 72 (February–April 2001): 44–49.

Wollen, Peter. "Julie Becker." *Afterall*, no. 2 (2000): 21–26.

Residencies

Stiftung Laurenz-Haus, Basel, Switzerland, 1998

Llyn Foulkes

Born in 1934 in Yakima, Washington

Education

Chouinard Art Institute, Los Angeles, 1957–59

Central Washington College of Education, Ellensburg, 1954

University of Washington, Seattle, 1953–54

Solo Exhibitions

1995 *Llyn Foulkes: Between a Rock and a Hard Place*, Laguna Art Museum, Laguna Beach, California; traveled to Contemporary Art Center, Cincinnati; Oakland Museum of California; Palm Springs Desert Museum, Palm Springs, California*

1984 *Llyn Foulkes: New Rocks, Postcards*, Los Angeles Institute of Contemporary Art

1974 *Llyn Foulkes: Fifty Paintings, Collages, and Prints from Southern California Collections: A Survey Exhibition, 1959–1974*, Newport Harbor Art Museum, Newport Beach, California*

1962 *Llyn Foulkes: Paintings and Constructions*, Pasadena Art Museum, Pasadena, California

1961 *An Introduction to the Paintings of Llyn Foulkes*, Ferus Gallery, Los Angeles

Group Exhibitions

2006 *Los Angeles, 1955–1985: Birth of an Art Capital*, Centre Pompidou, Paris

1997 *Sunshine and Noir: Art in L.A., 1960–1997*, Louisiana Museum of Modern Art, Humlebaek, Denmark*; traveled to Kunstmuseum Wolfsburg, Germany; Castello di Rivoli, Museo d'Arte Contemporanea, Turin, Italy; UCLA at the Armand Hammer Museum of Art and Cultural Center, Los Angeles

1992 *Proof: Los Angeles Art and the Photograph, 1960–1980*, Laguna Art Museum, Laguna Beach, California*; traveled to DeCordova Museum and Sculpture Park, Lincoln, Massachusetts; Friends of Photography, Ansel Adams Center, San Francisco; Montgomery Museum of Fine Arts, Montgomery, Alabama; Tampa Museum of Art, Tampa, Florida; Des Moines Art Center
Helter Skelter, Museum of Contemporary Art, Los Angeles*

1966 Ninth International São Paulo Bienal, Museum of Modern Art, São Paulo, Brazil*

Selected Publications

Desmarais, Charles. *Proof: Los Angeles Art and the Photograph, 1960–1980*. Los Angeles: Fellows of Contemporary Art; Laguna Beach, Calif.: Laguna Art Museum, 1992.

Friis-Hansen, Dana. *L.A. Hot and Cool*. Cambridge: List Visual Arts Center, Massachusetts Institute of Technology, 1987.

Llyn Foulkes: The Sixties. New York: Kent Fine Art, 1987.

Selz, Peter. *Art of Engagement: Visual Politics in California and Beyond*, 21, 67, 68. Berkeley: University of California Press, 2006.

Whiting, Cecile. *Pop L.A.: Art and the City in the 1960s*. Berkeley: University of California Press, 2006.

Selected Articles and Essays

Ayres, Anne. "Llyn Foulkes." In *Forty Years of California Assemblage*, 146–49. Los Angeles: Wight Art Gallery, University of California, 1989.

Ballatore, Sandy. "Llyn Foulkes, Commentary and Interview." *LAICA Journal* 3 (December 1974): 12–16.

Brooks, Rosetta. "Soul Searching." *Artforum* 28 (Summer 1990): 130–31.

Johnson, Ken. "Art in Review: Llyn Foulkes." *New York Times*, February 25, 2005.

McKenna, Kristine. "He's an Angry Man, but It Isn't Personal." *Los Angeles Times*, October 22, 1995.

Awards

1986 National Endowment for the Arts Grant

1977 Guggenheim Fellowship

1967 First Award for Painting, Fifth Paris Biennale, Musée d'art moderne de la ville de Paris

1964 First Los Angeles County Museum New Talent Purchase Grant

1959 First Award for Painting, Chouinard Art Institute, Los Angeles

Charles Irvin

Born in 1971 in Dallas, Texas

Education

MFA School of the Art Institute of Chicago, 1997

BFA University of Texas at Austin, 1994

Solo Exhibitions

2003 Daniel Hug Gallery, Los Angeles
Pruess Press, Los Angeles

Group Exhibitions

2008 *Some Paintings: The Third Annual LA Weekly Biennial*, Track 16, Santa Monica, California

2007 *One Foot High and Rising*, Balmoral, Los Angeles

2006 *Dream Show*, Circus of Books, West Hollywood, California

2005 *The Early Show*, White Columns, New York

2004 *Where Do We Come From...*, Champion Fine Arts, Los Angeles
Drunk vs. Stoned, Gavin Brown's Enterprise, New York

2002 *Rent-a-Bench*, Los Angeles

2001 *Charles Irvin, Michelle O'Marah, Otv*, Galleri Nicolai Wallner (project room), Copenhagen

Hirsch Perlman

Born in 1960 in Chicago

Education

BA Architecture, Yale University, New Haven, Connecticut, 1982

Solo Exhibitions

2006 Drammens Museum, Drammens, Norway

1996 *Projects 54*, Museum of Modern Art, New York

1995 Kunstraum, Vienna

1990 Shedhalle, Zurich, Switzerland*

1988 Renaissance Society, Chicago*

Group Exhibitions

2004 *Cinematic Video Works*, Berliner Kunstsalon, Berlin

2003 *Strange Days*, Museum of Contemporary Art, Chicago

2002 *Whitney Biennial*, Whitney Museum of American Art, New York*

2001 *(Tele)Visions*, Kunsthalle, Vienna

1990 *The Photography of Invention: American Pictures of the Eighties*, National Museum of American Art, Washington, D.C.*; traveled to Museum of Contemporary Art, Chicago; Walker Art Center, Minneapolis

Selected Articles and Essays

"Art: Hirsch Perlman." *New Yorker*, November 12, 2007, 15.

Avgikos, Jan. "Reviews: Hirsch Perlman." *Artforum* 46 (January 2008): 278.

Greene, David A. Review. *Frieze*, no. 102 (October 1996): 80–81.

Hapgood, Susan. "Hirsch Perlman at the Museum of Modern Art." *Art in America* 85 (January 1997): 99.

Iannaccone, Carmine. Review. *Art Issues*, no. 69 (September–October 2001): 52.

Miles, Christopher. "Hirsch Perlman." *Artforum* 42 (May 2004): 217–18.

Pagel, David. Review. *Los Angeles Times*, March 12, 2004, Calendar section.

Weissman, Benjamin. "Hirsch Perlman Saved from Avalanche." *Frieze*, no. 74 (April 2003): 74–79.

White, Roger. "Review: Hirsch Perlman." *Time Out New York*, November 15–21, 2007, 86.

Victoria Reynolds

Born in 1962 in Tyler, Texas

Education

MFA University of Nevada, Las Vegas, 1993

BFA University of Oklahoma, Norman, 1990

Solo Exhibitions

2008 *Drawn and Rendered*, Richard Heller Gallery, Santa Monica, California

2002 *Carne Vale*, Blue Star Arts Complex, Satellite Space, San Antonio, Texas

2001 *Rare and Well-Done (Blodig och genomstekt)*, Galleri Ahnlund, Umeå, Sweden

2000 *Bienvenido: The Living Desert*, Living Desert, Las Vegas

1994 *Stain of the Real*, The Cannery, Las Vegas

Selected Group Exhibitions

2008 *Mel's Hole*, Grand Central Art Center, Santa Ana, California*

Some Paintings: The Third Annual LA Weekly Biennial, Track 16, Santa Monica, California

2007 *Las Vegas Diaspora: The Emergence of Contemporary Art from the Neon Homeland*, Las Vegas Art Museum*; traveled to Laguna Art Museum, Laguna Beach, California

Art Auction = Stimulus, Laguna Art Museum, Laguna Beach, California

2004 *One Hundred Artists See God*, Contemporary Jewish Museum, San Francisco*; traveled to Laguna Art Museum, Laguna Beach, California; Institute of Contemporary Arts, London; Contemporary Art Center of Virginia, Virginia Beach; Albright College Freedman Art Gallery, Reading, Pennsylvania; Cheekwood Museum of Art, Nashville, Tennessee

Selected Articles and Essays

Duncan, Michael. Exhibition review. *Art in America* 90 (December 2002): 118.

Pagel, David. "'Vegas Show' Holds Mostly High Cards." *Los Angeles Times*, January 14, 1997.

Schwartzkoff, Louise. "Carnivorous Canvas." *Sydney Morning Herald*, March 15, 2008.

Swenson, Kirsten. "Sin City Slickers." *Art in America* 96 (February 2008): 62–63, 65, 67.

Verwoert, Jan. "The Magic Hour." *Frieze*, no. 65 (March 2002): 84.

Kaari Upson

Born in 1972 in San Bernardino, California

Education

MFA California Institute of the Arts, Valencia, 2007
BFA California Institute of the Arts, Valencia, 2004
New York Studio School, 1998

Solo Exhibitions

2007 *Hammer Project: Kaari Upson*, Hammer Museum, Los Angeles
The Larry Project, Chapter Two: The Honeymoon Period, D301 Gallery, California Institute of the Arts
2006 *Sampler Project*, L-Shape Gallery, California Institute of the Arts
2004 *Incidents*, D301 Gallery, California Institute of the Arts
2001 *Mental Mapping*, L-Shape Gallery, California Institute of the Arts

Group Exhibitions

2008 *Pretty Ugly*, curated by Alison Gingeras, Gavin Brown's Enterprise and Maccarone Gallery, New York
2007 *Internal Mechanisms*, High Energy Constructs, Los Angeles
For Ever, curated by Clara Kim and Eungie Joo, 915 Mateo, Los Angeles
The Juice Is Loose... a Big Painting Show, 507 Rose, Venice, California
2002 *New Victorians*, Stevenson Blanche Devereaux Gallery, California Institute of the Arts

Selected Articles and Essays

Holte, Michael Ned. "Kaari Upson." *Artforum* 46 (February 2008): 298–99.
Lacher, Irene. "The Art of Neighborly Obsession." *Los Angeles Times*, January 3, 2008.
"The Office." *Abitare*, October 2007, 292–93.
Williams, Maxwell. "Meet Larry." *Tokion*, Spring 2008, 122–25.

Jeffrey Vallance

Born in 1955 in Redondo Beach, California

Education

MFA Otis Art Institute of the Parsons School of Design, Los Angeles, 1981
BA California State University, Northridge, 1979

Solo Exhibitions

2008 *Blinky the Friendly Hen: Thirtieth Anniversary Exhibition*, Track 16 Gallery, Santa Monica, California
2007 *Relics and Reliquaries*, Grand Central Art Center, Santa Ana, California
2006 *Preserving America's Cultural Heritage*, California College of the Arts, San Francisco
1999 *Paranormal Diagrams: Heretical Theories*, Art Institute of Boston
1995 *The World of Jeffrey Vallance*, Santa Monica Museum of Art, Santa Monica, California

Group Exhibitions

2006 *Los Angeles, 1955–1985: Birth of an Art Capital*, Centre Pompidou, Paris*
2002 *(The World May Be) Fantastic*, Sydney Biennale 2002, Sydney, Australia*
1997 *Scene of the Crime*, UCLA at the Armand Hammer Museum of Art and Cultural Center, Los Angeles*
1985 *B & W*, Los Angeles Institute of Contemporary Art, Los Angeles
1982 *Critical Perspectives*, P.S.1 Contemporary Art Center, Long Island City, New York

Artist Books

Blinky the Friendly Hen. Published by the artist, 1979. Edition of 550.
My Life with Dick. Los Angeles: BükAmerica, 2005.
Thomas Kinkade: Heaven on Earth. By Jeffrey Vallance, Doug Harvey, and Thomas Kinkade. San Francisco: Last Gasp Books, 2004
The World of Jeffrey Vallance: Collected Writings, 1978–1994. Los Angeles: Art Issues Press, 1994.

Selected Articles and Essays

Knight, Christopher. "Exhibit Houses Modern Relics." *Los Angeles Times*, November 30, 2007.
Pincus, Robert L. "Mr. Vallance's World." *San Diego Union Tribune*, August 15, 1994.

Rugoff, Ralph. "Jeffrey Vallance." *Visions* 3 (Fall 1989): 28–29.

———. "Jeffrey Vallance's Strip Shows." *Artforum* 34 (May 1996): 84–85.

Schjeldahl, Peter. "L.A. Demystified! Art and Life in the Eternal Present." *Village Voice*, June 3, 1981, 33–35.

Awards

2004 John Simon Guggenheim Memorial Foundation Fellowship

2001 Stiftelsen Framtidens Kultur (The Foundation for the Culture of the Future), Uppsala, Sweden

2000 Distinguished Alumnus Award, Otis College of Art and Design, Los Angeles

Honorary Nobel, royal title conferred by the Tongan National Center, Nuku'alofa, Kingdom of Tonga

Charlie White

Born in 1972 in Philadelphia

MFA Art Center College of Design, Pasadena, California, 1998

BFA School of Visual Arts, New York, 1995

Solo Exhibitions

2008 *Charlie White: The Girl Studies*, Loock Gallery, Berlin

2006 *Everything Is American*, Center of Contemporary Art of Salamanca, Spain; Brändström & Stene, Stockholm; Wohnmaschine, Berlin, Germany; f a projects, London; Andrea Rosen Gallery, New York

2003 *And Jeopardize the Integrity of the Hull*, Andrea Rosen Gallery, New York

2001 *Understanding Joshua*, Andrea Rosen Gallery, New York

1999 *In a Matter of Days*, Andrea Rosen Gallery, New York; Santa Barbara Contemporary Arts Forum, Santa Barbara, California

Group Exhibitions

2007 *Sympathy for the Devil: Art and Rock and Roll since 1967*, Museum of Contemporary Art, Chicago

Between the Two Deaths, ZKM Museum für Neue Kunst, Karlsruhe, Germany

2006 *Dark Places*, Santa Monica Museum of Art, Santa Monica, California

2002 California Biennial, Orange County Museum of Art, Newport Beach, California*

2001 *My Reality: Contemporary Art and the Culture of Japanese Animation*, Brooklyn Museum of Art*; traveled to Contemporary Arts Center, Cincinnati; Tampa Museum of Art, Tampa, Florida; Chicago Cultural Center; Akron Art Museum, Akron, Ohio; Norton Museum of Art, West Palm Beach, Florida; Museum of Glass, Tacoma, Washington; Huntsville Museum of Art, Huntsville, Alabama

Selected Publications

And Jeopardize the Integrity of the Hull. Paris: Tdm Editions, 2003.

Charlie White, Monsters. New York: PowerHouse Books, 2007.

Charlie White: Photographs. Bonn, Germany: Goliath Verlagsgesellschaft, 2001.

Everything Is American. Salamanca, Spain: Da2—Domus Artium, 2002.

Selected Articles and Essays

Aletti, Vince. "Charlie White." *Village Voice*, May 7–13, 2003, 71.

Glueck, Grace. "Charlie White: Everything Is American." *New York Times*, February 10, 2006.

Kastner, Jeffrey. "Charlie White." *Artforum* 44 (March 2006): 290.

Rimanelli, David. "Charlie White." *Interview*, March 2001, 66.

Tatley, Roger. "Charlie White: Everything Is American." *Modern Painters* 18 (April 2006): 116.

Tumlir, Jan. "Sci-Fi Historicism, Part 3: Character Animation in Contemporary Los Angeles Art." *Flash Art*, no. 255 (July–September 2007): 121–24.

Acknowledgments

Over the course of the last two years, I've had the luxury of spending a substantial amount of time with each of the nine artists in this exhibition and have established an ongoing dialogue with them, which has furthered my own understanding of this city and, more importantly, their artwork. Each and every one of them is an inspiration to me for their incredible perseverance, their dedication, and their insatiable appetites for arcane knowledge: together these nine could write an encyclopedia of the weird and absurd.

Organizing this show was a group effort, and many individuals, organizations, and institutions were crucial to its realization. This exhibition and catalog would not have been possible without the exceptional support and assistance of the galleries and lenders. I want to extend my deepest thanks to everyone at the Hammer Museum who made this book and exhibition happen. I am deeply thankful to Dean Valentine for his honest friendship and for encouraging me to visit Llyn Foulkes, and to Llyn Foulkes for reminding me why I do what I do. I owe Ann Philbin a huge debt of gratitude for her endless support and enthusiasm. Gary Garrels has always had my back, and his honest and thoughtful opinion has been incredibly valuable. I owe thanks to everyone in the curatorial department, especially Cynthia Burlingham for her advice and encouragement, and Jessica Hough for helping me stay sane, along with Allegra Pesenti, April Lee, Elizabeth Cline, and Teresa Callahan, as well as former staff members Jenée Misraje and Claire de Dobay Rifelj. Thanks also to our amazing interns Sasha Bergstrom-Katz, Rachael Rebujio, Tiffany Smith, and Nina Viakhireva. Jennifer Wells Green and the entire development team at the museum—including Christine Lanoie, David Morehouse,

Janine Perron, Akiyaa Nickelson, Mary Ann Sears, and Laura Sils—have been absolutely essential to the success of this exhibition, and I am especially grateful to them all for their dedication and perseverance. Our amazing registrars—led by Portland McCormick with Julie Dickover, Olivia Caswell, and Kate Bergeron—have provided valuable support, and our remarkable installation crew—led by Peter Gould and including Franky Kong, Brian Sharp, and Mark Jones—have been wonderful to work with. Sarah Stifler, Morgan Kroll, Julia Luke, and Amanda Law have been stellar in their marketing and communications efforts.

To Purtill Family Business I extend my deepest gratitude and appreciation for their exceptional creativity, which made this book into more than just a catalog. Thanks also go to Karen Jacobson for her patience and diligence and her expert editing.

I am especially grateful to David Teiger and Dakis Joannou, two astoundingly generous and inspiring individuals whose passion for and support of the arts never cease to amaze me. I'm also extremely appreciative of Linda and Jerry Janger and their continuing support and encouragement.

I want to thank my partners in crime and sounding boards, Massimiliano Gioni and Maurizio Cattelan, as well as Michele Maccarone, Lauri Firstenberg, and Bettina Korek.

And finally I want to thank the artists: Lisa Anne Auerbach, Julie Becker, Llyn Foulkes, Charles Irvin, Hirsch Perlman, Victoria Reynolds, Kaari Upson, Jeffrey Vallance, and Charlie White. You've all made my life a lot more interesting, and working with you has been an absolute honor and delight.

Ali Subotnick

Photography Credits

Numbers refer to the page on which an image appears.

Jules Bates: 113
Mark Chamberlain: 110 (bottom left and right), 111 (bottom), 112
Tony Cuñha: 66
Brian Forrest: 54, 57 (top), 58 (bottom), 59, 60, 63, 64 (all three), 65 (all three), 69, 70, 71, 72, 73, 75, 81, 82 (top and bottom), 84 (top and bottom), 85 (bottom), 86 (top and bottom), 87
Courtesy Greene Naftali Gallery, New York: 38
Abigail Gumbiner © 2008: 19 (bottom)
Iva Hladis: 19 (top)
Peter Hunkeler: 36 (bottom)
Charles Irvin: 57 (bottom), 58 (top left and top right), 61 (all three)
Sean Meredith: 108 (top and bottom), 109 (top)
Douglas Parker: 110 (top)
Brian Pescador: 118
Victoria Reynolds: 74
Randel Urbauer: 20 (top)
Jeffrey Vallance: 111 (top)
Robert Wedemeyer: 25
Joshua White: 42, 45, 51, 105, 106–7